The Mayflower Migration

Immigrants to Plymouth, 1620

The Mayflower Migration

Immigrants to Plymouth, 1620

Robert Charles Anderson, FASG

NEW ENGLAND HISTORIC
GENEALOGICAL SOCIETY
AmericanAncestors.org

This work was sponsored by a generous grant
from The Hereditary Order of
Descendants of Colonial Governors
in commemoration of the 400th anniversary
of the landing of the *Mayflower* in 2020.

**HEREDITARY ORDER OF DESCENDANTS
OF COLONIAL GOVERNORS**
FOUNDED: 1896

ISBN: 978-0-88082-399-9

Library of Congress Control Number: 2020938661

Cover image: *The Arrival of the Pilgrim Fathers*; Gisbert, Antonio (1835–1901). Private Collection © Bonhams, London, UK/Bridgeman Images.

Cover design by Ellen Maxwell.

NEW ENGLAND HISTORIC
GENEALOGICAL SOCIETY
AmericanAncestors.org

TABLE OF CONTENTS

LIST OF SKETCHES

ACKNOWLEDGMENTS

Sketches for the passengers on the *Mayflower* have been published twice before by the Great Migration Study Project, first in 1995 in the volumes of *The Great Migration Begins: Immigrants to New England, 1620–1633,* and then in 2004 in *The Pilgrim Migration: Immigrants to Plymouth Colony, 1620–1633.* The years since the publication of *Pilgrim Migration* have seen a resurgence of new research on the *Mayflower* passengers, with the discovery of many new English origins and of other biographical information. A few years ago, with this new research in mind and in anticipation of the 400th anniversary of the sailing of the *Mayflower,* I had discussions with Brenton Simons, President and CEO of New England Historic Genealogical Society, and Ryan Woods, Executive Vice President and Chief Operating Officer of NEHGS. We agreed that a new volume covering just the *Mayflower* passengers would be an appropriate publication for the quadricentennial year. Since that decision, Brenton and Ryan have provided full support for this project.

 Mayflower expert Caleb Johnson and NEHGS staff members Lynn Betlock and Chris Child read and commented on the entire manuscript and in addition provided me with many clues to published and unpublished data that I had not been aware of. Genealogist Patricia Law Hatcher, FASG read the introductory essay with her usual insight. Historian Francis J. Bremer also read the essay and provided comments which clarified my thinking on an important point. Once the manuscript was complete I turned it over to Sharon Inglis, Publishing Director at NEHGS, who caught many errors and improved the presentation immensely by bringing consistency to my inadequate attempts to be consistent. Sharon also managed the project and edited the index prepared by Steve Csipke. In Sharon's office, Publications Design Manager Ellen Maxwell undertook the design and layout of the book and Assistant Publishing Director Cécile Engeln carefully checked the work of everyone who preceded her.

Several genealogical colleagues have provided assistance during the course of my writing. During visits to Leiden in 2018 and 2019 I had helpful and illuminating discussions with Jeremy Dupertuis Bangs, Director of the Leiden American Pilgrim Museum. Tamura Jones of Leiden has traced descendants of Moses Fletcher and James Chilton who remained behind in the Netherlands and has kindly shared some of his unpublished research. Scrooby historian Sue Allan shared with me portions of her recent research on William Bradford. Alicia Crane Williams, FASG clarified some issues relating to John Alden. Randy West of Salt Lake City was again kind enough to search out some documents that I could not otherwise access.

Any remaining errors and omissions are mine alone.

Robert Charles Anderson
Jaffrey, New Hampshire
24 May 2020

SCOPE

For the user of this volume to understand what is being presented, we must define carefully the scope of this phase of the Great Migration Study Project. Who were the participants in the *Mayflower* migration? What information is being collected on these people?

CRITERIA FOR INCLUSION IN
THE MAYFLOWER MIGRATION:
IMMIGRANTS TO PLYMOUTH, 1620

The Mayflower Migration attempts to identify and describe all the passengers who sailed to New England on the *Mayflower* in 1620. No passenger list was created when the *Mayflower* left England, but in 1651, in the course of writing his history of Plymouth Colony, William Bradford compiled a list of those who had been on the ship, and then a companion list which summarized the births, marriages, and deaths among the *Mayflower* passengers in the following three decades [Bradford 441–48]. In particular, we include the one passenger who died at sea (William Butten), the two children born aboard the *Mayflower* (Oceanus Hopkins and Peregrine White), and the crew members hired to remain at Plymouth when the *Mayflower* returned to England.

GOAL

The goal of the Great Migration Study Project may be stated very simply: to provide a concise, reliable summary of past research on the early immigrants to New England, which will reduce the amount of time which must be spent in discovering this past work, and will therefore serve as a foundation for future research.

The Project may be viewed, then, as an immense literature search, a scouring of the journals and books published in the last century and a half. This is not to say, however, that the Great Migration volumes contain no new research and no new discoveries.

A researcher interested in immigration to New England in the twenty years after the arrival of the *Mayflower* has had, until now, to look in dozens of places to learn what is known about any one immigrant. After 140 years, the first place to go is still James Savage's *Genealogical Dictionary of the First Settlers of New England*. This set was a marvel of its time and remains the only source attempting to cover all families in New England for the seventeenth century. But there have been many genealogical advances since the days of Savage, and we must also look in thousands of other books and periodicals when researching these early immigrants.

The purpose of the present volume is to summarize and, to a limited extent, evaluate what we know about the immigrants to Plymouth Colony in 1620. Modern researchers should not have to waste large amounts of time in searching out or, worse, redoing the research of earlier genealogists. With the current state of the genealogical literature this can be difficult. The Great Migration volumes aim to provide a solid base that researchers of the future can use as a stepping-off point for doing new research on a given immigrant.

The primary goal is to document each life as completely as possible. In some cases, this is a relatively easy task, since there may be only one or two records for the person in New England, and no clues to trace him or her back to England, or forward into a later career. In the majority of cases, however, an abundance of evidence exists, and a way must be found to bring it under control. After some experimentation, a standard format was developed to organize what is known about these participants in the Great Migration.

The standard sketch consists of three formatted sections: migration, biographical detail, and genealogical detail. In this volume we introduce a new section, **PREMIGRATION BIOGRAPHY**, which provides a brief narrative summary of the immigrant's life before departure for New England. This is followed by the **COMMENTS** section, which allows discussion of material not accommodated elsewhere, and also discussion of discrepancies or matters of dispute between various authorities. Some sketches conclude with a **BIBLIOGRAPHIC NOTE**. The contents of the standard sketch are demonstrated in more detail in the Sample Sketch below.

There are several things, though, that the standard sketch, and the Great Migration Study Project as a whole, does not attempt to accomplish.

If the parentage of the immigrant is known, that will be included. If a reasonably close relation to another immigrant is known, that will also be stated, perhaps naming other relatives who remained in England. But if the ancestry of the immigrant is known beyond his parents, it will usually not be presented or discussed, although a citation to anything published on the subject will be included.

Not every detail of the life of the immigrant will be incorporated into each sketch. If the subject of the sketch was one of the leaders of the colony, his lesser offices and day-to-day activities, as recorded in official records, will not be recorded here. If the immigrant was a land speculator, not every deed or land grant will be noted. In general, the more obscure and the more poorly recorded the immigrant in question, the greater will be the effort to find and include every known record.

The children of immigrants will not be traced until their deaths. We will attempt, of course, to identify every child, and to find the best evidence for that child's date and place of birth. After that we will look only for enough documentation to place that child beyond infancy, to distinguish him or her from others of the same name. Thus we will attempt to document the marriages of all children (although occasionally this may only be a first marriage). A death date will be sought for those who lived to adulthood and did not marry, and in these instances we may also include a probate record of the deceased, as it will frequently help in establishing the complete list of children of the immigrant. A death date may also be sought if it includes an age at death, and thus establishes an approximate year of birth.

METHODS

CONSTRUCTING A SKETCH

In most instances, the construction of a sketch begins with consultation of Savage's *Genealogical Dictionary of the First Settlers of New England* and Charles Henry Pope's *Pioneers of Massachusetts, 1620–1650.* The information from these brief accounts of the immigrants is entered into the appropriate categories in the sketches with the clear understanding that many changes and additions will be necessary before the sketch may be called complete. Sometimes problems in the presentations by Savage and Pope arise immediately, especially if the two sources are in clear contradiction. On other occasions problems appear only at a later stage in the process.

For the majority of the immigrants who were married, the next step is to consult Clarence Almon Torrey's "New England Marriages Prior to 1700." For present purposes, the complete transcript of this compilation, prepared by Robert J. Dunkle and published by the New England Historic Genealogical Society, is examined. This tertiary source includes for each marriage one or more citations to sources in which some mention of the married couple may be found. These citations may be to contemporary source documents or to secondary sources of many varieties. Torrey ceased work on his index in 1960, shortly before his death, and for the period after 1960 his work is supplemented by a privately generated card index, mostly to the periodical literature, covering the years from 1961 to the present.

As many as possible of the sources cited by Torrey are then collected and examined. At this point additional material from these sources may be added to the growing sketch. As the sketch continues to develop in this way, a number of things may happen. Points of dispute or controversy between two or more sources may appear, and they are noted so that they may be investigated and, if possible, resolved. Ideas for additional places to search may also come to light, and these are also added to the list of additional avenues of research.

Once the basic outline of the sketch has been created in this way, and many of the outstanding problems have been defined, research in primary sources begins. The vital records and church records are examined, deeds and wills are abstracted, and court records are surveyed. As will be explained in more detail later, the best source possible is sought for each fact and for each genealogical connection.

The form of a sketch, in which a defined set of categories is filled in for each immigrant, forces research into all necessary areas, so that the same documents used to answer the genealogical questions or to complete the information on *ESTATE* are also examined for evidence of *EDUCATION* or *OCCUPATION*.

The last step is to review the work done on the sketch, and return to Savage, Pope, and any other secondary sources of value to the immigrant under study. The *COMMENTS* section is then used to discuss the problem areas, in which two or more earlier researchers are in conflict. In many instances the conflict can be resolved, but, as this is not always possible, one can do no more than state the dispute, and perhaps suggest a path of research that might lead to a resolution.

This is also the stage at which the immigrant himself or herself may be evaluated. If the subject of the sketch was unusually contentious, or unusually innocuous, it might be reason for comment. The sketch should now be complete, with the immigrant's life outlined, using the best sources, and taking note of any remaining problems or of any unusual features of the person's life.

CHRONOLOGICAL ANALYSIS

Criteria for Approximating Dates

When we do not have an exact date for a vital event, such as a birth, baptismal, marriage, or death date, we will in all instances create an approximated date for that event. We do this for a number of reasons. Sometimes this type of chronological analysis will reveal an unsuspected contradiction in previous treatments of a family, indicating perhaps that not all the children of a man could have been born to his only known wife. Even when the analysis does not reveal anything of immediate import, it may help to narrow the parameters within which future research must be conducted.

The approximation of dates may be done in a variety of ways. The most desirable manner of approximating dates is from a piece of evidence that states an age, or in some other way describes a specific span of years. If an age at death or an age at the time of a deposition is available, then a year of birth may be estimated, and in such a case the entry will read "b. about

1634," indicating a date that is reliable within a relatively narrow span of years, perhaps just two years above or below the estimated date.

More frequently the evidence for estimating an age will be less precise, and we will have to state an age in a different way: saying that someone was "b. say 1634," meaning that this is our best estimate, but that it may be some years off in either direction. We may only have a date of first marriage, from which we will state a likely birth date based on the usual age at first marriage. There are many other indicators that help us to establish these broad ranges.

Although some of the dates approximated in this study will in the future be found to be wide of the mark, we believe that it is important to provide some context for future research, and at least try to get a feel for what is chronologically possible with some of these immigrants. As will be seen, when a birthdate is estimated through a long string of other estimations, the date arrived at will generally be the latest date that the birth could have taken place, or close to it. Thus, in examining English records we will ignore candidates of that name who were born some years after the suggested birth date.

The criteria for producing "say" dates are many and varied, and only a few will be mentioned here. As noted above, a likely time for first marriage will be assumed. In a large number of cases, men married for the first time in their early to mid-twenties, and so an age of twenty-five will be used in this study. Women married for the first time in their late teens or early twenties, so an arbitrary age at first marriage of twenty will be assumed for women in the absence of evidence to the contrary.

"Say" dates may also be generated by reliance on other milestones in life, such as the age at which one could choose a guardian, or sell real estate, or become a freeman. The particular criterion used in a given case will generally be stated explicitly.

Ordering Families

The next step in chronological analysis is the examination of whole families for the purpose of establishing birth-order for the children. This task poses no great problems when we have a complete set of birth or baptismal records, and when there are no internal inconsistencies among them.

When there are children without any precise date of birth, we begin, if possible, with those that do. This provides a framework around which we can attempt to place the others. We then look for those who have been assigned an "about" date of birth, based usually on age at death or age as given in a dated deposition. (If it happens that we do not have any children with known birth or baptismal dates, then we must erect our basic framework from those with "about" dates.)

We wish to fit the children with well-estimated years of birth into the framework at the most likely intervals. The first rule that we observe is that the births come about two years apart (unless we have strong evidence for multiple births, or for the employment of a wet nurse, which would allow the mother to conceive again soon after childbirth). We look, then, for gaps of three years or more into which a child might be placed (not enforcing the two-year interval rule too strictly).

At this point we will be left with children who have been assigned only "say" dates (based, perhaps, on a known date of first marriage, or on some other age-constrained life event), or for whom no clues on age are yet available. Those with "say" dates can be fitted into any remaining places. Those without any age information at all, perhaps children who died young with a known death date but no age at death, or unmarried children who died at a more advanced age, will now be placed into any plausible available slots.

Throughout this process we try to make the sequence of births as continuous as possible, for reasons that will emerge in a moment. We must be on the lookout for conflicts and contradictions, which may be indications that we have made an error in estimating or recording one of the dates. Also, by placing some of those without any age information into available gaps in the sequence, we should be able to assign "say" dates to most of the remaining children.

By making it our goal to place all the children in a single, compact sequence, we may obtain some useful information about other matters. If, after all our efforts, there remains a large gap, or more than one, in the list of children, we may wish to seek for an explanation. Such a gap may indicate nothing more than a string of stillbirths or deaths in infancy, but other possible explanations may direct our research into new channels.

One explanation for the gap might be that the immigrant had more than one wife, with an early group of children by a first wife, a gap before a second marriage, and then a second wife. Even without a gap, a second wife would be indicated if the sequence of children was spread out over much more than twenty years.

Another explanation, usually more difficult to verify, would be that the couple were separated for a number of years. Sometimes the immigrant head of household came to New England alone, while his wife was still of childbearing age, and did not send for her or return to fetch her until some years later.

The process of determining the order of birth of the children in a family, although time-consuming, frequently provides some of the best new data on that family. While some of the positions assigned to the children may turn out to be incorrect, the value of this process in pointing out conflicts and contradictions and in directing further research is worth the effort.

Form of Dates

Since England and the English colonies were still using the Julian calendar in the seventeenth century, a date that fell between 1 January and 24 March of the year could be ambiguous as to the year of the date. We employ various conventions in presenting these dates. If the doubledating is given explicitly in the record, or if the double-dated year can be deduced with confidence from the sequence of chronologically arranged records, the date will be given in the form "28 February 1636/7." If the double-dating can be deduced with reasonable but not complete confidence, the form will be "28 February 1637[/8]." If the double-dating cannot be determined with much assurance, the date will be given as "28 February 1637[/8?]." And, in some cases, when we are unable to resolve the double-dating, even tentatively, the date will be presented simply as "28 February 1637."

The use of "[NS]" to indicate New Style dates will be employed only for records created in jurisdictions already using the Gregorian calendar. Most of these will be from Leiden or New Amsterdam. In no case will a date created under the Julian calendar be adjusted to the Gregorian calendar.

DOCUMENTATION AND CITATION

Although the terms documentation and citation are sometimes used interchangeably, they are employed here to describe two distinct but related steps in the process of supplying evidence to support one's conclusions.

DOCUMENTATION is the inclusion of complete or partial copies of the records in a sketch, whether as lengthy extracts or brief abstracts.

CITATION is the presentation of that information that identifies a source or a record and allows the reader to find that source for himself or herself easily.

Documentation

In some instances, an abstract of a document or record may be sufficient. Perhaps only a small portion of the document is relevant to the matter at hand, or perhaps the document is burdened with much formulaic or legalistic language that does not in itself advance the argument. When an abstract is made, those portions of the record that have been used without change of verbiage are included in quotation marks, while the portions not in quotation marks have been abbreviated or paraphrased.

In other cases, a complete document, or large uninterrupted portions of a document, may be incorporated in the sketch. This may be because the entire document is important for making a specific point, or simply because it is intrinsically interesting, and gives an insight into the life and times of the immigrants we are studying. In some cases, the language of a document is so convoluted and complex that it is simply safer to produce a lengthy extract, as an attempted paraphrase might be just as long as the original, and not convey the point so well.

Whether a document is abstracted or transcribed in full, the modernized method of transcription is employed. In this technique, modern spelling, punctuation, and capitalization are used, and abbreviations are expanded. In the case of personal and place names, however, the spellings of the document itself are retained, and abbreviations are expanded in square brackets. The original author or scribe's choice and sequence of words are not disturbed. The edition of William Bradford's history of Plymouth Colony which we are most often using here, prepared by Samuel Eliot Morison, employs the modernized method. (See Frank Freidel, ed., *Harvard Guide to American History,* revised edition, two volumes in one, pp. 27–36, for a complete discussion of this subject, with examples.)

Citation

Most citations will be given in an abbreviated form in the text, with the expansion of these short forms presented in the **KEY TO TITLES** which follows this front matter. If a source is used in only a few sketches, the full citation may be given at each occurrence, in which case no entry will appear in the **KEY TO TITLES**. In some cases, generally a single-family genealogy, a source will be used, but the full citation will also appear in that sketch and nowhere else.

Vital records may sometimes appear without citation. In the case of entries from English parish registers, this means that the item has been taken directly from the original or a microfilm copy of the register, which has been examined in the course of preparing the sketches. When an English parish register entry has been taken from another source, that source will be given.

When citing New England town vital records, especially from Massachusetts, no citation will appear if the entry has been taken from a volume published in alphabetic order (unless the entry appears in an unlikely part of the alphabet).

SOURCES

Hundreds of sources were consulted for this study, in libraries, archives, and courthouses. Some were viewed in the original, some on microfilm, and some only in printed versions. We cannot describe in detail here every source consulted, but rather we will comment briefly on some of the more important documents employed in constructing these sketches. Many of these sources have been discussed in the pages of the *Great Migration Newsletter,* and where appropriate reference will be made to that publication.

We discuss here only those sources which are of broad application in the study of the *Mayflower* passengers. For information on a wider range of early New England sources (some of which are occasionally cited in this volume), consult the **SOURCES** section in the front matter of other volumes published by the Great Migration Study Project.

In 1966 George D. Langdon Jr. published an excellent bibliographic essay, covering both printed and manuscript sources, as part of his history of Plymouth Colony [George D. Langdon Jr., *Pilgrim Colony: A History of New Plymouth, 1620–1691* (New Haven 1966), pp. 247–66]. (This essay appears only in the paperback edition, and not in the hardback edition.)

PASSENGER LISTS

No passenger lists have survived for any of the ships which arrived in Plymouth Colony from 1620 to 1630. From other records, however, we are able to reconstruct lists of several of these ships, and for most of the passengers.

For the first and most important of these voyages, that of the *Mayflower* in 1620, we rely upon a record made about 1651 by William Bradford, in which he first cataloged those who arrived at Plymouth in 1620, and then recounted what had been the fate and progeny of each of these passengers in the succeeding decade. The most accessible version may be found in Morison's edition of Bradford.

LISTS OF FREEMEN

The status of freeman was primarily of political importance, for it gave one the right to vote for colony officers. In some colonies, though, freemanship was tied to church membership, and so the meaning was somewhat different. Massachusetts Bay and New Haven, the most puritan of the puritan colonies, made church membership a prerequisite for freemanship, while the rest of the New England colonies, including Plymouth Colony, did not.

Lists of freemen may be used for a number of purposes beyond providing biographical information about an immigrant. Like tax lists at a later time, a list of freemen provides basic information about the presence or absence of a person on a given date.

The Plymouth Colony court records include lists of men propounded for freemanship and of men subsequently admitted to freemanship. The records of being propounded are not found in other colonies and must, in Plymouth Colony, have taken the place of prior admission to a gathered church. As can be seen from examination of the periodic compiled lists of Plymouth Colony freeman, not all the men who were made free in the colony appear in the lists of admission to freemanship found in some court records.

The freemen of Plymouth Colony were recorded also in a different form, as lists of freemen as of a given date. Six of these lists were compiled during the independent existence of Plymouth Colony. In each case, these lists were augmented and annotated between their dates of compilation and the dates of compilation of the next lists in the series. The first two lists, for 1633 and for 7 March 1636/7, covered the entire colony in one undifferentiated list [PCR 1:3–4, 52–53]. The remaining four lists, for 1639, 1658, 29 May 1670, and 1 [blank] 1683/4, each have separate sections for each of the towns [PCR 5:274–279, 8:173–187, 197–209]. As men died, moved from one town to another within Plymouth Colony, or removed from Plymouth Colony entirely, these lists were annotated appropriately. (See GMN 5:17 for a more detailed discussion of the Plymouth records of freemen.)

COLONY AND COURT RECORDS

In the early colonies the full separation of executive, legislative, and judicial powers had not been attained, and the records of the General Court of the colony could encompass business of all varieties. The colonial court records for Plymouth Colony have been transcribed and published in volumes that are cited frequently here. (Full bibliographic detail for this set may be found in the **KEY TO TITLES** under PCR.)

The first six volumes of PCR (bound as four) include the court minutes from 1633 to 1691 in one chronological sequence.

The seventh volume of PCR contains the records of civil cases from 1633 to 1691. In addition to the summaries of the cases themselves, these records also contain many lists of the members of the petit juries which sat on these cases.

Volume eight of PCR comprises a miscellaneous group of records. The vital records and the lists of freemen are discussed in other sections of this front matter. Volume eight of PCR also includes the accounts of the colony treasurer.

The small quantity of loose court papers which have survived from Plymouth Colony have been published in Charles Henry Pope's *Plymouth Scrapbook*. Most of these documents pertain to probate matters.

TOWN RECORDS

Many of the town records of Plymouth Colony remained unpublished. More than in other colonies, the town clerks in Plymouth Colony had the habit of consolidating "useful" material from original record volumes that were only a few decades old and discarding the older volumes. Two sets of published town records deserve individual mention.

Three volumes of the records of the town of Plymouth were published in 1889, 1892, and 1903 [PTR]. The first of these, covering the years 1636 through 1705, has been exploited for the present volume.

More recently, Jeremy Dupertuis Bangs has prepared three volumes of transcriptions of records for the town of Scituate, these volumes having been published in 1997, 1999, and 2001 [ScitTR]. The first volume included a transcript of the earliest volume of town records, along with summaries of the records arranged by topic. The second volume covered the records of the Connihasset Partners. The third volume includes transcripts of some town record volumes from the latter part of the seventeenth century, along with some documents pertaining to Scituate but not generated by the town.

VITAL RECORDS

Like Massachusetts Bay Colony and Connecticut Colony, Plymouth Colony required that the town maintain records of births, marriages, and deaths, and submit copies to the central government for recording there. Also like those other colonies, compliance with this requirement was sporadic. What has survived from this process has been published in Volume Eight of the Plymouth Colony Records [PCR 8:3–89].

Many of the Plymouth Colony towns had their vital records published in the alphabetized, systematic series of volumes sponsored by the Commonwealth of Massachusetts in the early decades of the twentieth century. More recently, the laudable practice has arisen of publishing town vital records in their original order. This has been done for Plymouth, Marshfield, Swansea, Middleborough, Yarmouth, Falmouth, and some other towns.

In 1978 Robert S. Wakefield published a compilation of information on marriages (not necessarily marriage records) of all couples who had married in Plymouth Colony up to 1650 [Robert S. Wakefield, *Plymouth Colony Marriages to 1650* (Warwick, Rhode Island, 1978)].

PROBATE RECORDS

Plymouth Colony began to maintain a separate set of probate records in 1633 and by the time of the establishment of counties in Plymouth Colony in 1685 this category of records had reached four volumes [PCPR]. All of this material has been microfilmed and some has been printed. George Ernest Bowman published much of this material in *Mayflower Descendant* [MD]. He began a transcription of these documents in the order that they were recorded, but only reached into the third volume. He also published in the same periodical transcriptions or abstracts of some particular documents which pertained to specific families he was studying. In 1996 C. H. Simmons Jr. published transcriptions of the Plymouth Colony probate documents from 1633 through 1669, comprising volumes 1 and 2 of the originals [*Plymouth Colony Records, Volume 1, Wills and Inventories, 1633–1669* (Camden, Maine, 1996)].

In 1685 three counties were erected covering the territory of Plymouth Colony: Barnstable, Bristol, and Plymouth. Each of these counties immediately began its own series of probate records [cited in this volume as BarnPR, BrPR, and PPR].

In 1983 Ruth Wilder Sherman and Robert S. Wakefield compiled the *Plymouth Colony Probate Guide: Where to Find Wills and Related Data For 800 People of Plymouth Colony, 1620–1691* (Warwick, Rhode Island, 1983). The main part of this volume is an alphabetical inventory of "information concerning more than 725 men and 75 women—everyone for whom we found probate material in the Plymouth Colony records, and also every Colony resident for whom we could find probate records elsewhere." There is also an informative introduction, and an appendix listing published probate records for individuals from Barnstable, Bristol, and Plymouth counties.

LAND RECORDS

Since the town and colony of Plymouth were coextensive for more than a decade, the earliest grants of land from the government to the town may be found in the court records [PCR volumes 1 through 6 *passim*]. As the towns other than Plymouth were established, the government granted large tracts of land to the towns, and then the towns made grants to individuals, the classical proprietorial system of early New England.

Transfers of land from person to person could in the earliest years be recorded in either town or colony records. The separate series of Plymouth Colony deeds runs to six volumes (some of these volumes being in two parts) [PCLR]. The first of these volumes was transcribed and published as the twelfth volume of the Plymouth Colony Records [PCR 12]. Jeremy Dupertuis Bangs has transcribed the second volume and the first part of the third volume (*Plymouth Colony Records, Deeds &c., Volume II, 1651–1663* [Leiden 2016]; *Plymouth Colony Records, Deeds &c., Volume III, Part 1, 1664–1671* [Leiden 2017]). Scott Andrew Bartley has transcribed the second part of the third volume (*Records of the Colony of New Plymouth in New England, Deeds &c., Volume III, Part 2, 1671–1673* [Boston 2019]).

When the three counties of Plymouth, Barnstable, and Bristol were erected in 1685, they took over the recording of deeds. Unfortunately, the early Barnstable County deeds were lost in a fire in the early nineteenth century.

CHURCH RECORDS

Because religious conviction was the primary motivation for migration for most of those who came to New England during the Great Migration, establishing a church in each new settlement was one of the first matters attended to. Although the survival of records from these churches is spotty, what does survive provides some of the most important evidence we have for the immigrants to New England during this period. For some reason, the towns in Plymouth Colony had greater difficulty than did their neighbors in Massachusetts Bay in filling their pulpits, and so the church records in Plymouth Colony were not kept as diligently as those in Massachusetts Bay.

The town of Plymouth did not have a minister for most of its early history, and lay leaders such as William Brewster carried out many of the pastoral duties. The earliest Plymouth church records include a history of the early church, written many decades later. Death records for a few of the early immigrants appear here, but it is otherwise not very helpful for the years of the *Mayflower* migration. (See PChR in **KEY TO TITLES**.)

When Rev. John Lothrop arrived at Scituate, he organized a church, and kept records of that church during its few years at Scituate, and then for many more years after he and the church had removed to Barnstable [NEHGR 9:279–87, 10:37–43; GMN 5:12]. He recorded baptisms, marriages, burials, admissions, and disciplinary matters.

JOURNALS AND LETTERS

The sources discussed above are almost entirely official documents, which are generally of a formal nature and, with the exception of some court records, do not provide as much insight into individual character and behavior as we might like. There do exist a number of private documents, generally in the form of letters and diaries, which help to give us a more complete picture of the lives of the immigrants. The most important of these for Plymouth Colony are the writings of William Bradford and Edward Winslow. We also include here discussion of the documents created and collected by Governor John Winthrop of Massachusetts Bay, since he frequently took notice of events in Plymouth Colony.

Bradford's History of Plymouth

William Bradford wrote a history of the first twenty years of the existence of Plymouth Colony, prefaced by a history of the congregations in Scrooby and Leiden. This volume was written late in his life, relying heavily on correspondence which Bradford had retained. As a consequence, the chronology of the earlier years is sometimes muddled. Nevertheless, this is an essential source, the most accessible published version of which was prepared by Samuel E. Morison in 1952 as *Of Plymouth Plantation*. The edition published by Worthington C. Ford is also valuable. (As the present volume goes to press, a new edition prepared under the joint sponsorship of the Colonial Society of Massachusetts and the New England Historic Genealogical Society is nearing publication.)

Bradford Letterbook

William Bradford also kept a letterbook, into which he copied both incoming and outgoing correspondence. As with so many of Bradford's manuscripts, this volume had an unusual history, and only a small portion has been preserved, covering the years 1624 through 1630, the surviving portion beginning on page 339 of the original. Even this small remnant is filled with useful information.

These letters were first published in 1794, accompanied by an account of how they were rescued [MHSC 1:3:27–76]. George Ernest Bowman reprinted them more than a century later, and in the interim the original pages had been mislaid again [MD 5:5–16, 75–81, 164–71, 198–201, 6:16–17, 141–47, 207–15, 7:5–12, 79–82]. These several installments were then gathered into a separate publication in 1906 [*Governor William Bradford's Letter Book* (Boston 1906)].

Pamphlets of Edward Winslow

Edward Winslow authored or co-authored a number of detailed accounts of the earliest years of Plymouth Colony. The most important of these are *Mourt's Relation* and *Good News from New England* (for full biographical details see the **KEY TO TITLES** under Mourt and Good News).

Winthrop Journal

The most important diary is more than a diary: John Winthrop's *History of New England from 1630 to 1649* (also known as Winthrop's Journal, and referred to hereinafter as WJ). This lengthy record includes private items, matters relating to the development of Massachusetts Bay and all the other early New England colonies, events at court which did not make it into the official court records, and much more. Winthrop took notice of many Plymouth Colony events. (In the work of the Great Migration Study Project, we use the 1853 edition prepared by James Savage, which contains many useful annotations. The 1908 edition, part of the Original Narratives of Early American History series, was heavily bowdlerized, and should not be relied on. In 1996 Richard S. Dunn and Laetitia Yeandle published an updated version of *The Journal of John Winthrop, 1630–1649,* in which the readings are more accurate than those of Savage, but the annotations not as interesting [Cambridge 1996].)

Winthrop maintained his journal right up until his death in 1649, and so for the first two decades of Massachusetts Bay Colony this is an essential source for information about individuals and about the growth and change of New England communities and institutions, including the affairs of Plymouth Colony.

Winthrop Letters

Just as John Winthrop's journal is the most important diary for the earliest years in Massachusetts, so the vast archive of correspondence collected by the Winthrop family is the largest collection of letters for the period. The Massachusetts Historical Society has published the papers of the Winthrop family from 1498 through 1654 in six volumes, with more to come *(Winthrop Papers,* 6 volumes [Boston, 1925–1992], hereinafter WP). The Winthrop correspondence was also published much earlier in the *Massachusetts Historical Society Collections,* Fourth Series, Vol. 6 & 7, and Fifth Series, Vol. 1 & 8. In this earlier version the letters were arranged by correspondent rather than chronologically, and so for some purposes may be a more convenient source.

HOW TO USE THIS BOOK

This volume on the Mayflower Migration consists of sixty-one sketches comprising the one hundred and four individuals who sailed on the *Mayflower* in 1620. Each sketch follows a regular format, which is described in more detail in the next section, **Key to Sketch Headings**. Every statement in each sketch is supported by a citation to a document. Most of the citations appear in an abbreviated form, the abbreviations being expanded in the last part in this front matter, **KEY TO TITLES**.

Three additional conventions employed in these sketches will help the reader navigate through this book:

> For purposes of internal cross-reference, when a Mayflower passenger is referenced in the sketch of another passenger, he or she will be presented on the first occasion in that sketch in capital letters and italicized, without a page number. For example, *WILLIAM MULLINS* is mentioned in the sketch of John Carver.

> When a name is given all in capital letters but not italicized, this means that that person came to New England during the Great Migration (but not on the *Mayflower*), and is, or will be, the subject of a sketch elsewhere in the Great Migration volumes. The name will be followed by a year and a place, indicating the known or estimated year of migration, and the first residence in New England. If a sketch for this person has already been published in the Great Migration volumes, a volume and page citation will also be added. For example, SAMUEL COLE {1630, Boston} [GMB 1:430–35] represents a sketch published in the first Great Migration volume, while NICHOLAS BUSBY {1637, Dedham} represents a sketch to be published in a future volume.

> A string of citations of the form [Dawes-Gates 1:74, citing Perley 1:254, citing ELR 20:12] or [MD 16:181–82, citing PCLR 2:2:73] may serve one of two purposes. It may indicate a secondary

source that cites a document, when the document itself has not been examined; or it may indicate a published transcript of a document, followed by the citation of the document itself.

KEY TO SKETCH HEADINGS

Each of the persons treated in this volume is presented according to a fixed format, which forces research to answer a series of questions. There are three sections that are rigidly formatted, and then three additional sections which are more flexible in structure. Based on the volume of evidence available, not all of these sections will be included in all sketches.

The first section about migration asks questions related directly to the movements of the family or individual from the date of the last known residence in England to the end of his, her, or their lives. Entries in this section will generally be brief.

The second group of questions is of a biographical nature, attempting to provide answers about occupation, church membership, freemanship, education, officeholding, and wealth.

The third formatted section presents the specifically genealogical material: birth, death, spouses, children, as well as other associations.

These three sections may be followed by a brief **PREMIGRATION BIOGRAPHY**, a free-form space for **COMMENTS** in which a variety of matters may be discussed, and finally, a **BIBLIOGRAPHIC NOTE** for those families that have been frequently treated in print.

Sample Sketch

Below is a sketch of a fictional immigrant, pointing out what is likely to be found under each heading, and what is not.

PRESERVED PILGRIM

Each sketch begins with that portion of William Bradford's accounting of the passengers who sailed on the Mayflower *in 1620 which pertains to the subject of the sketch. This information has been published in a number of places, but we will use the version prepared by Samuel Eliot Morison for his edition of Bradford's history [Bradford 441–43].*

> *This will be followed by the equivalent information compiled*
> *by Bradford for the subject of the sketch in 1651. Again, we rely*
> *on Morison's version [Bradford 443–47].*

ORIGIN: The origin for our purposes is the last known residence in England or the Netherlands before migration. This will frequently be different from the place of birth, and knowledge of this difference can be important in assessing the motivation for migration and connecting the immigrant with others who made the move about the same time. The place of birth will be given as the place of origin only when no other residence in England is known.

An origin will be given only when there is solid evidence. If someone in the past has made a plausible suggestion, or if there is a leading clue, the entry here will be "Unknown," and there will be discussion of the possibilities in the **COMMENTS** section. (Information on place and date of birth, if known, will be given in the genealogical portion of the sketch, under **BIRTH.**)

Two additional criteria for determining **ORIGIN** are employed in this volume. First, in 2005 Caleb Johnson published a brief article analyzing the structure of Bradford's 1651 list of passengers. He discerned an arrangement in which those who came from the Leiden church and those who did not were organized in groups [TAG 80: 94–99]. Second, in 2009 Jeremy Bangs argued that any men or women who sailed on the *Mayflower* as servants to one of the Leiden families should be accounted as having been in Leiden in the 1610s [Strangers and Pilgrims 446–48, 727–28].

PREVIOUS RESIDENCES: This is a new category for Great Migration sketches. In past volumes, information on any residences in England or elsewhere prior to migration, not including the place of residence at the time of migration, might be scattered across other locations in the sketch, but was not gathered together and featured in one place. Adding this category makes that information easier to find and also provides a platform for deeper research into the motives for migration.

MIGRATION: Because this volume is devoted only to passengers on the *Mayflower*, the date of migration given here will in each case be 1620.

FIRST RESIDENCE: Except for those few passengers who died at sea or during the time that the *Mayflower* was anchored in what is now Provincetown Harbor, the place of first settlement is Plymouth.

REMOVES: If the subject of the sketch resided in more than one New England settlement, that information is given here. When the year of removal is known or can be deduced, the entry would say, for example,

"Hartford 1635"; in this instance, we would probably not have a record which explicitly stated that the person made the move in that year, but we would learn from the Cambridge records that the person had received land grants in 1633 and 1634, but did not appear in the land inventory taken in the fall of 1635, indicating early removal to Hartford, in advance of the main party. In many cases we will not be able to fix the date of migration so precisely, and the entry might then read "Windsor by 1648," indicating that the person was of record in Windsor in that year, but his or her last record in the prior place of residence was two or more years earlier.

RETURN TRIPS: This category encompasses movements in which the sometime New England resident returned to England temporarily or permanently, or moved on to a colony outside New England, whether on the mainland or in the Caribbean.

OCCUPATION: This heading will frequently be blank, as many of the early New Englanders left no direct evidence of occupation. Documents abstracted in the sketch, especially deeds, will sometimes state the occupation explicitly. Other evidence, especially probate inventories, will allow an inference as to occupation. For example, the possession of an unusually large number of woodworking tools will allow the conclusion that the immigrant was a carpenter. In most instances when no evidence is available and this category is omitted, we may assume that the person could be described as yeoman or husbandman.

CHURCH MEMBERSHIP: When we have direct evidence from surviving church records of membership in a given church, that knowledge will appear here. Jeremy Bangs has compiled a synthetic list of members of John Robinson's Leiden congregation [Strangers and Pilgrims 703–11]. For many Plymouth Colony settlements we have no surviving church records and no information on church membership. Most importantly, since no records exist for the early Plymouth church, and since no minister was settled there for a long period of time, we will only enter data on membership in Plymouth church for a few people who are mentioned directly in that context by Bradford or some other contemporary writer.

FREEMAN: For this volume this category will be used for two events related to citizenship not normally encountered for other participants in the Great Migration. First, for some of the men who came to Plymouth from Leiden, there is a record of admission to citizenship in Leiden. Second, most of the adult males signed the Mayflower Compact.

For some Plymouth Colony men, records of admission to freemanship were entered in the court minutes. Many freemen were not so recorded, but lists of freemen were compiled periodically, at first for the colony as a whole and then for the entire colony, but organized town by town. The court records also have some entries for men who were propounded for freemanship, but not admitted to that condition. There are also lists of men who took the oath of fidelity, and that data is also recorded here (see **SOURCES** section in this front matter for further discussion).

EDUCATION: The most direct evidence for education will be for those men, mostly ministers, who attended one of the universities in England—Cambridge or Oxford. The only *Mayflower* passenger known to have attended university was *WILLIAM BREWSTER*. Some immigrants also attended a grammar school in England. Beyond evidence of this sort, we will rely principally on three other sources to get some idea of the level of education and literacy reached by a given immigrant: holding an office that required reading and writing ability, such as town clerk; ownership of books, usually found in probate inventories; and ability to sign one's name. Evaluation of the importance of owning books has been augmented by Jeremy Bangs's careful study of books mentioned in probate inventories [Plymouth Libraries].

OFFICES: This category includes both civil service, whether at the town, county, or colony level, and military service. In most sketches we attempt to include all discoverable service, with the limitation that much of the evidence, especially for town offices, remains in manuscript form, not all of which has been searched. For those community leaders who held many higher offices, no attempt has been made here to collect evidence on all lesser offices.

All civil service will be presented first, usually with separate paragraphs for each colony, county, or town in which service has been found. All military service will then be grouped at the end. All ablebodied adult males were expected to serve in the local train band, and evidence of that service will be included in this category; this may amount to nothing more than an entry for a weapon or two in the probate inventory for that individual.

ESTATE: Most of the material included under this heading will be from land and probate records. Much of the evidence for the identities of the children of the immigrants, and the birth order, will be found here. When more detailed argumentation on these points is needed, it will be found under *COMMENTS*.

BIRTH: When we know the English origin of the immigrant, and have the baptismal record, that will be entered here, along with the names of the parents of the immigrant. More frequently, we will not have this information; nevertheless, in almost all cases, an attempt will be made to estimate a year of birth for the immigrant, however crudely. This will be based largely on certain assumptions about the minimum or average age at which certain life events occurred: fourteen to witness a document or choose a guardian; sixteen to become a church member; twenty-one to become a freeman; twenty-five as the approximate age of first marriage for most men; twenty as the approximate age of first marriage for most women.

DEATH: In the absence of a specific record of death, an estimate will be made based on the appearance of the subject in other records. This will frequently be based on probate documents, but there are many other possibilities. In such cases there may be no direct citation of the relevant documents here, as they will almost always be cited more directly under some other heading.

MARRIAGE: For each spouse, data on date and place of marriage, when known, is given, as well as the parents of the spouse, any previous or later spouses of that spouse, and a date of death.

CHILDREN: Evidence that allows us to compile a list of children born to a given couple, and to deduce their birth order, will be found mostly under **ESTATE, COMMENTS,** or both. The criteria for determining the order of birth of a couple's children and for estimating their dates of birth are discussed in detail in the **Chronological Analysis** section above.

We do not attempt here to outline the full career of each child. We wish only to determine whether the child died young, and if not, whether the child eventually married. All known marriages of the child will usually be given, although in a few cases we may only present the first marriage. We do not make a special effort to determine the date of death, although this may be included if it assists in estimating the year of birth.

ASSOCIATIONS: Two different types of information may appear here. First, when the subject of the sketch is related, whether by marriage or by blood, to some other immigrant to New England prior to 1640, and when that relationship existed prior to migration, that information will be shown here. This may simply demonstrate the influence of kinship on migration, or it may provide clues for further research in England. Second, if no such tie to another participant in the Great Migration is known, this will be the place to point out persistent associations with other immigrants, which may provide clues to English origins and group or chain migrations.

PREMIGRATION BIOGRAPHY: This section of the sketch is new to this volume. In compiling the introductory essay, "The Gathering of the *Mayflower* Passengers," identifying evidence that bears on the religious motivation of the passengers and the path that led each to cross the Atlantic in 1620 gained importance. The intent here is to create a brief narrative that describes that path and, where possible, the point where that passenger joined the religious reform movement, whether as a puritan or a separatist. Statements in this section will be documented only when they do not appear elsewhere in the sketch.

COMMENTS: This section provides an opportunity for discussing any matter that does not fit neatly into one of the categories described above. It may include, but is not restricted to, the following:

> Specific records that do not fall into any of the narrowly defined categories above, but which are thought to be of interest. The most common of these will be court appearances, whether in civil or criminal proceedings.

> Discussion of errors or discrepancies, whether in primary or secondary sources. If possible, the discrepancy will be corrected; if not, the arguments in favor of various positions will be presented.

> Evidence and arguments for specific genealogical conclusions. In some cases the records given under *ESTATE* will be sufficient, without further interpretation, to establish the list of children. But when this is not the case, further evidence and argumentation will be given here.

> Suggestions for further research. This will be the case when not all available records have been searched, or when some likely line of research suggests itself.

BIBLIOGRAPHIC NOTE: For some families, there has been sufficient material published to require separate discussion. This will be the case especially when a late-nineteenth-century genealogy has been corrected by more recent articles in the periodical literature, or when there are two or more published genealogies of greatly different value. This note will attempt to point out the relative value of what is in print, in hopes of deterring the continued reliance on outdated and incorrect claims. Although the organization here is generally chronological, in most sketches this section will begin with information on the volumes of the Five Generations Project of the General Society of Mayflower Descendants.

KEY TO TITLES

This listing includes all titles employed in more than one sketch in *The Mayflower Migration*. If a source is used in only one sketch, the full bibliographic details are given in that sketch.

Abandoning Susan Hardman Moore, *Abandoning America: Life-Stories from Early New England* (Woodbridge, Suffolk, 2013)

Austin John Osborne Austin, *The Genealogical Dictionary of Rhode Island ...* (Albany 1887; rpt. Baltimore 1969 [with *addenda et corrigenda* as published in TAG])

BA "A Book of All the Lands which Planters at First or by Alienation Since Possess[ed] Within New Haven Began by R[ichard] P[erry] 1645" [GMN 13:3–7, 9–16, 19–21]

BChR *The Records of the First Church in Boston, 1630–1868,* Publications of the Colonial Society of Massachusetts, Volumes 39, 40 and 41, Richard D. Pierce, ed. (Boston 1961)

Bodge George Madison Bodge, *Soldiers in King Philip's War being A Critical Account of That War with A Concise History of the Indian Wars of New England From 1620–1677* (Leominster, Massachusetts, 1896; rpt. Baltimore 1967)

Bradford William Bradford, *Of Plymouth Plantation, 1620–1647,* Samuel Eliot Morison, ed. (New York 1952)

Bradford LB *Governor William Bradford's Letter Book* (Boston, 1906; rpt. *from Mayflower Descendant,* 1904–6)

BrPR Bristol County, Massachusetts, Probate Records

BrVR *Records of the Town of Braintree, 1640 to 1793,* Samuel A. Bates, ed. (Randolph 1886), pp. 627–940

BVR *Boston Births, Baptisms, Marriages, and Deaths, 1630–1699,* Ninth Report of the Boston Record Commissioners (Boston 1883; rpt. Baltimore 1978)

Dawes-Gates	Mary Walton Ferris, *Dawes-Gates Ancestral Lines*, 2 volumes (n.p., 1943, 1931)
Dexter	Henry Martyn Dexter and Morton Dexter, *The England and Holland of the Pilgrims* (London, 1906; rpt. Baltimore 1978)
DuVR	Duxbury, Massachusetts, Vital Records
Edward Winslow	Jeremy Dupertuis Bangs, *Pilgrim Edward Winslow: New England's First International Diplomat, A Documentary Biography* (Boston 2004)
ELR	Essex County, Massachusetts, Deeds, microfilm copies
English Homes	Charles Edward Banks, *The English Ancestry and Homes of the Pilgrim Fathers ...* (New York c1929)
EPR	*The Probate Records of Essex County, Massachusetts, 1635–1681*, 3 volumes (Salem 1916–1920; rpt. Newburyport, Massachusetts, 1988). Citations to the unpublished probate records are to case numbers, or to register volumes (which begin with volume 301).
EQC	*Records and Files of the Quarterly Courts of Essex County, Massachusetts, 1636–1686*, 9 volumes (Salem 1911–1975)
ERO	Essex Record Office, Chelmsford, England
Ford	William Bradford, *History of Plymouth Plantation, 1620–1647*, Worthington Chauncey Ford, ed., 2 volumes (Boston 1912)
GDMNH	Sybil Noyes, Charles Thornton Libby, and Walter Goodwin Davis, *Genealogical Dictionary of Maine and New Hampshire* (Portland, Maine, 1928–1939; rpt. Baltimore 1972)
GM	Robert Charles Anderson, George F. Sanborn Jr., and Melinde Lutz Sanborn, *The Great Migration: Immigrants to New England, 1634–1635*, Volume I, A–B (Boston 1999); Volume II, C–F (Boston 2001); Volume III, G–H (Boston 2003); Volume IV, I–L (Boston 2005); Volume V, M–P (Boston 2007); Volume VI, R–S (Boston 2009); Volume VII, T–Y (Boston 2011)

GMB	Robert Charles Anderson, *The Great Migration Begins: Immigrants to New England, 1620–1633*, 3 volumes (Boston 1995)
GMN	*Great Migration Newsletter*, Volume 1 through 25 (1990–2016)
GMNJ	*Genealogical Magazine of New Jersey*, Volume 1 through present (1925+)
Good News	"Good Newes From New England: or a true Relation of things very remarkable at the Plantation of Plimoth in New England..." by E[dward] W[inslow], in Alexander Young, *Chronicles of The Pilgrim Fathers of The Colony of Plymouth, From 1602 to 1625 ...*, 2nd edition (Boston 1844; rpt. Baltimore 1974); pp. 271–375
Hubbard	William Hubbard, *A General History of New England from the Discovery to MDCLXXX* (Cambridge 1815)
LCVR	James N. Arnold, *Vital Record of Rhode Island, 1636–1850*, First Series, Volume 4, Part VI, Little Compton (Providence 1893)
Lechford	*Note-book Kept by Thomas Lechford, Esq., Lawyer, in Boston, Massachusetts Bay, from June 27, 1638, to July 29, 1641*, Edward Everett Hale Jr., ed. (Cambridge 1885; rpt. Camden, Maine, 1988). Citations herein refer to the pagination as printed (and not to the manuscript pagination) and will therefore differ from the index entries of the 1885 edition.
Leiden Pilgrims	Johanna W. Tammel, comp., *The Pilgrims and other People from the British Isles in Leiden. 1576–1640* (Isle of Man 1989)
LENE	Daniel Allen Hearn, *Legal Executions in New England, 1623–1960* (Jefferson, North Carolina, 1999)
Magnalia	Cotton Mather, *Magnalia Christi Americana ...*, 2 volumes (Hartford 1855)
MarVR	*Vital Records of Marshfield, Massachusetts, to the year 1850*, Robert M. Sherman and Ruth Wilder Sherman, eds. (n.p. 1970)

Mayflower Passengers	Caleb H. Johnson, *The Mayflower and Her Passengers* (n.p. 2006)
MBCR	*Records of the Governor and Company of the Massachusetts Bay in New England, 1628–1686*, Nathaniel B. Shurtleff, ed., 5 volumes in 6 (Boston 1853–1854)
MD	*Mayflower Descendant*, Volume 1 through present (1899–1937, 1985+)
MF	*Mayflower Families* (the "silver" books)
MFIP	*Mayflower Families in Progress* (the "pink" books)
MiddleVR	*Middleborough, Massachusetts Vital Records*, Barbara Lambert Merrick and Alicia Crane Williams, eds., 2 volumes (Boston 1986, 1990)
MJ	*Mayflower Journal*, Volumes 1 to 3 (2016–2018)
Morison	Samuel Eliot Morison, *The Founding of Harvard College* (Cambridge 1935) [especially for Appendix B, "English University Men Who Emigrated to New England Before 1646," pp. 359–410]
Morton	Nathaniel Morton, *The New-England's Memorial ...* (Plymouth 1826)
Mourt	*A Journal of the Pilgrims at Plymouth. Mourt's Relation. A Relation or Journal of the English Plantations Settled at Plymouth in New England, by Certain English Adventurers Both Merchants and Others*, Dwight B. Heath, ed. (New York 1963)
MQ	*Mayflower Quarterly*, Volume 1 to present (1935+)
NEA	*New England Ancestors*, Volumes 1 through 10 (2000–2009)
NEHGR	*New England Historical and Genealogical Register*, Volume 1 through present (1847+)
New English Canaan	Thomas Morton, *New English Canaan* (Amsterdam 1637; rpt. Boston 1883)
NGSQ	*National Genealogical Society Quarterly*, Volume 1 through present (1912+)
NHCR	*Records of the Colony and Plantation of New Haven, 1638–1649, 1653–1664*, 2 volumes, Charles J. Hoadly, ed. (Hartford 1857–1858)

NHLR	New Haven, Connecticut, Land Records
NHPR	New Haven, Connecticut, Probate Records
NJHSP	*New Jersey Historical Society Proceedings,* four series, 1845 to present
NYGBR	*The New York Genealogical and Biographical Record,* Volume 1 through present (1869+)
ODNB	*Oxford Dictionary of National Biography*
OED	*Oxford English Dictionary*
PCC	Prerogative Court of Canterbury, England
PChR	*Plymouth Church Records, 1620–1859, Part 1 and Part 2* in Publications of the Colonial Society of Massachusetts, Volumes 22 and 23 (Boston 1920, 1923)
PCLR	Plymouth Colony Deeds (from microfilm; Volume 1 has been published as Volume 12 of PCR)
PCPR	Plymouth Colony Probate Records (from microfilm)
PCR	*Records of the Colony of New Plymouth in New England,* Nathaniel B. Shurtleff and David Pulsifer, eds., 12 volumes in 10 (Boston 1855–1861)
Phoebe Tilton Anc	Walter Goodwin Davis, *The Ancestry of Phoebe Tilton, 1775–1847, The Wife of Capt. Abel Lunt of Newburyport, Massachusetts* (Portland 1947)
Plooij	D. Plooij and J. Rendel Harris, *Leyden Documents Relating to the Pilgrim Fathers: Permission to Reside at Leyden and Betrothal Records; together with Parallel Documents from the Amsterdam Archives* (Leiden 1920)
PLR	Plymouth County, Massachusetts, Deeds (from microfilm)
Plymouth Libraries	Jeremy Dupertuis Bangs, ed., *Plymouth Colony's Private Libraries, as Recorded in Wills and Inventories, 1633–1692,* revised edition (Leiden 2018)
PM	Robert Charles Anderson, *The Pilgrim Migration: Immigrants to Plymouth Colony, 1620–1633* (Boston 2004)

PNQ	*Pilgrim Notes and Queries,* Volume 1 through 5 (1913–1917)
PPR	Plymouth County, Massachusetts, Probate Records (from microfilm)
Prince	Thomas Prince, *A Chronological History of New England ...,* Samuel G. Drake, ed., third edition (Boston 1852)
PTR	*Records of the Town of Plymouth,* Volume 1, 1636 to 1705 (Plymouth 1889)
PVR	*Vital Records of Plymouth, Massachusetts, to the Year 1850,* Lee D. van Antwerp, comp., and Ruth Wilder Sherman, ed. (Camden, Maine, 1993)
RICT	*Rhode Island Court Records: Records of the Court of Trials of the Colony of Providence Plantations, 1647–1662,* Volume I (Providence 1920) [RICT 1]; *Rhode Island Court Records: Records of the Court of Trials of the Colony of Providence Plantations, 1662–1670,* Volume II (Providence 1922) [RICT 2]; Jane Fletcher Fiske, trans., *Rhode Island General Court of Trials, 1671–1704* (Boxford, Massachusetts, 1998) [RICT 3]
Savage	James Savage, *A Genealogical Dictionary of the First Settlers of New England,* 4 volumes (Boston 1860–1862; rpt. Baltimore 1965)
SChR	*The Records of the First Church in Salem, Massachusetts, 1629–1736,* Richard D. Pierce, ed. (Salem 1974)
Scrapbook	*The Plymouth Scrap Book, The Oldest Original Documents Extant In Plymouth Archives ...,* Charles Henry Pope, ed. (Boston 1918)
Sewall	*The Diary of Samuel Sewall,* Volume 1, 1674–1708, Volume 2, 1709–1729, M. Halsey Thomas, ed. (New York 1973)
SJC	Supreme Judicial Court, Massachusetts
Small Gen	Lora Altine Woodbury Underhill, *Descendants of Edward Small of New England and the Allied Families with Tracings of English Ancestry,* revised edition, 3 volumes (Boston and New York, 1934)

SPR	Suffolk County, Massachusetts, Probate Records
Strangers and Pilgrims	Jeremy Dupertuis Bangs, *Strangers and Pilgrims, Travellers and Sojourners: Leiden and the Foundations of Plymouth Plantation* (Plymouth, Massachusetts, 2009)
Stratton	Eugene Aubrey Stratton, *Plymouth Colony: Its History & People, 1620–1691* (Salt Lake City 1986)
SwVR	*Vital Records of Swansea, Massachusetts to 1850,* transcribed by H. L. Peter Rounds (Boston 1992)
TAG	*The American Genealogist,* Volume 9 to present (1932+)
TG	*The Genealogist,* Volume 1 to present (1980+)
Three Visitors	Sydney V. James, Jr., *Three Visitors to Early Plymouth* (Plymouth 1963)
Venn	John Venn and J. A. Venn, *Alumni Cantabrigienses, Part I (From the Earliest Times to 1751),* 4 volumes (Cambridge 1922–1927)
Waterhouse Anc	Walter Goodwin Davis, *The Ancestry of Joseph Waterhouse, 1754–1837, of Standish, Maine* (Portland 1949)
Waters	Henry FitzGilbert Waters, *Genealogical Gleanings In England,* 2 volumes (Boston 1901)
WJ	John Winthrop, *The History of New England from 1630 to 1649,* James Savage, ed., 2 volumes (Boston 1853). Citations herein refer to the pagination of the 1853 and not the 1826 edition, even though the index to the 1853 edition continues to use the 1826 pagination.
WP	*Winthrop Papers, 1498–1654,* 6 volumes, various editors (Boston 1925–1992)
Young's Pilgrim Fathers	*Chronicles of the Pilgrim Fathers of the Colony of Plymouth ...,* Alexander Young, ed. (Boston 1844; rpt. Baltimore 1974)

THE GATHERING OF THE
MAYFLOWER PASSENGERS

When the *Mayflower* finally set sail from Plymouth on 6 September 1620, there were just over a hundred passengers on board. How did this complement of migrants come together? How many were members of the Leiden congregation and how many had joined the ship directly from England? How many of them shared the religious beliefs of Reverend John Robinson and the other core members of the Leiden congregation and how many did not?

For centuries the answers to those questions have been formulated in the context of the history of the separatists of Scrooby, Nottinghamshire, and vicinity, and their removal to the Netherlands for a dozen years and then their decision to depart for the New World. Presenting that story of the gathering of the *Mayflower* families still has its value, but the blossoming over the last quarter century of new research on the origins of these migrants is revealing another approach to answering these questions. The discovery of English origins for many of the *Mayflower* passengers is also uncovering hidden pockets of separatism in late Elizabethan and early Jacobean England. In some cases these subterranean communities of separatism had existed for many years before the members of the Scrooby congregation had chosen to leave the Church of England. In the final accounting, the number of members of the Scrooby group who sailed on the *Mayflower* was a small minority of the total passenger complement.

With the new information now in hand, we learn that of the hundred or so passengers on the *Mayflower*, about two-thirds had been members of the Leiden congregation and many of these had earlier belonged to a variety of separatist communities in England. The remaining third of the passengers apparently joined the Leiden Pilgrims at Southampton after the *Speedwell* arrived from Delfshaven, and many of these shared some of the religious beliefs held by those who had just spent a decade in the Netherlands, perhaps not as fully fledged separatists, but many with some degree of reformed puritan inclinations. Indeed, the boundary between puritan and separatist was quite porous. A person who remained nominally within the Church of England but who also frequently attended private puritan meetings might differ little in practice and belief from another person who had made the decision to leave the Church of England. There is a growing tendency to extend the term "puritan" to include "separatists."[1] The passenger complement of the *Mayflower* had slowly accreted over the decade of the 1610s from many locations, and a new version of the Pilgrim story can now be told on the basis of this amalgamation of separatists and nonconformists from many corners of England.[2]

The original intention of the Pilgrims was to cross the Atlantic in two vessels. The smaller of these two ships was the *Speedwell*, which the migrants had acquired in the Netherlands and which they boarded at Delfshaven in July 1620. The *Speedwell* carried most of the members of the Leiden congregation who would eventually sail on the *Mayflower*. On the other hand, the *Speedwell* carried at least three Leiden congregation families who were planning to make the voyage for the New World but in the end, as we shall see, were forced to remain behind and migrate at a later date.

While the *Speedwell* was making its way to Southampton, the *Mayflower* was taking on provisions and probably passengers at London. The latter ship soon made its way down the Thames to the English Channel and then on to its rendezvous with the *Speedwell* at Southampton. Other English passengers may have boarded the vessels directly at Southampton. The various passengers who had never been at Leiden but who ended up on the *Mayflower* are described as being "of London," although they may never have resided in the metropolis.

The two vessels soon set off on their voyage to the New World, but the *Speedwell* proved not to be seaworthy. The small convoy put into Dartmouth and then into Plymouth for repairs, but the *Speedwell* had to be abandoned. The *Mayflower* by itself was unable to carry all the passengers who had been on both vessels, so the passenger complements were reshuffled and a number of families were left behind, some of whom had come from and now returned to Leiden. Those known to have been left behind were the families of Robert Cushman, William Ring, and Thomas Blossom, all of whom eventually migrated to Plymouth.

---

[1] Robert Charles Anderson, *Puritan Pedigrees: The Deep Roots of the Great Migration to New England* (Boston 2018) 2–6.

[2] Jeremy Dupertuis Bangs, "Strangers on the *Mayflower* – Part One," NEA 1:1:60.

PATHWAYS TO THE *MAYFLOWER*

For three-quarters of a century, since its publication at the end of World War II, the ruling paradigm for interpretation of the composition of the passenger complement of the *Mayflower* was that presented by George Willison in *Saints and Strangers*.[3] In his 2009 magnum opus, *Strangers and Pilgrims*, Jeremy Bangs characterized that paradigm as "pitting the original Leiden religious fanatics (as [Willison] considered them and whom he called 'Saints') against the group recruited in England (whom he designated 'Strangers')." Bangs further quotes Willison as stating that "little more than a third of those on board came from Leyden —forty-one to be exact." Bangs then presented his own estimate, noting that there was evidence for a Leiden residence for some of those that Willison had not counted among the Leiden group. He then came up with a new estimate by first observing that the "total number of *Mayflower* passengers who can be identified as having joined from London is seventeen, plus the four Moore children and John Alden." Then, apparently by simple subtraction, he concluded that "leaves 80 of the 102 passengers who were either from Leiden or of uncertain origin but likely to have been from Leiden."[4]

Three developments during the first two decades of this century allow us to undertake an updated accounting of the number of passengers who came from Leiden and the number who came from "London."[5] First, in 2005 Caleb Johnson published a brief article analyzing the structure of Bradford's 1651 list of passengers. He discerned an arrangement in which those who came from the Leiden church and those who did not were organized in groups. We differ with Johnson in only one of his identifications; he assigned Myles Standish to the category of "Leading 'Strangers'" but the evidence shows that Standish and Robinson had a close relationship prior to 1620, which strongly implies that the former was in Leiden before migration. Further research may lead to tweaks in Johnson's analysis, but for the present purposes, and with the one exception noted above, we employ Johnson's results in our new accounting.[6]

Second, in 2009 Jeremy Bangs argued that any men or women who sailed on the *Mayflower* as servants to one of the Leiden families should be

---

[3] George F. Willison, *Saints and Strangers* (New York 1945).

[4] Jeremy Dupertuis Bangs, *Strangers and Pilgrims, Travellers and Sojourners: Leiden and the Foundations of Plymouth Plantation* (Plymouth, Massachusetts, 2009) 613–18.

[5] "London" is placed in quotes in recognition that not all the passengers who joined the *Mayflower* at London or at Southampton were necessarily from London itself. Some of these passengers presumably did have connections with London, but most have not yet been proven.

[6] Caleb Johnson, "New Light on William[1] Bradford's Passenger List of the *Mayflower*," TAG 80:94–99.

accounted as having been in Leiden in the 1610s.[7] In most cases, we have no information about the English origin of these servants, so we cannot tell when and where the servants became associated with the Leiden families. In one case, that of John Howland of Fenstanton, Huntingdonshire, we do have some evidence, not yet fully proved, but suggestive enough to make his placement in Leiden before 1620 and his association with his master a reasonable conclusion. John Carver and Randall Thickens of Leiden had married sisters, daughters of Alexander White. Randall Thickens had a brother in London, Ralph Thickens, who had dealings with a Mr. John Howland, citizen and salter of London. No genealogical connection between the two John Howlands has yet been made, but if such a relationship can be demonstrated, then the presence of the former John Howland in the household of John Carver would be understandable.[8]

Third, over the last two decades many new discoveries of English origins for *Mayflower* passengers, both from Leiden and directly from England, have been published. Several researchers have provided us with this new information, but the most extensive work in this regard has been done by the team of Sue Allan, Caleb Johnson, and Simon Neal.

Different researchers use different numbers for the *Mayflower* passenger contingent that finally left Plymouth in September 1620. The number we will work with is 104, including William Butten who died just before landfall and Oceanus Hopkins and Peregrine White who were born on the *Mayflower*, as well as the two hired hands at the end of Bradford's list, William Trevor and "one Ely."

LEIDEN CONTINGENT [69][9]

Scrooby, Nottinghamshire [6]

The Scrooby, Nottinghamshire, contribution to the *Mayflower* passenger list comprised only six individuals: William Brewster, his wife and two sons, along with William Bradford and Susanna (Jackson) White, the wife of William White (see next group). Brewster (with his family) and Bradford (as yet unmarried) departed England in 1608, spent a year in Amsterdam, and then moved to Leiden in 1609. When Susanna Jackson travelled to the Netherlands is unknown.

7   Bangs, *Strangers and Pilgrims*, 446–48, 727–28. This same principle is applied here to the servants of William White as coming from Amsterdam.
8   Caleb Johnson and Simon Neal, "A 1623 Indenture That References John Howland, Citizen and Salter of London," MD 63:225.
9   The numbers in square brackets represent the number of *Mayflower* passengers in each group and subgroup.

Wisbech, Cambridgeshire [6]

Henry May and his wife and children, along with his sister Jacomine May and half-brother William White, all of Wisbech, Cambridgeshire, migrated to Amsterdam in the summer of 1608, where they joined the Ancient Church led by Francis Johnson. This was about the same time members of the Scrooby congregation were arriving there as well. Before the Scrooby group departed for Leiden a year later, William Bradford would have had the opportunity to become acquainted with Henry May's daughter Dorothy, who would have been eleven years old. Five years later Bradford returned to Amsterdam and married Dorothy. None of the records for a William White in Leiden can be associated with Dorothy's uncle of that name, so he may have remained in Amsterdam until 1620 and joined the Leiden migrants as they departed for Delfshaven, or he may have joined his niece in Leiden at or soon after her marriage, but managed to escape capture in the surviving records.[10] William White's wife, Susanna (Jackson) White, has been included with the Scrooby group, so the six from Wisbech are William White and his two sons (Resolved and Peregrine), his two servants William Holbeck and Edward Thomson, and Dorothy (May) Bradford, the wife of William Bradford.

Southeast Suffolk Separatists [15]

Several of the *Mayflower* passengers belonged to a concentration of "sectary recusants" (separatists) scattered across a string of parishes in an arc to the west of Ipswich, Suffolk. This cluster of families constituted one-seventh of the passenger complement of the *Mayflower*, by far the largest contribution from any one geographical area.

Isaac Allerton was from East Bergholt, Suffolk, and brought with him three children and his servant John Hooke [NEHGR 173:197–205]. (His wife is accounted separately below.) John Allerton of the *Mayflower* was possibly his brother. [6]

John Carver was baptized in 1581 at Great Bealings, Suffolk, and he brought with him his kinswoman Desire Minter, along with four servants: John Howland, Roger Wilder, William Latham and a maidservant [NEHGR 174:5–20]. (John Carver's wife and a fifth servant, Jasper More, are accounted separately below.) [6]

Elizabeth (Barker) Winslow, the first wife of Edward Winslow, was from Chattisham, Suffolk [NEHGR 173:5–17]. (Edward Winslow and his two sons are accounted separately below.) [1]

---

[10] TAG 89:81–94, 168–88.

John Crackstone, who sailed with son John, was married at Stratford St. Mary, Suffolk [TAG 80:100]. [2]

Mary (Norris) Allerton, wife of Isaac Allerton [1]

On 4 November 1611 [NS] at Leiden, Isaac Allerton married Mary Norris, "single woman from Newbury in England." She may have been from Newbury, Berkshire, or from some other English town of that name. Mary Norris may have been a member of John Robinson's Leiden congregation before her marriage, but she certainly belonged to it after that event.

Catherine (White) (Leggatt) Carver, wife of John Carver [1]

About 1609 John Carver married Catherine (White) Leggatt, daughter of Alexander White of Sturton-le-Steeple, Nottinghamshire. Sturton-le-Steeple was also the home parish of Rev. John Robinson, leader of the Leiden congregation.

John Turner [3]

John Turner of England had arrived in Leiden by 1610 when he was made a citizen. At some point during the next decade he became a member of the Leiden congregation. Nothing is known about his English origin or his religious inclinations prior to 1610. When he sailed on the *Mayflower*, Turner was accompanied by his two sons.

Francis Cooke [2]

Francis Cooke, born in England, was already in Leiden in 1603 when he married Hester Mahieu of the Walloon church there. A few years later they travelled back and forth between Leiden and Norwich, Norfolk, where they attended the Walloon church in that city. Sometime after 1611 the couple joined John Robinson's Leiden congregation.

Fuller Brothers, Redenhall, Norfolk [5]

Brothers Edward Fuller (who sailed with his wife and a son) and Samuel Fuller (who sailed with a servant) were born at Redenhall, Norfolk. Edward was born in 1575 and Samuel in 1580. Samuel had moved to Leiden by 1611, where he became a leading member of the Robinson congregation and was in that year chosen as deacon. As discussed in Samuel's sketch, several clues suggest that he may already have belonged to a separatist congregation before his departure from England. Edward may have accompanied his brother to Leiden. Further research in English records might enhance our understanding of the religious evolution of the two brothers.

Degory Priest [1]

Degory Priest of London had arrived in Leiden by 1611 when he married the widow Sarah Vincent, who was the sister of Isaac Allerton. For the remainder of the decade, prior to departing for New England, Priest was associated with various members of John Robinson's Leiden congregation, and Jeremy Bangs accounts him a member of that church [Strangers and Pilgrims 709]. When Degory sailed for New England in 1620, he left his wife and two daughters behind, but they migrated to Plymouth in 1623.

Sandwich Separatists [4]

Before migrating to Leiden, the families of James Chilton and Moses Fletcher had resided at Sandwich, Kent, where they were members of the parish of St. Peter. In 1609 Moses Fletcher and James Chilton's wife were excommunicated for objecting to the burial practices of the Church of England, and Moses Fletcher was excommunicated again in 1610. Neither family is seen at Sandwich after 1610. Fletcher had arrived in Leiden by 1613 and the Chiltons were there by 1615. Many other Sandwich families moved to Leiden and became active in John Robinson's congregation, including Richard Masterson, Roger Wilson and John Ellis [NEHGR 153:407-12, 154:353-69; MJ 2:38-44]. The Sandwich contingent on the *Mayflower* consisted of James Chilton, his wife, his daughter Mary, and Moses Fletcher (whose wife and children remained behind in Leiden).

Thomas Rogers, Watford, Northamptonshire [2]

Thomas Rogers, who sailed with his son, was born at Watford, Northamptonshire, about 1572 and resided there at least until 1613 when his sixth and last known child was born. By 1617 he had settled at Leiden, where he bought a house. Nothing is known of his or his wife's religious inclinations before their arrival in the Netherlands.

Tilley Brothers, Henlow, Bedfordshire [7]

John Tilley (with his wife and daughter) and his brother Edward (with his wife and her niece Humility Cooper and nephew Henry Samson) all derived from Henlow, Bedfordshire. In early 1618 Edward Tilley first appears in Leiden records, in a document that was signed by Robert Cooper, almost certainly Humility Cooper's father. In the absence of further evidence, we assume that all members of this family group migrated from England to Leiden together, arriving no later than the spring of 1618. Nothing is known about the religious inclinations of any of them before their arrival in the Netherlands.

Myles Standish [2]

Myles Standish, who sailed with his wife Rose, was born in the early 1580s, probably on the Isle of Man. As a young man he became a soldier and served in the Dutch wars during the early years of the seventeenth century. This service placed him in Leiden frequently, and when John Robinson and his group arrived there in 1609, Standish became acquainted with them, becoming a good friend of Robinson. Jeremy Bangs has argued "that there is no evidence that Standish was not a member of the Pilgrim congregation, and that there are several circumstances strongly suggesting that he was a member" [MQ 72:139–43].

Edward Winslow, Droitwich, Worcestershire [4]

Edward Winslow was born at Droitwich, Worcestershire, in 1595. After attending the King's School of Worcester Cathedral from 1606 to 1611, he was apprenticed to John Beale, stationer and citizen of London, "for the term of eight years, from the 19th day of August, 1613." Jeremy Bangs lists a number of volumes that Beale published that had been written by puritan authors and comments that "these Puritan works may have influenced Winslow's religious thinking." In 1617 Winslow removed to Leiden where he worked with William Brewster in his publishing ventures and also joined John Robinson's congregation [Winslow 3-5]. (Edward Winslow's wife is accounted above with the Southeast Suffolk Separatists.) Although Caleb Johnson's analysis did not include Edward's brother Gilbert Winslow among the Leiden contingent, the probability is high that he made the voyage with the encouragement of his brother, and so we include him here, along with Edward's two servants, George Soule and Elias Story.

Thomas Tinker [3]

Thomas Tinker, Englishman, was made a citizen of Leiden in 1617. Nothing is known about his English origin or his religious inclinations prior to 1617. When he sailed on the *Mayflower*, Tinker was accompanied by his wife and a son.

Francis Eaton, Bristol [3]

Francis Eaton was born 1596 in Bristol, where he probably grew to adulthood and served an apprenticeship as a carpenter. Other than this speculation, nothing is known of his life in England thereafter. In his analysis of Bradford's list of *Mayflower* passengers, Caleb Johnson included Francis Eaton, his wife, and his son among those who came from Leiden, although no record of the family has been found there [TAG 80:99]. Nothing is known about the religious inclinations of Francis Eaton before he arrived in Leiden.

John Rigdale [2]

In his analysis of Bradford's list of *Mayflower* passengers, Caleb Johnson included the Rigdales among those who came from Leiden, although no record of the family has been found there [TAG 80:99]. Nothing is known about the English origin or the religious inclinations of John Rigdale and his wife before they boarded the *Mayflower*.

John Goodman [1]

Nothing is known of the English origin of John Goodman or his religious beliefs. He is included among the Leiden contingent based on Caleb Johnson's analysis of Bradford's list of passengers.

Thomas Williams [1]

Nothing is known of the English origin of Thomas Williams or his religious beliefs. He is included among the Leiden contingent based on Caleb Johnson's analysis of Bradford's list of passengers.

"LONDON" CONTINGENT [35]

Dorking, Surrey [6]

William Mullins (who brought a wife, two children, and a servant) and Peter Brown were both from Dorking, Surrey, and presumably boarded the *Mayflower* in London or, perhaps, at Southampton. No evidence has been found of their religious inclinations prior to 1620.[11] But Dorking must have been a center of some sort of nonconformist activity, as several other families from that town migrated to New England over the next decade. John Brown, brother of Peter, settled at Duxbury, Massachusetts, by 1632 [PM 80–82]. Christopher Hussey migrated in 1633 and went first to Lynn, Massachusetts [GMB 1048–52; TAG 79:177–78]. In 1635 two other Dorking families, headed by William Bassett and Hugh Burt, sailed to

---

[11] In 1929 Charles Edward Banks wrote that in 1616 "the Privy Council issued a 'warrant to John Manington, to apprehend and bring one William Mollins before their lordships,'" suggesting that this document might have referred to the *Mayflower* passenger and might have involved a religious infraction. Caleb Johnson observed that the name William Mullins was not that uncommon and the record as presented by Banks does not refer to any religious problem [MD 61:24].

New England on the *Abigail* and joined Hussey at Lynn [GM 2:1:190–95, 501–4; TAG 79:181–83]. Hugh Mason, who also came to New England in 1635 and settled at Watertown, had come from Maldon, Essex, but he had been born at Dorking [GM 2:5:74–81]. Finally, Stockdale Coddington from Dorking had arrived in New England by 1641 and resided at Roxbury, Massachusetts [TAG 79:179–80]. In his work on William Mullins, Caleb Johnson demonstrated many connections among all these families when they were living at Dorking.

Normally when one encounters this many Great Migration families deriving from the same town, one expects that they constituted what is referred to as a clerical company, that is, a group of families associating with and migrating with a charismatic puritan minister. But this does not seem to be the case with these Dorking families. First, they did not arrive in the space of just two or three years, as was common with most clerical companies, but came to New England over a period of two decades. Second, they did not all settle in the same town upon arrival in New England. Third, they do not seem to have been accompanied to New England by a minister, and there does not seem to have been a puritan minister at Dorking in the early seventeenth century.

There is, however, substantial evidence of puritan activity in the immediate vicinity of Dorking. In the early decades of the seventeenth century, Dorking and the nearby town of Guildford hosted combination lectures, a regular series of sermons in which preachers from neighboring towns took turns in the pulpit; these lectures were not necessarily dominated by puritan ministers, but this seems to have been the case for both Dorking and Guildford.[12] Just a few miles to the south of Dorking was the parish of Ockley, Surrey, where the rector from 1618 to 1638 was Henry Whitefield, a prominent puritan who himself led a clerical company to Guilford, Connecticut, in the late 1630s [Morison 406]. Further research in Surrey records might teach us more about this cluster of migrants from Dorking.

Christopher Martin, Billericay, Great Burstead, Essex [4]

Christopher Martin was born about 1582 and was from 1607 to 1620 active as a merchant in the town of Billericay in the parish of Great Burstead, Essex. In 1612 and 1620 he was presented in the church courts for activities that indicate he held puritan views. Presumably because of his mercantile connections with London, he was chosen in 1620 to work with John Carver and Robert Cushman in preparing for the voyage to New England. He failed to follow instructions and angered the leaders of the Leiden contingent. When he sailed on the *Mayflower*, he was accompanied by his wife and by two servants, Solomon Prower (his stepson) and John Langmore.

---

[12] Patrick Collinson, *Godly People: Essays on English Protestantism and Puritanism* (London 1983) 485.

Richard Warren, Great Amwell, Hertfordshire [1]

Richard Warren was born about 1585 and married Elizabeth Walker at Great Amwell, Hertfordshire, in 1610. When Richard Warren sailed for New England in 1620 he left his wife and five daughters behind; they arrived at Plymouth in 1623. Soon after arrival in New England Richard was said to be of London; although no records placing him in that city have been discovered, he had known connections to the city by marriage [TAG 78:274–75]. Nothing definitive is known about the religious inclinations of Richard Warren and his wife. There are, however, some hints of puritan connections that would be worth pursuing. First, Great Amwell was a known center of puritan activity in the 1620s that sent a number of migrants to New England and may have been so at the time of Richard Warren's marriage.[13] Second, Richard Warren's wife was aunt to Rev. Simon Adams of Aston-le-Walls, Northamptonshire, another parish with known puritan activity (although nothing has been discovered about the religious beliefs of Simon Adams).[14]

Richard More and Siblings, Shipton, Shropshire [4]

Samuel More married his cousin Catherine More in 1611 and over the next five years the couple had four children: Elinor, Jasper, Richard and Mary. By 1616 Samuel had come to the conclusion that some or all of these children were not biologically his and that the father was actually a man named Jacob Blakeway. Samuel then decided to divorce Catherine, a process which dragged on for the next four years. At the end of these proceedings, Samuel More sought to find a new home for the children, and through his London connections approached Thomas Weston about getting them on the ships that the latter was organizing for a voyage to Virginia. Weston then turned the problem over to Robert Cushman and John Carver, who placed the four children with the Carver, Brewster, and Winslow families on the *Mayflower*. The four children in 1620 were aged from four to eight years old and presumably did not have any firm religious convictions of their own. Interestingly, however, Samuel More's father Richard More of Linley was a man of "firm, if not radical, puritan sympathies," suggesting that "religious considerations influenced the Mores in choosing this particular means of disposing of the children."[15]

---

13 Anderson, *Puritan Pedigrees*, 274–80.

14 W. J. Sheils, *The Puritans in the Diocese of Peterborough, 1558–1610* (Northampton 1979) 65.

15 MD 43:123–32, 44:11–20, 109–18, especially 44:113.

Stephen Hopkins, Hursley, Hampshire [8]

Stephen Hopkins was born in Upper Clatford, Hampshire, and was raised there and in the city of Winchester. He married his first wife by 1604 and with her had three children born at Hursley, Hampshire, where he ran a shop in town. In 1609 he sailed for Virginia but was shipwrecked on Bermuda; a year later he reached Virginia where he lived for several years. By early 1618 he was back in England where he married a second time, and soon joined with other London merchants who were assisting in the financing of the Pilgrims' voyage to New England. Based on Hopkins's activities on Bermuda in 1609-10, Jeremy Bangs describes him as "a non-Separatist whose notable piety, literacy, and familiarity with the Bible brought him to the attention of the minister who accompanied the ship of Sir George Somers on its ill-fated attempt to reach Virginia" [Strangers and Pilgrims 616–18]. This minister who fetched up on Bermuda along with Hopkins and others was described as a "godly preacher," suggesting that Hopkins himself had puritan tendencies at least. The eight members of this household were Stephen himself, his wife Elizabeth, his four children Giles, Constance, Damaris, and Oceanus, and servants Edward Doty and Edward Leister.

John Alden [1]

John Alden was hired as the company's cooper when the *Mayflower* and the *Speedwell* were at Southampton in the summer of 1620. Nothing is known about his English origins or about his religious inclinations before 1620.

John Billington, Spalding, Lincolnshire [4]

John Billington was born about 1579 and married about 1604. In 1612 he and his family were residing at Spalding, Lincolnshire, but nothing else is known about them prior to 1620. Billington and his wife, who travelled with two sons, were apparently recruited for the voyage by Robert Cushman, but their residence at this time is unknown. Nothing is known about the religious inclinations of John Billington and his wife, but the persistent antisocial behavior of this family once they arrived in New England suggests they did not share the religious beliefs of most of the other *Mayflower* passengers.

Miscellaneous [7]

There remain seven single men about whom little can be said. There is no evidence that any of them resided at Leiden and nothing is known about their English origins or their religious inclinations: Richard Britteridge,

Richard Clarke, Thomas English, _____ Ely, Richard Gardiner, Edmund Margesson, and William Trevor.

SUMMARY

We propose that, in the current state of research and given the parameters we have stated above, there were sixty-nine passengers who were from or had some close definable relationship with Leiden and thirty-five who did not, almost exactly a two-thirds versus one-third split. This comes in shorter on the Leiden side than does Bangs's accounting. The explanation for this is two-fold, on the one side our reliance on Johnson's analysis of Bradford's list and on the other side Bangs's inclusion in his estimate of eighty of those "of uncertain origin but likely to have been from Leiden." Our result is therefore somewhat more conservative than Bangs's, but future research will undoubtedly change both our numbers.

The new research of the last two decades has produced two discoveries beyond the straightforward demonstration of new English origins, and each of these discoveries should stimulate further investigations. The first of these finds is that a number of the Leiden Pilgrims had belonged to separatist communities in late Elizabethan and early Jacobean England, communities that have not previously had much attention from historians or genealogists. The most important of these is the one labeled above as the Southeast Suffolk Separatists. Most histories of religion in Suffolk have not taken notice of this group. Only in 2004 did historian Joy Rowe publish an article describing them and pointing to the diocesan list of sectary (or Brownist) recusants that the team of Allan, Johnson, and Neal exploited in making their discoveries.[16]

One path for further research on this front could be the brothers Samuel and Edward Fuller. Samuel Fuller was in Leiden by 1611 and at that date appears as deacon of John Robinson's congregation, only two years after that gathering had been founded. This would suggest that upon arrival in Leiden Fuller was known or recognized as someone who already had experience with separatism. The long-noted failure to find marriage records and baptismal records for the children of the Fuller brothers would be explained if they belonged to separatist meetings in England, long before leaving for Leiden. Further research with this in mind could be fruitful.

---

[16] Joy Rowe, "Protestant Sectaries and Separatists in Suffolk 1594–1630," *The Journal of the United Reformed Church History Society* 7 (2004):225–34.

The second new discovery of recent decades is the information elicited about the premigration religious activities of some members of the non-Leiden group, which, although they did not necessarily extend to separatism, in some cases exhibited something approaching radical puritanism. As noted at the beginning of this essay, there could be little difference between nonconformists who remained within the Church of England and separatists who had cut their associations with the national church. More directly related to the position of the Leiden Pilgrims, during the 1610s their religious leader, John Robinson, had moved away from a strict separatist position which barred communion with those who still remained within the Church of England. In 1610, just a year after Robinson and his congregation had moved from Amsterdam to Leiden, three leading English puritans—William Ames, Henry Jacob, and Robert Parker—appeared in Leiden, where they resided for some months and engaged in discussions with Robinson. In part because of these conversations, by 1620 Robinson had moved to a much more moderate position, in which he recognized and valued the positions of many of the reformers who had not moved to separatism and was willing to have religious interactions with them.[17] In this context, the religious activities of many of the "London" passengers who joined the *Mayflower* in England, even if those activities did not extend to a strict separatism, were not so far from the beliefs and practices of the Leiden Pilgrims.

One example of reformist activity among the "London" passengers would be the appearances of Christopher Martin before the church courts. Other examples that deserve further research on these grounds would be William Mullins and Richard Warren, as described above. In general, research on the English origins of those who arrived during the Great Migration should include investigations of the church court records, in hope of learning about their religious inclinations on the verge of migration.

Finally, we return to the theme of two different ways to tell the Pilgrim story. In this essay we have attempted to show how John Robinson's congregation at Leiden grew by accretion during the 1610s, acting as a magnet for other English men and women with separatist sympathies. The original core of the Scrooby contingent was enlarged by separatists from southeast Suffolk and from Sandwich and elsewhere. One result of that development was that once the decision was made to migrate to the New World, the passenger list for the *Mayflower* included relatively few who had started out in Scrooby.

---

[17] Michael P. Winship, *Godly Republicanism: Puritans, Pilgrims, and a City on a Hill* (Cambridge, Massachusetts, 2012), Chapter 4, "The Triumphs and Trials of the Lord's Free People."

Willison was aware of this, pointing out that "only three of the company were from Scrooby—William and Mary Brewster and William Bradford."[18] Presumably Willison implicitly included in his accounting the two Brewster children, but the only change to this number in the last three-quarters of a century has been the discovery that Susanna (Jackson) White, the wife of William White, was daughter of Richard Jackson of Scrooby.[19]

Even with this modern change of focus, however, the older, Scrooby-based narrative still has considerable force and relevance.[20] The leaders of the Leiden congregation and then the new settlement at Plymouth were members of the Scrooby separatist meeting: William Brewster, John Robinson, and William Bradford. John Robinson, who joined Richard Clifton as minister at Scrooby, probably in 1607, became the clerical leader of the Leiden congregation in 1609, when the Scrooby contingent made the move from Amsterdam to Leiden, and Richard Clifton chose to remain in Amsterdam. At the last minute, as preparations were being made for the 1620 voyage, the decision was made that Robinson would stay behind in Leiden to care for those who could not leave at that time. He hoped and planned to join the Plymouth settlers, but this plan failed when he died in 1625.

William Bradford of Austerfield probably joined the Scrooby congregation in 1606 or 1607, after hearing Clifton preach at Bawtry, a market town between Austerfield and Scrooby. He was at the time still a teenager, and although he must already have shown promise of having leadership potential, it would take some years for him to grow into this role. When the *Mayflower* sailed in 1620, Bradford was thirty years old, and when Governor John Carver died at Plymouth in the spring of 1621, Bradford was chosen to succeed him and became the most important political figure in the colony until his death.

William Brewster is the unbroken thread in the whole story. As early as 1598 he was called before the church courts to answer for "repeating of sermons"; historian Ronald Marchant suggested that "it is likely that [this practice] existed in a similar form for a number of years before and after that date, and at least from the time Brewster returned home" in 1589.[21] In 1606 he was instrumental in organizing the Scrooby separatist congregation and hosting its meetings at Scrooby Manor. In 1609 when the Scrooby

---

[18] Willison, *Saints and Strangers*, 129.
[19] Sue Allan, Caleb Johnson, and Simon Neal, "The Origin of *Mayflower* Passenger Susanna[1] (Jackson) (White) Winslow," TAG 89 (2017):241–64.
[20] The best survey of the Scrooby story is Jeremy Bangs's comprehensive accounting in *Strangers and Pilgrims, Travellers and Sojourners: Leiden and the Foundations of Plymouth Plantation* (Plymouth, Massachusetts, 2009).
[21] Marchant, *Puritans and the Church Courts*, 141–42.

congregation arrived at Leiden, Brewster was made ruling elder, the leading layman of the group. And in 1620, when the decision was made that John Robinson would remain in Leiden for a few more years, Brewster as ruling elder became the leader of the church at Plymouth.

Plymouth Colony would not have happened if the leadership of the Scrooby-Leiden congregation, leadership that was dominated by founders of the Scrooby congregation, had not made a series of decisions of critical importance. First, of course, was the decision to leave England for the Low Countries to escape the pressures of the Church of England authorities. Second, the decision to move to Leiden from Amsterdam in 1609, just a year after their arrival in the latter city, was made at least in part to escape the fractious nature of the Ancient Church at Amsterdam. And finally, the third decision was to leave Leiden and sail for the New World, at least in part because they feared that the younger generation would become so assimilated into the Dutch population that they might lose their distinct identity.

When Bradford wrote about the organization of the separatist communities in Nottinghamshire and vicinity in 1606 and 1607, he briefly told the story of the church gathered by John Smyth at Gainsborough, Lincolnshire. Bradford relates that in "one of these churches (besides others of note) was Mr. John Smith, a man of able gifts and a good preacher, who afterwards was chosen their pastor. But these afterwards falling into some errors in the Low Countries, there (for the most part) buried themselves and their names."[22] The decisive actions of the Scrooby core of the Leiden congregation ensured that the Pilgrims did not bury themselves and their names.

---

[22] Bradford, *Of Plymouth Plantation*, 9.

GENEALOGICAL SKETCHES

JOHN ALDEN

John Alden was hired for a cooper at Southampton where the ship victualled, and being a hopeful young man was much desired but left to his own liking to go or stay when he came here, but he stayed and married here.

John Alden married with Priscilla, Mr. Mullins's daughter, and had issue by her as is before related.

ORIGIN: Southampton.
MIGRATION: 1620 on the *Mayflower.*
FIRST RESIDENCE: Plymouth.
REMOVES: Duxbury.

OCCUPATION: Cooper. Hired as a cooper at Southampton in 1620. His inventory included "coopers tools" valued at £1 2s. [PPR 1:10; MD 3:10].
FREEMAN: On 11 November 1620, John Alden signed the Mayflower Compact [Morton 26].

In the 1633 Plymouth list of freemen, among those admitted prior to 1 January 1632/3 [PCR 1:3] and in the list of 7 March 1636/7 [PCR 1:52]. In the Duxbury sections of the Plymouth Colony lists of 1639 and 1658 [PCR 8:174, 198].
EDUCATION: Although there is no direct evidence for his literary and educational attainments, his extensive public service, including especially his appointments as colony treasurer and to committees on revising the laws, certainly indicates that he must have been well educated. He signed his name to legal documents [MD 60:146–47].
OFFICES: Assistant, 6 February 1631/2 [WP 3:65], 1 January 1632/3, 1 January 1633/4, 1 January 1634/5, 5 January 1635/6, 3 January 1636/7, 6 March 1637/8, 4 March 1638/9 [PCR 1:5, 21, 32, 36, 48, 79, 116 (the assistants elected on 3 March 1639/40 were not sworn until 2 June 1640, so John Alden continued to serve as assistant at a few courts in early 1640)]. Assistant each year from 1650 to 1686 [PCR 2:153, 166, 3:7, 30, 48, 77, 99, 114, 134, 162, 187, 214, 4:13, 36, 60, 90, 122, 147, 179, 5:17, 34, 55, 90, 112, 143, 163, 194, 229, 256, 6:9, 34, 58, 83, 106, 127, 164, 185].

Acted as Deputy Governor on two occasions, in absence of Governor, 7 March 1664/5, 30 October 1677 [PCR 4:81, 5:245]. Treasurer, 3 June 1656, 3 June 1657, 1 June 1658 [PCR 3:99, 115, 135]. Council of War, 27 September 1642, 10 October 1643, 2 June 1646, 6 April 1653, 12 May 1653, 1 June 1658, 2 April 1667 [PCR 2:46, 63, 100, 3:26, 28, 138, 4:145].

Committee to revise laws, 4 June 1645, 3 June 1657 [PCR 2:85, 3:117]. Committee on Kennebec trade, 3 March 1645/6, 7 June 1648, 8 June 1649, 5 March 1655/6 [PCR 2:96, 127, 144, 3:96]. Appointed to numerous other minor posts and committees by Plymouth General Court.

Deputy for Duxbury to Plymouth General Court 1641, 1642, 1644, and 1646 to 1649, and also at courts of 20 August 1644, 28 October 1645, and 3 March 1645/6 [PCR 2:16, 40, 72, 75, 94, 95, 104, 117, 123, 144].

"Mr. John Alden Senior" is in the Duxbury section of the 1643 list of men able to bear arms [PCR 8:189]. His inventory included "2 old guns" valued at 11s. [PPR 1:10; MD 3:10].

ESTATE: In the 1623 Plymouth land division granted an unknown number of acres as a passenger on the *Mayflower* in 1620 [PCR 12:4]. (Robert S. Wakefield suggests that this is four acres, for John Alden, Priscilla (Mullins) Alden, and her deceased parents [MQ 40:13].) In the 1627 Plymouth cattle division, included in company of John Howland, along with wife Priscilla, daughter Elizabeth, and son John [PCR 12:10].

John Alden was one of the Purchasers, those who acquired the rights to land distributions in Plymouth Colony as a consequence of the agreement made between the London merchants and the Plymouth settlers in 1627 [Ford 282–88].

Assessed £1 4s. in Plymouth tax lists of 25 March 1633 and 27 March 1634 [PCR 1:9, 27].

Assigned mowing ground for the year, 14 March 1635/6, 20 March 1636/7 [PCR 1:40, 56].

On 6 March 1636/7, "[a] parcel of land containing a knoll, or a little hill, lying over against Mr. Alden's land at Blewfish River, is granted by the Court unto the said Mr. John Alden in lieu of a parcel of land taken from him (next unto Samuel Nash's lands) for public use" [PCR 1:51].

Granted "certain lands at Green's Harbor," 5 February 1637/8 [PCR 1:76]. Granted to Myles Standish and John Alden three hundred acres "on the north side of the South River," 2 July 1638 [PCR 1:91]. Granted "a little parcel of land ... lying at the southerly side of his lot," 3 September 1638 [PCR 1:95].

On 3 June 1657, "liberty is granted unto Mr. John Alden to look out a portion of land to accommodate his sons withal, and to make report thereof unto the Court, that so it may be confirmed unto him" [PCR 3:120]. On 13 June 1660, "[i]n regard that Mr. Alden is low in his estate, and occasioned to spend much time at the courts on the country's occasions, and so hath done this many years, the Court have allowed him a small gratuity, the sum of ten pounds, to be paid by the Treasurer" [PCR 3:195].

Granted "a competency of land" at Namasskett, 7 June 1665 [PCR 4:95]. Granted one hundred acres at Teticutt, 4 March 1673/4 [PCR 5:141].

On 8 July 1674, John Alden of Duxbury "for love and natural affection and other valuable causes and considerations" deeded to "David Alden his true and natural son all that his land both meadow and upland that belongs unto him situate or being at or about a place called Rootey Brook within the Township of Middleborough ... excepting only one hundred acres," containing about three hundred acres [PLR 3:330]. On 1 April 1679, "John Alden of Duxborough ..., gentleman," deeded to "Joseph Alden my true and natural son ... all that my share of land ... within the township of Bridgewater" [PLR 3:194].

A description of a parcel of land of "Mr. John Aldin, of Duxbery," is entered under date of 4 December 1637, but with the modern annotation that this is a later entry, and with the internal statement that one of the abutters was "Philip Delano, deceased," which means that the entry must have been made in 1687 or later; this is immediately followed by an entry for another parcel of land which Alden bought of Edward Hall in 1651 [PCR 1:71, 73].

On 1 January 1684[/5] [36 Charles II], John Alden Sr. of Duxbury for "that real love and parental affection which I bear to my beloved and dutiful son Jonathan Alden" deeded to him all my upland in Duxbury, for which "see old book of grants and bounds of land anno 1637 folio 137," and all other lands at Duxbury whether granted by court at Plymouth or town of Duxbury [PLR 6:53].

On 13 January 1686[/7] [2 James II], John Alden Sr. of Duxbury for "that natural love and affection which I bear to my firstborn and dutiful son John Alden of Boston" deeded him one hundred acres at Pekard Neck *alias* Pachague with one-eighth of the meadow belonging to that place, and one hundred acres at Rootey Brook (brother David Alden is to have first right of purchase if John should wish to sell this hundred acres), together with a sixteen shilling purchase being the fifteenth lot, all in Middleborough, and one hundred acres, the first in a division of one thousand acres in Bridgewater [PLR 5:427].

On 19 August 1687, "John Alden Senior of Duxborough ..., cooper," deeded to "my two sons Jonathan & David Alden ... five acres of saltmarsh at Duxbury" and "my whole proportion in the Major's Purchase commonly so-called being the thirty-fifth part of said purchase" [MD 9:145, citing PLR 4:65].

The inventory of the estate of John Alden, taken 31 October 1687, totaled £49 17s. 6d., all moveables. On 13 June 1688, the heirs of John Alden Sr. of Duxbury signed a release in favor of Jonathan Alden, stating that they had received their portion of the estate; those signing were Alexander Standish (in the right of his wife Sarah deceased), John Bass (in the right of his wife Ruth deceased), Mary Alden, Thomas Delano, John Alden, Joseph Alden, David Alden, Priscilla Alden, and William Pabodie [PPR 1:10, 16; MD 3:10–11].

BIRTH: About 1599 (deposed on 6 July 1682 "aged 83 years or there abouts" [PCR 7:256; MD 3:120]; in his 89th year at death on 12 September 1687 [MD 9:129]; "about eighty-nine years of age" at death on 12 September 1687 [MD 34:49]).

DEATH: Duxbury 12 September 1687 [Sewall 150; MD 9:129, 34:49].

MARRIAGE: Plymouth about 1623 Priscilla Mullins, daughter of *WILLIAM MULLINS*. She died after 1651, when she is mentioned in Bradford's summary of *Mayflower* passengers.

CHILDREN:

    i ELIZABETH ALDEN, b. about 1624; m. Plymouth 26 (or 20) December 1644 William Pabodie [PCR 2:79; DuVR]; she d. Little Compton 31 May 1717 [LCVR 143], "a. 92" [*Boston News-Letter*]. (Her tombstone at Little Compton gives her age at death as "in the 94th year of her age," but as the current monument was erected in 1882, this information may not have been on the original stone.)

    ii JOHN ALDEN, b. about 1626; m. Boston 1 April 1660 "Elizabeth Everill, widow, relict of Abiell Everill, deceased" (although the correct date should probably be 1659, as a child was born to John and Elizabeth Alden on 17 December 1659 [BVR 69], and in the original form of the vital records, given in the second of the following citations but not in the first, this birth record is imbedded among others for 1659) [BVR 76; NEHGR 18:333; but see NEHGR 52:162 and Munsey-Hopkins 55, which interpret the 1659 birth record to imply that John Alden had had an earlier wife, also named Elizabeth]; she was born before 1640, daughter of WILLIAM PHILLIPS {1639, Charlestown}, and m. Boston 6 July 1655 Abiel Everill [BVR 52], son of

JAMES EVERILL {1634, Boston} [GM 2:2:469–76]; John Alden d. 14 March 1701/2 [Sewall 463].

iii JOSEPH ALDEN, b. about 1627 (in list of men able to bear arms in 1643, and therefore at least 16 [PCR 8:189]); m. by about 1660 Mary Simonson, daughter of MOSES SIMONSON {1621, Plymouth} [MD 31:60; GMB 3:1681–83; PM 419].

iv PRISCILLA ALDEN, b. say 1630; living unm. in 1688 [PPR 1:16].

v JONATHAN ALDEN, b. about 1632; m. Duxbury 10 December 1672 Abigail Hallett, daughter of ANDREW HALLETT {1635, Dorchester} [GM 2:3:195–200]. Jonathan Alden d. Duxbury 14 February 1696/7 "in the 65 year of his age" [MD 9:159; NEHGR 52:365]. (The date on the tombstone is 14 February 1697, but the double-dating problem is resolved by the probate papers, as administration on the estate was granted on 8 March 1696/7 [MD 6:174–78].)

vi SARAH ALDEN, b. say 1634; m. by about 1660 Alexander Standish (date based on approximated birthdates of children [NEHGR 52:363–65]), son of *MYLES STANDISH*.

vii RUTH ALDEN, b. say 1636; m. Braintree 3 February 1657/8 John Bass [BrVR 716], son of SAMUEL BASS {1633, Roxbury} [GMB 1:122–27].

viii MARY ALDEN, b. say 1638; living unm. in 1688 [PPR 1:16].

ix REBECCA ALDEN, b. say 1640; subject of unfounded rumor that she was "with child," 1 October 1661 [PCR 4:7]; m. in 1667, before 30 October, Thomas Delano [PCR 4:168, 8:122; NEHGR 102:83, 86], son of PHILIP DELANO {1621, Plymouth} [PM 165].

x DAVID ALDEN, b. say 1642; m. by 1674 Mary Southworth, daughter of CONSTANT SOUTHWORTH {1628, Plymouth} [PM 437] (in his will, dated 27 February 1678, Constant Southworth bequeathed to daughter Mary Alden [PCPR 4:1:18–20]).

COMMENTS: Many suggestions have been made as to the English origin of John Alden. Alicia Crane Williams has examined all the relevant evidence carefully and exhaustively, and came to the conclusion that, although one or two of the suggested origins are "tempting," all are far from proved [MD 39:111–22, 40:133–36, 41:201]. By entering "Southampton" under **ORIGIN** above, we are only taking note of Bradford's statement that Alden was hired at that port; we are not implying that he was born or raised there.

In 1651 Bradford stated under his account of William Mullins that "his daughter Priscilla survived, and married with John Alden; who are both living and have eleven [*sic*] children. And their eldest daughter is married and hath five children" [Bradford 445]. (As the marginal annotation for this entry gives the "increasing" as fifteen, and the eldest daughter already had five children, the correct number of children for John and Priscilla is more likely ten, which conforms with our overall knowledge of the family [MD 39:111].)

The present account differs somewhat from other accounts in the birth order of the children and the approximated ages. The estimated dates of birth for the first two children (Elizabeth and John) are reasonably well defined because they fell between the 1623 land division and the 1627 cattle division. The third child (Joseph) must have been born late in 1627 to appear on the 1643 list of men able to bear arms. The next date that we are able to fix is that of Jonathan, who was said at his death early in 1697 to be in his sixty-fifth year, and so born in 1632 (or possibly early in 1633); note that this gives us a gap of about five or six years between Joseph and Jonathan. We arbitrarily place one of the unmarried daughters, Priscilla, in this gap, although it might as well be Mary who fits here. The remainder of the children are then ranged after Jonathan at two-year intervals. This makes Ruth about twenty-two when she married John Bass, and Rebecca about twenty-one when she was the subject of the unfortunate rumor. Given the paucity of solid evidence on many of these points, other plausible arrangements may be easily constructed.

Some accounts of the family of John Alden include a son Zachariah, who had a daughter Anne Alden who married in 1699 Josiah Snell. In 1948 Hallock P. Long demonstrated that this son never existed, and that Anna Alden was almost certainly the daughter of John Alden's son Jonathan [NEHGR 102:82–86; see also MF 16:1:45, 122–23].

Attempts have been made to include Henry Alden of Billerica, Roxbury, and Dedham as a descendant of John Alden, but this cannot be. Henry Alden was rated in Billerica in 1688 [NEHGR 31:303], so he must have been born no later than 1667. The wills of John Alden's sons John and Joseph make it clear that neither of them had a son Henry. John Alden's son Jonathan did not marry until 1672, and his son David apparently even later than that. Henry Alden must have been a late migrant to New England, with no known genealogical connection with John Alden of Plymouth and Duxbury [MD 42:21ff.].

In 1627, pursuant to the renegotiation of the financial agreement between the London merchants and the Plymouth settlers, John Alden became one of the eight Undertakers who agreed to oversee the liquidation of Plymouth Colony's debts [Bradford 194–96; Bradford LB 38–40].

As noted above, John Alden was frequently a member of the committee on the Kennebec trade. He had actively participated in the trade himself, and in early 1634 he became involved in an incident in which a party of Plymouth men led by himself and John Howland became embroiled with a group of men from the Piscataqua settlement which would grow into Dover. One man on each side was killed, and in the aftermath Alden was detained at Boston as security against the final resolution of the conflict. [For particulars of this incident, see WJ 1:155–56, 162–63; WP 3:167–68; MBCR 1:119; and Bradford 262–68.] The results of a 1960 season of digging at the site of this incident are given by Roland Wells Robbins in *Pilgrim John Alden's Progress: Archaeological Excavations in Duxbury* (Plymouth: The Pilgrim Society 1969).

BIBLIOGRAPHIC NOTE: The Five Generations Project of the General Society of Mayflower Descendants has so far published five volumes to cover the descendants of John Alden, prepared by Esther Littleford Woodworth-Barnes. The first volume was issued in 1999 and covers the first four generations. The remaining four volumes cover the fifth-generation descendants of the children of John and Priscilla (Mullins) Alden, except for daughter Rebecca (Alden) Delano and son David Alden [2002, 2004, 2015, 2016]. Alicia Crane Williams and John Bradley Arthaud served as editors for the Alden volumes.

In 1998, prior to the publication of the first Alden volume of the Five Generations Project, Alicia Crane Williams prepared a brief overview of the first four generations [MD 48:107–10].

ISAAC ALLERTON

Mr. Isaac Allerton and Mary his wife, with three children, Bartholomew, Remember and Mary. And a servant boy John Hooke.

Mr. Allerton his wife died with the first, and his servant John Hooke. His son Bartle is married in England but I know not how many children he hath. His daughter Remember is married at Salem and hath three or four children living. And his daughter Mary is married here and hath four children. Himself married again with the daughter of Mr. Brewster and hath one son living by her, but she is long since dead. And he is married again and hath left this place long ago. So I account his increase to be eight, besides his sons in England.

ORIGIN: Leiden.
PREVIOUS RESIDENCES: East Bergholt, Suffolk; London.
MIGRATION: 1620 on the *Mayflower*.
FIRST RESIDENCE: Plymouth.
REMOVES: Marblehead, New Amsterdam, New Haven.
RETURN TRIPS: Frequent trips to England, especially in the 1620s and 1630s, on personal and colony business.

OCCUPATION: Merchant.
CHURCH MEMBERSHIP: "Mr. Allerton" and "Sister Allerton" were assigned pews in New Haven meetinghouse, 10 March 1646/7 [NHCR 1:302, 304].
FREEMAN: On 17 February 1614 [NS], Isaac Allerton was made a citizen of Leiden [Leiden Pilgrims 28].

On 11 November 1620, Isaac Allerton signed the Mayflower Compact [Morton 26].

In the 1633 Plymouth list of freemen, immediately after Assistants, and well before those admitted on 1 January 1632/3 [PCR 1:3]. In the Plymouth list of 7 March 1636/7 [PCR 1:52].
EDUCATION: Although there is no direct evidence of Isaac Allerton's education, he must have been well educated to engage in business, political, and diplomatic activities as extensively as he did. His inventory

included, in a list of miscellaneous items, "1 old book." Allerton did sign his name to some documents [MD 57:97–104].

OFFICES: In early 1621, after the death of John Carver, William Bradford was chosen Governor, and "Isaac Allerton was chosen to be an assistant unto him who, by renewed election every year, continued sundry years together" [Bradford 86]. Chosen Assistant, 1 January 1633/4 [PCR 1:21].

ESTATE: In the 1623 Plymouth land division, "Mr. Isaak Alerton" received seven acres [PCR 12:4; MQ 40:10]. In the 1627 Plymouth cattle division, Mr. Isaac Allerton, his wife Feare Allerton, Bartholomew Allerton, Remember Allerton, Mary Allerton, and Sarah Allerton were the first six persons in the second company [PCR 12:9].

Isaac Allerton was one of the Purchasers, those who acquired the rights to land distributions in Plymouth Colony as a consequence of the agreement made between the London merchants and the Plymouth settlers in 1627 [Ford 282–88].

Assessed £3 11s. in Plymouth tax list of 25 March 1633 and £1 16s. in list of 27 March 1634 [PCR 1:9, 27].

Assigned mowing ground for year, 1 July 1633 [PCR 1:14].

On 6 May 1635, the Massachusetts Bay General Court noted that "Mr. Ollerton hath given to Moses Maveracke, his son-in-law, all his houses, buildings, & stages, that he hath at Marble Head, to enjoy to him & his heirs forever" [MBCR 1:147].

On 27 October 1646, "Isacke Allerton" of New Amsterdam in the province of New Netherland, merchant, confirmed to son-in-law Thomas Cushman of New Plymouth a debt of one hundred pounds owed to Isaac by John Coombe [PCR 2:133].

In the New Haven Book of Alienations, in an entry from 1646, "Isaack Allerton" held four parcels of land "bought of Lawr[ence] Ward": "6 acres ½ upland in the first division"; "1 acre ¼ & 8 rods in the neck"; "2 acres ½ of meadow"; and "10 acres in the 2d division" [BA 5].

In his "will," undated and proved 19 October 1659, "Isaac Alerton, late of New Haven, deceased," devoted most of the space to a list of debts owing to him, and then ordered "my son Isaac Allerton and my wife, as trustees to receive in my debts, & to pay what I owe, as far as it will go & what is overplus I leave to my wife and my son Isaac, as far as they receive the debts to pay what I owe" [MD 2:155–56, citing NHPR 1:1:82].

The inventory, taken 12 February 1658/9, totaled £118 5s. 2d., of which £75 was real estate: "the dwelling house, orchard & barn with two acres of meadow," £75 [MD 2:156–57, citing NHPR 1:1:83].

On 4 May 1680, "[w]hereas there was agreements between Mr. Isaac Allerton sometime of New Haven in the Colony of Connecticut now deceased and Will[iam] Holt of the aforesaid New Haven respecting a small quantity of land granted to the lots that butted on the Oystershell Field which proportion of land the said Will[iam] Holt did make and pass over to the said Allerton ... and there having not yet been any written or recorded deed to declare the same now I Johanah the widow and relict of the said Allerton ... and well knowing the agreement with the said Holt and John Holt son of the said William ... do both of them ratify and confirm the said agreement" [NHLR 1:38]. On 19 May 1684, "Elizabeth Eyer, formerly Elizabeth Allerton now wife of Simon Eyre of New Haven ..., having the reversion of a house that my grandmother Mrs. Johanna Allerton now dwells in situate in New Haven aforesaid with the appurtenances thereunto belonging ... when it was in the possession of my deceased grandfather ... together with the house was bought by my father of my grandfather's creditors and given to me by my father Mr. Isaac Allerton to be possessed thereof as my propriety and right given me by my father after the death of my grandmother Mrs. Johanna Allerton which reversion ... I the said Elizabeth Eyre for good consideration me thereunto moving do give, grant and alienate ... unto my dear and loving husband Simon Eyre" [NHLR 1:265].

BIRTH: About 1587, son of Bartholomew and Mary (_____) Allerton of East Bergholt, Suffolk [NEHGR 173:197–205].

DEATH: New Haven between 1 February 1658/9 (court appearance) and 12 February 1658/9 (date of inventory).

MARRIAGE: (1) Leiden 4 November 1611 [NS] Mary Norris "single woman from Newbury in England" [Plooij IX; Leiden Pilgrims 27–28; MD 7:129–30]. She died at Plymouth on 25 February 1620/1 [Prince 289].

(2) Plymouth between 1623 and 1627 Fear Brewster, daughter of *WILLIAM BREWSTER*. She died not long before 12 December 1634, presumably at Plymouth [MD 30:97–98; WP 3:177].

(3) By 1644 Joanna Swinnerton, almost certainly the "Mrs. Swinnerton" who received a grant of land at New Haven on 17 March 1640/1 [NHCR 1:50; NEHGR 124:133; MD 42:124, 63:214–24]. On 17 February 1644/5, "Mr. Allerton coming from New Haven in a ketch, with his wife and diverse other persons, were taken in a great storm at northeast with much snow, and cast away at Scituate, but the persons all saved" [WJ 2:258]. She was living on 19 May 1684 [NHLR 1:265].

CHILDREN:

With first wife

    i BARTHOLOMEW ALLERTON, b. say 1613; he served as vicar of Knocktemple and Liscarroll parishes in County Cork, Ireland, from 1641 to about 1644 and as vicar of Bramfield, Suffolk, from 1644 to his death in 1658; m. (1) Margaret _____; m. (2) Sarah Fairfax, dau. of Benjamin Fairfax; and had at least four children [MD 40:7–10; MJ 3:1:63–79, 3:2:24–50].

    ii REMEMBER ALLERTON, b. say 1615; m. by 6 May 1635 Moses Maverick [MBCR 1:147], son of Rev. JOHN MAVERICK {1630, Dorchester} [GMB 2:1241–43; MD 5:129–41; NEHGR 96:358–61; Small Gen 669–80].

    iii MARY ALLERTON, b. say 1617; m. by about 1636 Thomas Cushman, son of ROBERT CUSHMAN {1621, Plymouth} [MD 4:37–42; PM 158]. A late annotation to Bradford's 1651 list indicated that "Mary Cushman the daughter of Mr. Allerton" was still alive in 1690 [Bradford 448]. She d. Plymouth 28 November 1699 [PVR 136; MD 16:63], the last of the *Mayflower* passengers to die.

    iv Child ALLERTON, bur. Pieterskerk, Leiden, 5 February 1620 [NS] [Dexter 601; NEA 3:2:48].

    v Son ALLERTON, stillborn aboard the *Mayflower* 22 December 1620 in Plymouth Harbor [Mourt 41].

With second wife

    vi SARAH ALLERTON, b. about 1626; listed with rest of family in 1627 cattle division [PCR 12:9]; no further record.

    vii ISAAC ALLERTON, b. Plymouth say 1630; Harvard 1650 [Sibley 1:253–56]; m. (1) about 1652 Elizabeth _____ [NEHGR 124:83–84 argues that she was a daughter of Joanna Swinnerton, third wife of Isaac's father]; m. (2) in Virginia about 1663 Elizabeth (Willoughby) (Overzee) Colclough, dau. of Capt. Thomas Willoughby and widow of Simon Overzee and George Colclough [MF 7:6–7]. (All modern authorities agree that the Isaac Allerton born at New Haven in 1655, son of this Isaac Allerton with his first wife, died without issue, and some other origin must be found for the Allertons who appear in New Haven late in the seventeenth century [MQ 45:23; MD 42:117].)

ASSOCIATIONS: Brother of Sarah Allerton, wife successively of John Vincent, *DEGORY PRIEST,* and GODBERT GODBERTSON {1623, Plymouth} [PM 226]. On 2 December 1633, as part of the settlement of the estate of Godbert Godbertson, it was noted that "the greater part of his debts are owing to Mr. Isaack Allerton, of Plymouth, merchant, late brother of the said Zarah" [PCR 1:20].

Possibly brother of *JOHN ALLERTON* of the *Mayflower.*

PREMIGRATION BIOGRAPHY: Isaac Allerton was born at East Bergholt, Suffolk, about 1587. His parents, Bartholomew and Mary Allerton, appeared in the diocesan lists of sectary or Brownist recusants (that is, separatists) from 1597 through 1603 [NEHGR 173:203]. On 21 June 1609, Isaac Allerton was apprenticed to "James Glyn, Citizen and Black Smith of London for seven years" [MQ 75:54–56]. Allerton did not complete his apprenticeship, for by 1611 he was in Leiden where he married Mary Norris, with whom he had four children by 1620. He was made a citizen of Leiden in 1614. On 9 January 1619 [NS], Allerton took on "Jan Houck" as an apprentice [Leiden Pilgrims 28]; this was the John Hooke who sailed with Allerton on the *Mayflower* as his servant. As members of the Leiden congregation made preparations to sail to the New World, Allerton was one of the leaders at Leiden who was closely involved in this work [Bradford 360–61].

COMMENTS: On 12 June 1609, "Isack Allerton son of Bartholomew Allerton of Ipswich in County Suffolk tailor" was apprenticed to James Glyn of the Blacksmiths' Company of London [Blacksmiths' Company, Court Minutes, 1605–1611 (translated from the Latin; reference courtesy of Leslie Mahler)].

In 1627, pursuant to the renegotiation of the financial agreement between the London merchants and the Plymouth settlers, Isaac Allerton became one of the eight Undertakers who agreed to oversee the liquidation of Plymouth Colony's debts [Bradford 194–96; Bradford LB 38–40].

Isaac Allerton was one of the busiest and most complicated men in early New England, and no attempt is made here to cover his career comprehensively. A full-scale biography would be needed for that, and an outline of what is available in print is given in the next section. Records for Allerton may be found in virtually every colony on the Atlantic seaboard and in the Caribbean, including Newfoundland, New Netherland, New Sweden, Virginia, Barbados, and Curaçao.

In noting his various residences above, we do not estimate years of removal, as he seems to have maintained residences simultaneously at more than one location. Also, the attempt made above to describe the estate of Allerton does not come close to showing the magnitude and intricacy of his business activities. No one has yet tried to survey comprehensively this, the major part of Allerton's life.

Since Moses Maverick, the husband of Remember Allerton, received Isaac Allerton's estate at Marblehead, and Isaac Jr. received his father's estate at New Haven, it is likely that Thomas and Mary (Allerton) Cushman were at some time given Allerton's property at Plymouth (assuming that there was more at Plymouth than the debt assigned by Allerton to Cushman in 1646 [PCR 2:133]).

BIBLIOGRAPHIC NOTE: The descendants of Isaac Allerton were treated extensively by Walter S. Allerton about a century ago, but this account is now obsolete [*A History of the Allerton Family in the United States, 1585 to 1885* ... (New York 1888, rev. 1900)].

More recently Lora Underhill published an extremely detailed account of Isaac Allerton and his children [Small Gen 756–851]. Although this version of the life of Isaac Allerton has been shown to have errors, and although many new discoveries have been made, it has great value because it attempts to cite every record in which Allerton ever appeared (as available in 1934), and prints many of the records in full.

Much of the modern research on Allerton has been carried out by Newman Hall, presented in a series of periodical articles [NEHGR 124:133; MQ 45:23–24, 47:14–18; *Virginia Genealogist* 32:83–92, 171–78, 287–96; MD 40:7–10]. More recently Robert S. Wakefield has prepared the Mayflower Five Generations Project volume on Isaac Allerton, as Volume Seventeen of the series [*Mayflower Families Through Five Generations ... Family of Isaac Allerton* (Plymouth 1998)].

In 2006 Caleb Johnson prepared a substantial summary of the life of Isaac Allerton [Mayflower Passengers 59–70]. In 2019 Caleb Johnson, Sue Allan, and Simon Neal published the evidence for the parentage and English origin of Isaac Allerton [NEHGR 173:197–205].

For a different interpretation of the character of Isaac Allerton, see Michael McGiffert, "Religion and Profit Do Jump Together: The First American Pilgrim," *Reflections* 87 (Summer 1992):15–23 (a publication of Yale Divinity School).

JOHN ALLERTON

John Allerton and Thomas English were both hired, the latter to go master of a shallop here, and the other was reputed as one of the company but was to go back (being a seaman) for the help of others behind. But they both died here before the ship returned.

Thomas English and John Allerton died in the general sickness.

ORIGIN: Leiden.
MIGRATION: 1620 on the *Mayflower.*
FIRST RESIDENCE: Plymouth.

FREEMAN: On 11 November 1620, John Allerton signed the Mayflower Compact [Morton 26].

BIRTH: By about 1591 (based on estimated date of marriage), possibly son of Bartholomew and Mary (_____) Allerton of East Bergholt, Suffolk [NEHGR 173:197–205].
DEATH: Plymouth before 5 April 1621 (date of return of the *Mayflower* to England).
MARRIAGE: By 1616 _____ _____.
CHILD:

> i Child ALLERTON, bur. Pieterskerk, Leiden, 21 May 1616 [NS] (father's name given as "Jan Alaerton") [NEA 3:2:48].

ASSOCIATIONS: Possibly a brother of *ISAAC ALLERTON* [NEHGR 173:204].

COMMENTS: The genealogical detail given above is based solely on the 1616 burial record at Leiden and the assumption that that record pertains to the *Mayflower* passenger.

John Allerton was a member of the exploratory party that left Provincetown Harbor on 6 December 1620 and selected the site for the town of Plymouth [Mourt 32].

JOHN BILLINGTON

John Billington and Ellen his wife, and two sons, John and Francis.

John Billington, after he had been here ten years, was executed for killing a man, and his eldest son died before him but his second son is alive and married and hath eight children.

ORIGIN: Spalding, Lincolnshire or vicinity (but see **PREMIGRATION BIOGRAPHY**).
MIGRATION: 1620 on the *Mayflower*.
FIRST RESIDENCE: Plymouth.

FREEMAN: On 11 November 1620, John Billington signed the Mayflower Compact [Morton 26].
ESTATE: In 1620 John Billington's homelot was on the south side of the street [PCR 12:1].

In the 1623 Plymouth land division John Billington received three acres as a passenger on the *Mayflower* [PCR 12:4]. (There is a discrepancy with this entry, as the family of John Billington on the *Mayflower* consisted of four persons [MQ 40:10]. Caleb Johnson suggests that the younger John Billington may have been residing with the Richard Warren family in 1623 [Mayflower Passengers 75].)

In the 1627 Plymouth cattle division John Billington Senior, Hellen Billington, and Francis Billington were the eleventh through thirteenth persons in the seventh company (headed by Stephen Hopkins), and John Billington [Jr.] was the tenth person in the ninth company (headed by Richard Warren) [PCR 12:11, 12].

"_____ Billington" (presumably the heirs of John Billington) was one of the Purchasers, those who acquired the rights to land distributions in Plymouth Colony as a consequence of the agreement made between the London merchants and the Plymouth settlers in 1627 [Ford 282–88].

On 8 January 1637/8, "Mrs. Elinor Billington, widow," deeded to "Francis Billington my natural son ... all and singular those my land, meadows, pastures and commons with all and singular the appurtenances thereunto belonging situate, lying and being near Plain Dealing within the government of New Plymouth" [PCR 12:28–30]. On 21 September 1638, "Gregory Armestronge, Ellinor his now wife and Francis Billington her natural son" sold to "Mr. William Bradford ... one acre & a half of land lying on the north side of the lands of the said Will[ia]m Bradford upon the lowest division next the water side in the field on the north side of the town of Plymouth" [PCR 12:37–38].

BIRTH: By about 1579 (based on estimated date of marriage).

DEATH: Hanged September 1630 at Plymouth [Bradford 234; WJ 1:43].

MARRIAGE: By about 1604 Elinor _____. She married (2) between 14 and 21 September 1638 GREGORY ARMSTRONG {1638, Plymouth} and was living as late as 2 March 1642/3 [MF 21:3–4; PCR 12:33–34].

CHILDREN:

> i JOHN BILLINGTON, b. say 1604; d. Plymouth between 22 May 1627 and September 1630 [PCR 12:12; Bradford 446].
>
> ii FRANCIS BILLINGTON, b. about 1606 (deposed 10 July 1674 "68 years of age" [MD 2:46, citing PLR 1:81]); in the Plymouth tax lists of 25 March 1633 and 27 March 1634 assessed 9s. [PCR 1:10, 27]; m. Plymouth [blank] July 1634 "Christian Eaton" [PCR 1:31]. She was CHRISTIAN (PENN) EATON {1623, Plymouth}, widow of *FRANCIS EATON*.

PREMIGRATION BIOGRAPHY: Based on the 1650 survey of the manor of Spalding, Lincolnshire, John Billington and his family resided in or near the parish of Spalding in 1612. Whether Billington had been born in that area or moved from some other location is unknown. In describing the execution of John Billington for murder in 1630, William Bradford stated that the Billington family "came from London, and I know not by what friends shuffled into their company." In this and other instances, we see that Bradford was not fully informed about the *Mayflower* passengers from England who joined the Leiden company at Southampton in July 1620, and so this claim of origin in London might extend to quite a wide range of places in southern England. The Billington family might thus have left Spalding at any time in the fifteen years before 1620 and moved to a more southerly location in England before joining the *Mayflower* company. Bradford's suggestion that the Billingtons were "shuffled into their company" and his report to Robert Cushman in 1625 that "Billington still rails against you" opens the possibility that the Billingtons had been recruited for the voyage by Cushman and that John Billington was not satisfied with the outcome of whatever arrangements had been made for his and his family's participation. The association of members of the Billington family in the 1627 division of cattle with other "London" families (Hopkins and Warren) might provide clues for further research.

COMMENTS: In a Survey of 1650 for the manor of Spalding in Lincolnshire is a lease for three lives in which one of the lives is "Francis Billington son of John Billington." The original lease was dated 7 February 1611/2. In the Survey of 1650, we are told that "the lives are all in being" (meaning that all three of the principals named in the original indenture were alive) and that "Francis Billington (as it is informed) was living about a year since in New England aged forty years or thereabouts" [NEHGR 124:116–18]. This estimated age for Francis Billington is probably less accurate than his own deposition in 1674, but this record does provide an excellent clue for further research on the English origin of the family.

The Billington family was a constant source of concern to the company of immigrants. On 5 December 1620, "we, through God's mercy, escaped a great danger by the foolishness of a boy one of Francis [*sic*] Billington's sons, who, in his father's absence, had got gunpowder and has shot off a piece or two, and made squibs, and there being a fowling-piece charged in his father's cabin, shot her off in the cabin, the fire being within four feet of the bed between decks, and many flints and iron things about the cabin, and many people about the fire, and yet, by God's mercy, no harm done" [Mourt 31]. On 8 January 1620/1, "Francis Billington, having the week before seen from the top of a tree on a high hill a great sea as he thought, went with one of the master's mates to see it" [Mourt 44]. This body of water was the large pond in Plymouth now called Billington Sea.

In late March of 1621, Bradford reported "the first offense since our arrival is of John Billington who came on board at London, and is this month convented before the whole company for his contempt of the captain's [i.e., Standish's] lawful command with opprobrious speeches, for which he is adjudged to have his neck and heels tied together; but upon humbling himself and craving pardon, and it being the first offense, he is forgiven" [Prince 189]. (The bulk of this passage was taken from a book of early Plymouth records maintained by William Bradford and which by the eighteenth century had come into the possession of the antiquary Thomas Prince, but has now been lost. The short passage "who came on board at London," however, is indicated by Prince as being interpolated by himself from Bradford's "Of Plymouth Plantation." This must be from the account of Billington's execution for murder, where the actual language is that the Billingtons "came from London," not that they boarded the ship at London [Bradford 234].)

Late in July of 1621, "John Billington lost himself in the woods, and wandered up and down some five days, living on berries and what he could find. At length he light on an Indian plantation twenty miles south of this place, called Manomet; they conveyed him further off, to Nauset among those people that had before set upon the English when they were coasting whilst the ship lay at the Cape" [Bradford 87–88; Mourt 69–72]. This was John Billington, the son of the immigrant.

In 1624 John Billington Sr. was implicated in the short-lived rebellion of Rev. John Lyford and John Oldham against the Plymouth leaders. When confronted with his actions, "Billington and any whom [Lyford] named denied the things and protested [Lyford] wronged them and would have drawn them to such and such things which they could not consent to, though they were sometimes drawn to [Lyford's] meetings" [Bradford 157]. In a letter to Robert Cushman dated 9 June 1625, William Bradford observed that "Billington still rails against you, and threatens to arrest you, I know not wherefore; he is a knave, and so will live and die" [Bradford LB 13].

John Billington's troubled life at Plymouth came to an end in September 1630, when "John Billington the elder, one that came over with the first, was arraigned, and both by grand and petty jury found guilty of willful murder, by plain and notorious evidence. And was for the same accordingly executed. This, as it was the first execution amongst them, so was it a matter of great sadness unto them. They used all due means about his trial and took the advice of Mr. Winthrop and other the ablest gentlemen in Bay of the Massachusetts, that were then newly come over, who concurred with them that he ought to die, and the land to be purged from blood. He and some of his had been often punished for miscarriages before, being one of the profanest families amongst them; they came from London, and I know not by what friends shuffled into their company. His fact was that he waylaid a young man, one John Newcomen, about a former quarrel and shot him with a gun, whereof he died" [Bradford 234; Hubbard 101; New English Canaan 216; PM 344; LENE 5–6].

BIBLIOGRAPHIC NOTE: The family of John Billington has been treated thoroughly by Harriet Woodbury Hodge (as revised by Robert S. Wakefield) in the twenty-first volume of the Five Generations Project of the General Society of Mayflower Descendants. They list the many occasions on which John Billington or his sons were in trouble with the Plymouth authorities in the first decade of the colony's existence [MF 21:1–4].

In 1982 Robert S. Wakefield published a detailed account of each of the children of Francis Billington, son of John Billington [TG 3:228–48].

WILLIAM BRADFORD

William Bradford and Dorothy his wife, having but one child, a son left behind who came afterward.

William Bradford his wife died soon after their arrival, and he married again and hath four children, three whereof are married.

ORIGIN: Leiden.
PREVIOUS RESIDENCES: Austerfield, Yorkshire; Amsterdam.
MIGRATION: 1620 on the *Mayflower.*
FIRST RESIDENCE: Plymouth.

OCCUPATION: Fustian-worker (in Leiden) [Leiden Pilgrims 57].
  Magistrate.
CHURCH MEMBERSHIP: As a member of the Scrooby congregation, Bradford was also prominent in the churches at Leiden and Plymouth.
FREEMAN: On 11 November 1620, William Bradford signed the Mayflower Compact [Morton 26].

In the 1633 list of Plymouth freemen, prior to those admitted on 1 January 1632/3 [PCR 1:3]. In the list of 7 March 1636/7 [PCR 1:52]. "Mr. William Bradford" (as governor) was in the Plymouth section of the list of 1639 [PCR 8:173].
EDUCATION: Bradford probably attended grammar school at Tickhill, Yorkshire [Sue Allan, *In Search of William Bradford* (n.p. 2020) 51–53]." Like many of the ministers, Bradford had knowledge of many languages, including Hebrew [Isidore S. Meyer, *The Hebrew Exercises of Governor William Bradford* (Plymouth, Massachusetts, 1973)]. In 2010 Jeremy Dupertuis Bangs discussed the "sources for Dutch legal precedents" that Bradford deployed in his history of Plymouth Colony [MQ 76:24–35]. His education was also on display in his many writings (see *BIBLIOGRAPHIC NOTE*).

His inventory included a detailed listing of his extensive library, valued at £14 3s. and comprising two Bibles, thirty books or sets of books (mostly theological) listed by title, and a parcel described as "three and fifty small books" [MD 2:232–33, citing PCPR 2:1:57–58; Plymouth Libraries 216–32 (identifying and providing full titles for most of the volumes)]. The inventory of his widow's estate included a similar list, stated to be located in "the study," valued at £14 7s. and comprising the same listing as in her husband's inventory, with the exception of four specific titles which she no longer held [MD 3:146–47, citing PCPR 3:1:3; Plymouth Libraries 268–82].

OFFICES: Governor of Plymouth Colony, 1621–32, 1635, 1637, 1639–43, 1645–56 [Bradford 86; PCR 1:32, 48, 116, 140, 2:8, 33, 52, 83, 100, 115, 123, 139, 153, 166, 3:7, 30, 48, 77, 99 (note that this gives Bradford thirty-one terms as governor, an accounting at odds with a number of secondary sources)]. Assistant, 1633, 1634, 1636, 1638, 1644 [PCR 1:5, 21, 36, 79, 2:71]. Plymouth Commissioner to United Colonies, 1647–49, 1652, 1656 [PCR 2:115, 123, 139, 3:99, 9:84, 109 (elected president), 150, 10:71, 153 (elected president)].

"Mr. Bradford" appeared in the Plymouth section of the 1643 Plymouth Colony list of men able to bear arms [PCR 8:188]. His inventory included "3 matchcock muskets" valued at £2 2s., "a snaphance musket" valued at £1, "a birding piece and another small piece" valued at 18s., "a pistol and cutlass" valued at 12s., "a corslet and one headpiece" valued at £1 10s., and "1 fowling piece without a lock, 3 old barrels of guns, one pair of old bandoliers and a rest" valued at 16s. [MD 2:229–34, citing PCPR 2:1:54–59]. The inventory of his widow's estate included "2 guns and a pair of bandoliers" valued at £1 and "a rest and some other odd things" valued at 2s. [MD 3:145–49, citing PCPR 3:1:3–5].

ESTATE: In the 1623 Plymouth land division William Bradford received three acres as a passenger on the *Mayflower,* and Alice Bradford received one acre as a passenger on the *Anne* [PCR 12:4, 6; MD 40:9]. In the 1627 Plymouth cattle division "the Governor Mr. William Bradford and ... his wife Alles Bradford," William Bradford Junior, and Mercy Bradford were the first four persons in the eleventh company [PCR 12:12].

William Bradford was one of the Purchasers, those who acquired the rights to land distributions in Plymouth Colony as a consequence of the agreement made between the London merchants and the Plymouth settlers in 1627 [Ford 282–88].

Assessed £1 16s. in the Plymouth tax list of 25 March 1633 and £1 7s. in the list of 27 March 1634 [PCR 1:9, 27].

In his nuncupative will, dated 9 May 1657 and proved 3 June 1657, "Mr. William Bradford Senior being weak in body, but in perfect memory having deferred the forming of his will in hopes of having the help of Mr. Thomas Prence therein," stated that he had "disposed to John and William already their proportions of land, which they are possessed of," asked "that my son Joseph be made in some sort equal to his brethren out of my estate," made "my dear and loving wife Allice Bradford" executrix and for "her future maintenance my will is that my stock in the Kennebecke trade be reserved for her comfortable subsistence," appointed "my well-beloved Christian friends Mr. Thomas Prence, Captain Thomas Willett and Lieutenant Thomas Southworth" as supervisors, to whose wisdom he commended "some small books written by my own hand to be improved as you shall see meet; in special I commend to you a little book with a black cover, wherein there is a word to Plymouth, a word to Boston, and a word to New England, with sundry useful verses" [MD 2:228–29, citing PCPR 2:1:53].

The inventory of "the estate of Mr. Will[i]am Bradford Sr. lately deceased," taken 22 May 1657, was not totaled; it included several parcels of real estate, not all of which were valued: "the house and orchard and some small parcels of land about the town of Plymouth," £45; "one parcel at Eastham and another at Bridgwater," not valued; and "a small parcel about Sawtuckett and his purchase land at Coaksett with his rights in the town's land at Punckatessett," not valued [MD 2:229–34, citing PCPR 2:1:54–59].

In her will, dated 29 December 1669 and proved 7 June 1670, "Allis Bradford Senior of the town of Plymouth ..., widow," requested that "my body may be interred as near unto my deceased husband, Mr. William Bradford, as conveniently may be" and bequeathed to "my dear sister Mary Carpenter" moveables; to "my son Mr. Constant Southworth my land at Paomett"; to "my said son Constant Southworth and unto my son Mr. Joseph Bradford the one-half of my sheep to be equally divided betwixt them and the other half to my son Captain Will[i]am Bradford"; to "my said son Joseph Bradford" livestock; to "my honored friend Mr. Thomas Prence one of the books that were my dear husband's library, which of them he shall choose"; to "my dear grandchild Elizabeth Howland, the daughter of my dear son Captain Thomas Southworth deceased, the sum of seven pounds, for the use and benefit of her son James Howland"; to "my servant maid Mary Smith a cow calf"; residue equally divided to "my sons Mr. Constant Southworth, Captain Will[i]am Bradford and Mr. Joseph Bradford" [MD 3:144–45, citing PCPR 3:1:2].

The inventory of the estate of "Mistress Allice Bradford Senior late deceased," taken 31 March 1670, totaled £162 17s., with no real estate included [MD 3:145–49, citing PCPR 3:1:3–5].

BIRTH: Baptized Austerfield, Yorkshire, 19 March 1589/90, son of William and Alice (Hanson) Bradford [MD 7:65–66; NEHGR 84:10–11].
DEATH: Plymouth 9 May 1657 [Hull 180; MD 2:228–29].
MARRIAGE: (1) Amsterdam, 10 December 1613 [NS] Dorothy May, daughter of Henry and Katherine (_____) May of Wisbech, Cambridgeshire

[MD 9:115–17, 22:63–64; Plooij XXVII, LXX; TAG 89:81–94, 168–88]. She died on 7 December 1620 by drowning in Provincetown Harbor [Prince 165 (and see **COMMENTS**)].

(2) Plymouth 14 August 1623 Alice (Carpenter) Southworth [Prince 221], daughter of Alexander Carpenter and widow of Edward Southworth [Sue Allan, *In Search of Separatist Edward Southworth of Leiden* (n.p. 2019); PM 92, 437]). She died at Plymouth on 26 March 1670 [MD 18:68].

CHILDREN:

With first wife

> i JOHN BRADFORD, b. say 1617; m. by 1650 Martha Bourne, daughter of Thomas Bourne [Waterman Gen 615–19, 625].

With second wife

> ii WILLIAM BRADFORD, b. Plymouth 17 June 1624 [Prince 227, MD 30:4]; m. (1) by 1650 Alice Richards, daughter of THOMAS RICHARDS {1633, Dorchester} [GMB 3:1575–79], d. Plymouth 12 December 1671 [MD 18:68]; m. (2) by 1675 Sarah (_____) Griswold, widow of Francis Griswold [NEHGR 155:245–50]; m. (3) after 7 March 1675/6 Mary (Wood) Holmes, daughter of John Wood and widow of John Holmes [PCR 5:188, 6:163; PLR 4:20, 11:156, 14:93; NEHGR 144:26–28].

> iii MERCY BRADFORD, b. by 1627; m. Plymouth 21 December 1648 Benjamin Vermayes [PCR 8:5].

> iv JOSEPH BRADFORD, b. about 1630; m. Hingham 25 May 1664 Jael Hobart [NEHGR 121:116], daughter of the Reverend Peter Hobart, and granddaughter of EDMUND HOBART {1633, Charlestown} [GMB 2:958–60].

ASSOCIATIONS: Dorothy (May) Bradford, first wife of William Bradford, was niece of *WILLIAM WHITE* [TAG 89:81–94, 168–88].

PREMIGRATION BIOGRAPHY: William Bradford was born at Austerfield, Yorkshire, in 1590. His father died when he was only a year old, and his mother when he was seven. After his mother's remarriage, he resided with his paternal grandfather until the latter's death in 1596, and then with his uncles Robert and Thomas Bradford. While living with his uncles, he probably attended grammar school at Tickhill, Yorkshire.

Cotton Mather tells us of William Bradford's conversion and his consequent association with the Scrooby congregation:

> When he was about a dozen years old, the reading of the scriptures began to cause great impressions upon him; and those impressions were much assisted and improved, when he came to enjoy Mr. Richard Clifton's illuminating ministry, not far from his abode; he was then also further befriended, by being brought into the company and fellowship of such as were then called professors [Magnalia 1:110].

Bradford was twelve years old in 1602, when Rev. Richard Clifton was minister at Babworth, Nottinghamshire, about ten miles from Austerfield. Although it would not be impossible that Bradford audited one or more of Clifton's sermons at Babworth in 1602, Mather's story does not require that all the events described therein occurred simultaneously. More likely, the separate elements of the story should be read as sequential, with some time elapsing between each episode. Thus, the connection between the two men probably happened in late 1606 or early 1607 when Clifton was preaching illegally at Bawtry, the parish immediately adjacent to Austerfield. Bradford would then have been sixteen or seventeen. The separatist congregation at Scrooby was then less than a year old, with Clifton as its leading minister, and Bradford probably became a member of that gathering soon after hearing Clifton preach.

COMMENTS: George Ernest Bowman debunked the story claiming that Dorothy (May) Bradford had committed suicide [MD 29:97–102, 31:105], and Eugene A. Stratton summarized the literature on her death [Stratton 324–26]. Both concluded that her death was an accidental drowning.

William Bradford was a member of the party that explored the Outer Cape from 15 to 17 November 1620 [Mourt 19]. He was also a member of the exploratory party that left Provincetown Harbor on 6 December 1620 and selected the site for the town of Plymouth [Mourt 32].

In 1627, pursuant to the renegotiation of the financial agreement between the London merchants and the Plymouth settlers, William Bradford became one of the eight Undertakers who agreed to oversee the liquidation of Plymouth Colony's debts [Bradford 194–96; Bradford LB 38–40].

BIBLIOGRAPHIC NOTE: In 2004 the Five Generations Project of the General Society of Mayflower Descendants published five generations of the descendants of William Bradford in Volume Twenty-two of the series, compiled by Ann Smith Lainhart and Robert S. Wakefield.

The best information on William Bradford is found in his own writings. Most important of these, of course, is his history of Plymouth Colony, and of its antecedents. There are many editions of this work, of which four are useful in various ways:

> *History of Plymouth Plantation 1620–1647. By William Bradford,* ed. Worthington C. Ford, 2 volumes (Boston 1912).
>
> *Of Plymouth Plantation 1620–1647,* ed. Samuel Eliot Morison (New York 1952).
>
> *Of Plymouth Plantation,* ed. Caleb H. Johnson (n.p. 2006).
>
> *Of Plimoth Plantation by William Bradford: The 400th Anniversary Edition,* eds. Kenneth P. Minkema, Francis J. Bremer, and Jeremy D. Bangs (Boston 2020).

In 2003 Douglas Anderson undertook a textual analysis of Bradford's history: *William Bradford's Books*: Of Plimmoth Plantation *and the Printed Word* (Baltimore 2003).

Sargent Bush Jr. prepared a sketch of William Bradford for the *Oxford Dictionary of National Biography*. In 2020 Sue Allan examined the early life of Bradford [*In Search of William Bradford* (n.p. 2020)]. Brief popular biographies of Bradford have been published, such as Perry D. Westbrook's *William Bradford* in 1978. Bradford deserves a full, modern biography.

WILLIAM BREWSTER

Mr. William Brewster, Mary, his wife, with two sons, whose names were Love and Wrestling. And a boy was put to him called Richard More, and another of his brothers. The rest of his children were left behind and came over afterwards.

Mr. Brewster lived to a very old age; about 80 years he was when he died, having lived some 23 or 24 years here in the country. And though his wife died long before, yet she died aged. His son Wrestling died a young man unmarried. His son Love lived till this year 1650 and died and left four children, now living. His daughters which came over after him are dead but have left sundry children alive. His eldest son is still living and hath nine or ten children; one married who hath a child or two.

Richard More's brother died the first winter, but he is married and hath four or five children, all living.

ORIGIN: Leiden.
PREVIOUS RESIDENCES: Scrooby, Nottinghamshire.
MIGRATION: 1620 on the *Mayflower.*
FIRST RESIDENCE: Plymouth.
REMOVES: Duxbury.

OCCUPATION: Postmaster (at Scrooby) [MD 60:52–60].
Publisher (in Leiden). (See R. Breugelmans, ed., *The Pilgrim Press, a bibliographical & historical memorial of the books printed at Leyden by the Pilgrim Fathers by Rendel Harris & Stephen R. Jones, With a chapter on the location of the Pilgrim Press in Leyden by Dr. Plooij, Partial reprint with new contributions by R. Breugelmans, J. A. Gruys & Keith Sprunger* [Nieuwkoop 1987].)
CHURCH MEMBERSHIP: Morison summarized Brewster's church activities prior to 1620: "One of the original members of the separatist congregation at Scrooby which became the nucleus of the Pilgrim church, he emigrated with them to Holland in 1608, and became elder and teacher of their church at Leyden" [Morison 368]. With no minister at the Plymouth church for most of the years before Brewster's death, he was the lay leader

and preached to the congregation regularly, and continued in this manner after his move to Duxbury. In the course of relating the controversy surrounding John Lyford, Bradford recounts how "our reverend Elder hath labored diligently in dispensing the Word of God to us, before he came: and since, hath taken equal pains with himself, in preaching the same" [Bradford 162; PM 309–13]. Included in the inventory of his library were "7 sermons by W B," which may have been his notes for some of his own sermons.

FREEMAN: On 11 November 1620, William Brewster signed the Mayflower Compact [Morton 26].

In 1633 Plymouth list of freemen, prior to those admitted on 1 January 1632/3 [PCR 1:3]. In list of 7 March 1636/7 [PCR 1:52]. In Plymouth section of Plymouth Colony list of 1639 (later annotated "dead") [PCR 8:173].

EDUCATION: Entered Peterhouse, Cambridge, 3 December 1580, but did not graduate [Venn 1:213; Morison 368]. Within the inventory of William Brewster separate listings were made of his Latin and English books, with nearly four hundred titles included; "the total of both Latin & English books amounts to the sum of £42 19s. 11d." [MD 3:27; Plymouth Libraries 38–178 (identifying and providing full titles for most of the volumes)].

ESTATE: In the list of Plymouth "meersteads & garden plots of [those] which came first laid out 1620" Mr. W[illia]m Brewster is on the south side of the street, at the corner of the highway, and next to John Goodman [PCR 12:3].

In the 1623 Plymouth land division Mr. William Brewster received six acres as a passenger on the *Mayflower,* and his children "Pacience & Fear Brewster" received two acres as passengers on the *Anne* [PCR 12:4, 6; MD 40:9]. In the 1627 Plymouth cattle division "Mr. Will[ia]m Brewster," Love Brewster, and Wrestling Brewster were the first three names in the fifth company [PCR 12:10].

William Brewster was one of the Purchasers, those who acquired the rights to land distributions in Plymouth Colony as a consequence of the agreement made between the London merchants and the Plymouth settlers in 1627 [Ford 282–88].

Assessed £1 7s. in the Plymouth tax lists of 25 March 1633 and 27 March 1634 [PCR 1:9, 27].

Administration on the estate of William Brewster was granted on 5 June 1644 to Jonathan Brewster and Love Brewster [MD 3:15, citing PCR 2:101]. The inventory of the estate of William Brewster, taken 18 May 1644, totaled £150 7d., with no real estate included [MD 3:15–27, citing PCPR 1:53–59].

"Whereas William Brewster late of Plymouth, gent., deceased left only two sons surviving viz: Jonathan the eldest and Love the younger and whereas the said William died intestate for ought can to this day appear," the two sons requested William Bradford, Edward Winslow, Thomas Prence, and Myles Standish to assist them in coming to an agreement, and on 20 August 1645 a division was made. Jonathan Brewster was excused the debt he had owed to his father, except £4 "in consideration of the wintering of some cattle which the said Jonathan had the summering upon the division and for the diet of Isaack Allerton a grandchild of the said William which he had placed with his son Love to table and because he was the first born of his father we gave him his father's arms and also a two year old heifer over and above his part of the dividables of the said estate," and Love received his father's dwelling house. The lands were divided equally, except for a dispute over the lands at Duxbury, of which sixty-eight acres went to Jonathan (along with a "dwellinghouse which the said Jonathan had built on the said land by leave of his said father") and forty-three acres went to Love "and the reason wherefore we gave Love the less quantity was and is because the quality of Love's land in goodness is equal to the quantity of Jonathan's as we judge"[MD 3:27–30, citing PCLR 1:198–99; PCR 12:115–17].

BIRTH: About 1567 (deposed 25 June 1609 [NS] "aged 42 years" [NEHGR 18:20]), probably at Scrooby, son of William and Mary (Smith) (Simkinson) Brewster [Sue Allan, *The Making of a Pilgrim*]).
DEATH: Duxbury 10 April 1644 [MD 1:7].
MARRIAGE: By 1593 Mary _____. She died at Plymouth on 17 April 1627 [MD 1:7]. (See **COMMENTS** for discussion of her identity.)
CHILDREN:

    i JONATHAN BREWSTER, b. Scrooby, Nottinghamshire, 12 August 1593 [MD 1:7]; m. Plymouth 10 April 1624 "Lucretia Oldam of Darby" [MD 1:8]; she was bp. All Saints, Derby, Derbyshire, 14 January 1600/1, and was sister of JOHN OLDHAM {1623, Plymouth} [PM 345].

    ii PATIENCE BREWSTER, b. say 1603; m. Plymouth 5 August 1624 THOMAS PRENCE {1621, Plymouth} [PM 374], "the ninth marriage at New Plymouth" [Prince 229].

    iii FEAR BREWSTER, b. say 1605; m. Plymouth by 1627 *ISAAC ALLERTON* [Bradford 218, 242; PM 10].

    iv LOVE BREWSTER, b. say 1607; m. Plymouth 15 May 1634 Sarah Collier [PCR 1:30], daughter of WILLIAM COLLIER {1633, Plymouth} [PM 128].

    v Child BREWSTER, bur. Hooglandsekerk, Leiden, 20 June
        1609 [NS] [Dexter 605; NEA 3:2:49].
   vi WRESTLING BREWSTER, b. say 1611; d. unm. after 1627
        and by 1651 [Bradford 444; GDMNH 109; MD 43:13,
        62:123–28; Waterhouse Anc 67].

PREMIGRATION BIOGRAPHY: William Brewster was born at Scrooby, Nottinghamshire, about 1566. Scrooby Manor was an estate of the Archbishop of York, and William's father, also named William, resided there as bailiff and postmaster. William probably attended grammar school at Doncaster, just across the county border in Yorkshire. In 1580 he entered Peterhouse College at Cambridge University, but apparently left within a year or two without receiving his degree [Sue Allan, *William Brewster: The Making of a Pilgrim* (n.p. 2016)].

In 1583 William Brewster entered the service of Elizabethan diplomat William Davison and remained with him until 1589. While travelling with Davison on the Continent, Brewster had the opportunity of visiting Leiden in 1585 and 1586 [Jeremy Dupertuis Bangs, "Young William Brewster in Leiden, 1585–86," NEA 1:3:36–41; Sue Allan, *William Brewster: The Making of a Pilgrim* (n.p. 2016), 89–109]. Upon leaving Davison's service, Brewster returned to Scrooby where he resided at Scrooby Manor until his departure for the Low Countries two decades later. By about 1593 Brewster had married Mary, maiden name unknown, and eventually had at least six children with her. At the Archdeaconry Court for Easter 1598, William Brewster was presented for "repeating of sermons publicly in the church without authority for anything they know" [MQ 72:239–41].

When, in the wake of the Coventry conference, probably in late 1605, a separatist congregation was founded with Richard Clifton and John Robinson as the leaders, William Brewster hosted their meetings in Scrooby. When the members of this congregation made their first attempt to remove to the Low Countries, in 1607, they were intercepted by the authorities and the leaders, including Brewster, were imprisoned for a time at Boston, Lincolnshire. A second attempt to migrate in 1608 was successful and Brewster was among those who settled for a year in Amsterdam, joining the separatist English church there led by Francis Johnson.

After a year, many of those from Scrooby and vicinity who had come to Amsterdam decided to leave the fractious separatist meeting there and move on to Leiden. In the English separatist church organized at Leiden under John Robinson, Brewster became ruling elder, the leading layman in the congregation, and would retain that position for the remainder of his life, both at Leiden and at Plymouth.

In 1616 or 1617 the Pilgrim Press was established by William Brewster and Thomas Brewer, an English merchant living at Leiden. At about this time Edward Winslow arrived from England and worked with Brewster in this enterprise. They published a variety of books supporting the reformed position, some reprints and some new works. By 1619 Sir Dudley Carleton, the English ambassador to the Netherlands, had been instructed to identify the printer of a pamphlet that had displeased James I. Carleton soon identified Brewster as the printer but reported that Brewster had left Leiden and was in London [Strangers and Pilgrims 542–45, 555–68]. Brewster had in fact left Leiden but may not have left the Netherlands before departing for New England [Jeremy Dupertuis Bangs, "William Williamson, the Englishman," NEA 4:2:55–56, 59].

COMMENTS: The quest for the identity of Mary, the wife of William Brewster, has attracted the attention of many genealogists, but as yet without a definitive result. For some time she had been thought to be Mary Wentworth, daughter of Thomas Wentworth of Scrooby, and in 1965 John G. Hunt presented his case in favor of this identity [TAG 41:1–5, 63], but this claim was rejected by Rubincam and others, and Hunt himself gave up this position. Hunt, however, published a pamphlet claiming that she was a certain Mary Wyrrall, based on the appearance in a will of a bequest to "Mary Butho," which Hunt took be a variant of Brewster resulting from a speech defect in the person dictating the will [John G. Hunt, *Of Mary Brewster: The Identity of Mary, Wife of Elder William BREWSTER of the Mayflower Voyage of 1620 from Plymouth, England, to New Plymouth, New England* (Bowling Green, Virginia, 1984)]. Eugene A. Stratton reviewed this volume negatively in 1985 [*Detroit Society for Genealogical Research Magazine* 48:135–36], to which Hunt responded with a supplement to his pamphlet [*Of Mary Brewster, part two* (Bowling Green, Virginia, August 1985)]. The maiden surname of Mary, wife of Elder Brewster, remains unknown. (Hunt published other articles on various aspects of William Brewster's life, which, as with all of Hunt's work, need to be used with caution: "'Master Williamson' of the *Mayflower*" [NGSQ 62:88–90]; "The Mother of Elder William Brewster of the *Mayflower*" [NEHGR 124:250–56]; "Mary Stubbe – A Connection of Elder William Brewster?" [NEHGR 128:288–90].) In 2012 Jeremy D. Bangs revisited the problem of Mary's identity and reported his negative results from comprehensive surveys of

London and Nottinghamshire marriage records and some court records; along the way he discovered some new details of the life of William Brewster's brother James [MQ 78:145–47].

In 1627, pursuant to the renegotiation of the financial agreement between the London merchants and the Plymouth settlers, William Brewster became one of the eight Undertakers who agreed to oversee the liquidation of Plymouth Colony's debts [Bradford 194–96; Bradford LB 38–40].

A number of other children have been proposed for William Brewster, although there is no reason to accept any of these proposals. Jacobus in 1936 disposed of the claimed connections between William Brewster of Plymouth and Francis Brewster of New Haven and his son Nathaniel [TAG 12:199–210, 13:8–21, 113–116]. Mary Walton Ferris proposed a son Edward, for whom there is no evidence [Dawes-Gates 2:151].

BIBLIOGRAPHIC NOTE: The General Society of Mayflower Descendants has published three volumes on William Brewster as part of its Five Generations Project. The first volume, covering the first four generations and issued in 2014, was prepared by Barbara Lambert Merrick and edited by Scott Andrew Bartley [MF 24:1]. The second and third volumes, covering the fifth generation and issued in 2019, were prepared by Merrick and edited by John Bradley Arthaud [MF 25:2 and MF 25:3]

Emma C. Brewster Jones published early in the twentieth century a serviceable genealogy of the family [*The Brewster Genealogy, 1566-1907* ..., 2 volumes (New York 1908)]. Among the many versions of the family published in all-my-ancestor volumes the most complete is that of Mary Walton Ferris [Dawes-Gates 2:142–56].

In 1985 and 1986 Jeremy D. Bangs published a three-part article presenting and discussing all known documents naming Jonathan Brewster in Leiden [MQ 51:161–67, 52:6–16, 57–63]. Bangs examined the claim made by Morton Dexter that Jonathan Brewster had an earlier wife and child while residing in Leiden; Bangs determined that the records cited by Dexter did not pertain to Jonathan Brewster. In 2011 Bangs surveyed the evidence demonstrating that Brewster succeeded his father as postmaster at Scrooby Manor after the latter's death; Bangs also shows the interactions between Brewster and Richard Jackson, who served as bailiff at Scrooby, and was an early member of the separatist congregation there [MD 60:52–60]. (Richard Jackson was the father of Susanna Jackson, who was wife of William White and then of Edward Winslow.)

Sue Allan has produced biographical studies of William Brewster's brother James and of William Brewster's early life [*James Brewster, Bawtry Chapel & "A Trybe of Wicked People"* (n.p. 2014); *William Brewster: The Making of a Pilgrim* (n.p. 2016)].

In 2019 Caleb H. Johnson published a full, annotated edition of the "Brewster Book," a manuscript volume which contains material written by many members of the Brewster family (Caleb H. Johnson, *The Brewster Book Manuscript* [n.p. 2019]).

RICHARD BRITTERIDGE

Moses Fletcher, John Goodman, Thomas Williams, Digory Priest, Edmund Margesson, Peter Browne, Richard Britteridge, Richard Clarke, Richard Gardiner, Gilbert Winslow.

Moses Fletcher, Thomas Williams, Digory Priest, John Goodman, Edmund Margesson, Richard Britteridge, Richard Clarke, all these died soon after arrival in the general sickness that befell. But Digory Priest had his wife and children sent hither afterwards, she being Mr. Allerton's sister. But the rest left no posterity here.

ORIGIN: England.
MIGRATION: 1620 on the *Mayflower.*
FIRST RESIDENCE: Plymouth.

FREEMAN: On 11 November 1620, Richard Britteridge signed the Mayflower Compact [Morton 26].

BIRTH: By 1599 (assuming he was at least twenty-one when he signed the Mayflower Compact).
DEATH: Plymouth 21 December 1620 ("Dec. 21 [1620], dies Richard Britteridge, the first who dies in this harbor" [Prince 168]).
MARRIAGE: None known.
CHILDREN: None known.

COMMENTS: Caleb Johnson notes the baptism of Richard Brightridge, son of Anthony Brightridge, at Crowhurst, Sussex, on 31 December 1581 as a potential match for this immigrant, but no more than a possibility [Mayflower Passengers 101].

PETER BROWN

Moses Fletcher, John Goodman, Thomas Williams, Digory Priest, Edmund Margesson, Peter Browne, Richard Britteridge, Richard Clarke, Richard Gardiner, Gilbert Winslow.

Peter Browne married twice. By his first wife he had two children who are living and both of them married; and the one of them hath two children. By his second wife he had two more. He died about sixteen years since.

ORIGIN: Dorking, Surrey [TAG 79:161–78].
MIGRATION: 1620 on the *Mayflower.*
FIRST RESIDENCE: Plymouth.

FREEMAN: On 11 November 1620, Peter Brown signed the Mayflower Compact [Morton 26].

In the 1633 Plymouth list of freemen, ahead of those made free on 1 January 1632/3 [PCR 1:4].

EDUCATION: His inventory included "1 Bible" valued at 3s. [MD 1:79–82, citing PCPR 1:7–8; Plymouth Libraries 21].
OFFICES: His inventory included "1 fowling piece" valued at £1 10s. and "12 oz. of shot" valued at 2s. [MD 1:79–82, citing PCPR 1:7–8].
ESTATE: In the list of Plymouth "meersteads & garden plots of [those] which came first laid out 1620" on south side of street next to John Goodman [PCR 12:3].

In the 1623 Plymouth land division "Peter Browen" received one acre as a passenger on the *Mayflower* [PCR 12:4; MD 40:10]. In the 1627 Plymouth cattle division Peter Brown, Martha Brown, and Mary Brown were the fourth, fifth, and sixth persons in the eighth company [PCR 12:11].

Peter Brown was one of the Purchasers, those who acquired the rights to land distributions in Plymouth Colony as a consequence of the agreement made between the London merchants and the Plymouth settlers in 1627 [Ford 282–88].

"Peter Browne" was assessed 18s. in the Plymouth tax list of 25 March 1633 [PCR 1:10]. "Widow Browne" was assessed 9s. in the list of 27 March 1634 [PCR 1:28].

The inventory of the estate of "Peter Browne of New Plymouth deceased," taken 10 October 1633, was untotaled, and presented at court on 28 October 1633, on which date the widow, Mary Brown, was granted administration [MD 1:79–82, citing PCPR 1:7–8; PCR 1:17].

On 11 November 1633, a court of assistants at Plymouth ordered that "whereas Peter Browne died without will, having diverse children by diverse wives, his estate amounting to an hundred pounds, or thereabouts, it is ordered, that Mary, his wife, who is allowed the administratrix of the said Peter, forthwith pay down fifteen pounds for the use of Mary Browne, daughter of the said Peter, to Mr. Joh. Done, of Plymoth aforesaid, with whom the said Court have placed the said Mary for nine years; at the end whereof the said John is to make good the said fifteen pounds to her or her heirs, if in case she die. Also it is further ordered, that the said widow Mary Browne pay or cause to be paid into the hands of Mr. Will[iam] Gilson the full sum of fifteen pounds, for the use of Prisilla Browne, another of the daughters of the said Peter, the Court having placed the said Prisilla with the said Will[iam] for 12 years, at the end whereof the said Will[iam] is to make good the same unto her, as her father's legacy as aforesaid; & to that end the said John & Will[iam] either stand bound for other for performance of the several payments, as also for such other performances of meat, drink, clothing, &c., during the said term, as is meet.

"And for the rest of the estate, the widow having two children by the said Peter, together with her own 3d, it is allowed her for bringing up the said children, provided that she discharge whatsoever debts shall be proved to be owing by the said Peter, & the legacies given by the Court. For performance whereof she & Mr. Will[iam] Brewster bound in two hundred pounds" [PCR 1:18–19].

BIRTH: Baptized Dorking, Surrey, 26 January 1594/5, son of William Brown [TAG 79:165].
DEATH: Plymouth between 25 March 1633 (tax list) and 10 October 1633 (inventory).
MARRIAGE: (1) By 1626 widow MARTHA FORD {1621, Plymouth}, who died in 1630 or 1631 [TAG 42:35–42; PM 211].

(2) By 1631 Mary _____, who survived her husband by at least one year [PCR 1:28] but was probably dead by 1647 when one of her daughters sold land without referring to the widow's dower rights.
CHILDREN:
With first wife
> i MARY BROWN, b. about 1626 (and certainly before the division of cattle on 22 May 1627); m. by 27 October 1647 Ephraim Tinkham [PCLR 1:146; PCR 12:146].
> ii PRISCILLA BROWN, b. about 1628; m. Sandwich 21 March 1649 William Allen [PCR 8:9].

With second wife

    iii REBECCA BROWN, b. about 1631; m. by about 1654 William Snow [PCLR 5:197].

    iv Child BROWN, b. by 1633; d. by 1647 (when this child's three surviving sisters sold their inherited land).

ASSOCIATIONS: Peter Brown was brother of JOHN BROWN {1632, Duxbury} [TAG 79:161–78; PM 80–82].

Caleb Johnson has assembled evidence demonstrating that Peter Brown was associated in England with *WILLIAM MULLINS*, also of Dorking, and through Mullins to several other later Great Migration immigrants [TAG 79:161–78].

PREMIGRATION BIOGRAPHY: Peter Brown was born at Dorking, Surrey, in 1595, son of William Brown. Little is known of William Brown, including his occupation. Peter Brown presumably passed the first quarter century of his life as a single man in Dorking, where he certainly was acquainted with William Mullins [TAG 79:171].

COMMENTS: The evidence for the marriages of Peter Brown's three daughters is largely from deeds in which his land was sold by his sons-in-law, with the consent of his daughters. The earliest and best treatment in print on this point is an article published in 1966 by Florence Barclay [TAG 42:35–42, citing PCLR 1:146, 186, 5:197 (bis)].

The claim has also been made that Peter Brown of Windsor was son of the Plymouth Peter, but these same deeds, showing that each of the three daughters controlled one-third of their father's real estate, provide the best evidence that there was no such son; Robert S. Wakefield argued this in greater detail in 1979 [NGSQ 67:253–54].

Barbara Merrick has argued for some estimated dates slightly different from those used here [MQ 53:10–13].

BIBLIOGRAPHIC NOTE: The seventh volume of the Five Generations Project of the General Society of Mayflower Descendants, prepared by Robert S. Wakefield and published in 1992, with a revised second edition published in 2002, covers the descendants of Peter Brown [Robert S. Wakefield, *Mayflower Families Through Five Generations: Volume Seven, Peter Brown* (Plymouth 2002)].

In 2004 Caleb Johnson published data that establishes with a high degree of certainty that the brothers John and Peter Brown were baptized at Dorking, Surrey [TAG 79:161–78].

WILLIAM BUTTEN

Mr. Samuel Fuller and a servant called William Button. His wife was behind, and a child which came afterwards.

Mr. Fuller his servant died at sea.

ORIGIN: Leiden (as servant of *SAMUEL FULLER*).
MIGRATION: 1620 on the *Mayflower*.
FIRST RESIDENCE: Died at sea.

OCCUPATION: Servant to *SAMUEL FULLER*.

BIRTH: Born say 1605.
DEATH: At sea 6 November 1620 ("In all this voyage there died but one of the passengers, which was William Butten, a youth, servant to Samuel Fuller, when they drew near the coast" [Bradford 59; Prince 161]).
MARRIAGE: None.
CHILDREN: None.

COMMENTS: Caleb Johnson notes a William Butten, son of John Butten, baptized at Worksop, Nottinghamshire, on 13 March 1605 as possibly being this passenger. Worksop was not far from Scrooby and briefly had a separatist gathering in 1607. Some members of the Worksop congregation had joined with members of the Scrooby separatist congregation in the migration to the Netherlands in 1608 and soon after. Johnson also observes that another William Butten was baptized at Austerfield, Yorkshire, on 12 September 1589, but that man would have been too old to be considered a "youth" in 1620 [Mayflower Passengers 105].

ROBERT CARTER

Mr. William Mullins and his wife and two children, Joseph and Priscilla, and a servant, Robert Carter.

Mr. Mullins and his wife, his son and his servant died the first winter.

ORIGIN: Unknown (but see **COMMENTS**).
MIGRATION: 1620 on the *Mayflower*.
FIRST RESIDENCE: Plymouth.

OCCUPATION: Servant to *WILLIAM MULLINS*.

BIRTH: Born say 1600.
DEATH: Early 1621 at Plymouth (after his master, *WILLIAM MULLINS*, dictated his nuncupative will in mid-February 1620/1).
MARRIAGE: None.
CHILDREN: None.

COMMENTS: As a servant of William Mullins, Robert Carter may also have been from Dorking, Surrey, or vicinity. Caleb Johnson has collected some records that might lead to identifying Carter's English origin [Mayflower Passengers 106; TAG 79:166].

In his will, William Mullins asked that his overseers "have a special eye to my man Robert which hath not so approved himself as I would he should have done" [MQ 34:10; Waters 254–55; MD 1:230–32 (all citing PCC 68 Dale)].

JOHN CARVER

Mr. John Carver, Katherine his wife, Desire Minter, and two manservants, John Howland, Roger Wilder. William Latham, a boy, and a maidservant and a child that was put to him, Jasper More.

Mr. Carver and his wife died the first year, he in the spring, she in the summer. Also, his man Roger and the little boy Jasper died before either of them, of the common infection. Desire Minter returned to her friend and proved not very well and died in England. His servant boy Latham, after more than 20 years' stay in the country, went into England and from thence to the Bahama Islands in the West Indies, and there with some others was starved for want of food. His maidservant married and died a year or two after, here in this place. His servant John Howland married the daughter of John Tilley, Elizabeth, and they are both now living and have ten children, now all living, and their eldest daughter hath four children; and their second daughter one, all living, and other of their children marriageable. So 15 are come of them.

ORIGIN: Leiden.
PREVIOUS RESIDENCES: Great Bealings, Suffolk.
MIGRATION: 1620 on the *Mayflower*.
FIRST RESIDENCE: Plymouth.

CHURCH MEMBERSHIP: Deacon of John Robinson's congregation at Leiden [PChR 1:51].
FREEMAN: On 11 November 1620, John Carver signed the Mayflower Compact [Morton 26].
EDUCATION: Drafted the will of *WILLIAM MULLINS* [Waters 255; MD 1:230–32]. Although no letters written by Carver exist, he must have written many while serving as the congregation's agent in England in 1620, judging by the number of letters he received [Bradford 42–46, 360–61, 367].
OFFICES: Governor from landing at Plymouth until his death in early 1621 [Bradford 76].

ESTATE: John Carver had substantial landholdings in the manor of Seckford Hall, Great Bealings, in the first decade of the seventeenth century, land which he had inherited from his father [NEHGR 174:12]. Nathaniel Morton described Carver as "being one also of a considerable estate spent the main part of it, in this enterprise" [PChR 1:52].

BIRTH: Baptized Great Bealings, Suffolk, 12 March 1580/1, son of John and Margaret (_____) Carver [NEHGR 174:16].

DEATH: "In this month of April [1621], whilst they were busy about their seed, their Governor (Mr. John Carver) came out of the field very sick, it being a hot day. He complained greatly of his head and lay down, and within a few hours his senses failed, so as he never spake more till he died, which was within a few days after. Whose death was much lamented and caused great heaviness amongst them, as there was cause. He was buried in the best manner they could, with some volleys of shot by all that bore arms. And his wife, being a weak woman, died within five or six weeks after him" [Bradford 86].

MARRIAGE: (1) By 1603 Martha Rose, daughter of William Rose of Tuddenham St. Martin, Suffolk. She died in 1608 or soon after [NEHGR 174:16].

(2) By 1609 Catherine (White) Leggatt, daughter of Alexander White [NEHGR 174:16–17]. She died at Plymouth about five or six weeks after her husband, so in late May or early June 1621 [Bradford 86].

CHILD:
With first wife
> i MARGARET CARVER, bp. Great Bealings 26 April 1603 [NEHGR 174:18]; living on 4 November 1604 when named in grandfather's will; no further record.

ASSOCIATIONS: Through his wife, John Carver was uncle of ISAAC ROBINSON {1631, Plymouth} [PM 391–95]. John Carver was related through marriage to *DESIRE MINTER* [NEHGR 174:5–20]. ROBERT CARVER {1638, Marshfield} was not related to John Carver of the *Mayflower*, and was probably from Whitechapel, Middlesex [NEHGR 174:19–20].

PREMIGRATION BIOGRAPHY: John Carver was born at Great Bealings, Suffolk, in 1581. He certainly attended grammar school, perhaps at Woodbridge, Suffolk. John Carver appeared frequently in the manorial rolls of Seckford Hall, Great Bealings, and sold off all his holdings there between 1605 and 1608, after which he disappears from English records.

The Carver family had arrived in Leiden by 1615, where he was made deacon of John Robinson's congregation [NEHGR 174:17–18]. As the plans to migrate to the New World developed over the next few years, Carver joined Robert Cushman [PM 158–60] as an agent for the congregation in England, dealing with the London adventurers [Bradford 42–46, 360–61, 367].

COMMENTS: Dexter published burial records of two children at Hooglandsekerk, Leiden, one in 1609 and one in 1617, as children of John Carver [Dexter 608–9]. Dexter misread these burial records, which pertain to other families [private communication from Jeremy D. Bangs].

John Carver was a member of the exploratory party that left Provincetown Harbor on 6 December 1620 and selected the site for the town of Plymouth [Mourt 32].

BIBLIOGRAPHIC NOTE: In 2020 Sue Allan, Caleb Johnson, and Simon Neal published the evidence establishing the English origin of John Carver [NEHGR 174:5–20].

DOROTHY _____
(JOHN CARVER'S MAIDSERVANT)

Mr. John Carver, Katherine his wife, Desire Minter, and two manservants, John Howland, Roger Wilder. William Latham, a boy, and a maidservant and a child that was put to him, Jasper More.

His maidservant married and died a year or two after, here in this place.

ORIGIN: Leiden (as servant of *JOHN CARVER*).
MIGRATION: 1620 on the *Mayflower*.
FIRST RESIDENCE: Plymouth.

ESTATE: Whether she was dead or alive in 1623, one acre of land was granted to Francis Eaton in Dorothy's right in the land division of that year [PCR 12:4; MQ 40:13].

BIRTH: By about 1602 (based on estimated date of marriage).
DEATH: Plymouth soon after 1622 (and certainly before Eaton married his third wife about 1626).
MARRIAGE: Dorothy married about 1622 *FRANCIS EATON* as his second wife.
CHILDREN: None.

COMMENTS: This identification depends on a single document, a Bristol record of 4 December 1626 in which "Francis Eaton of the City of Gloucester carpenter and Dorothy his wife" took on John Morgan of Bristol as an apprentice; a marginal note for this apprenticeship places "the Master at New England." This identification has been discussed by Caleb Johnson and Neil Thompson [Mayflower Passengers 263–65; TAG 72:301–4].

JAMES CHILTON

James Chilton and his wife, and Mary their daughter; they had another daughter that was married, came afterward.

James Chilton and his wife also died in the first infection, but their daughter Mary is still living and hath nine children; and one daughter is married and hath a child. So their increase is ten.

ORIGIN: Leiden.
PREVIOUS RESIDENCES: Canterbury, Kent; Sandwich, Kent.
MIGRATION: 1620 on the *Mayflower*.
FIRST RESIDENCE: Died before *Mayflower* reached Plymouth.

OCCUPATION: Tailor [NEA 8:2:40; MQ 75:139–40].
FREEMAN: On 11 November 1620, James Chilton signed the Mayflower Compact [Morton 26].
ESTATE: In the 1623 Plymouth land division "Marie Chilton" received an unknown number of acres (perhaps three) as a passenger on the *Mayflower* [PCR 12:4; MD 40:13]. In the 1627 Plymouth cattle division Mary, now the wife of John Winslow, is listed as the sixth person in the sixth company [PCR 12:11].

BIRTH: About 1556 (aged 63 in 1619 [Bangs 34]), probably at Canterbury, Kent, son of Lionel and Edith (_____) Chilton [TAG 38:244; MD 62:69–77].
DEATH: 8 December 1620 in Provincetown Harbor [Prince 165].
MARRIAGE: By 1584 _____ _____. On 12 June 1609, "[blank] the wife of James Chilton" was excommunicated from St. Peter, Sandwich, Kent. [NEHGR 153:407–12]. She died at Plymouth early in 1621 [Bradford 446]. (John G. Hunt suggested that she was Susanne Furner, James Chilton's stepsister [TAG 38:244–45], but there are serious chronological problems with this identification [NEHGR 153:408–9; NEA 8:2:40].)
CHILDREN:

> i JOEL CHILTON, bp. St. Paul, Canterbury, 16 August 1584 [NEA 8:2:39–40]; bur. St. Martin, Canterbury, 2 November 1593 [MF 15:3].

ii ISABELLA CHILTON, bp. St. Paul, Canterbury, 15 January 1586/7 [MF 15:3]; m. Leiden 21 July 1615 [NS] ROGER CHANDLER {1632, Plymouth} [Leiden Pilgrims 142; MD 11:129; PM 101].

iii JANE CHILTON, bp. St. Paul, Canterbury, 8 June 1589 [MF 15:3]; no further record.

iv MARY CHILTON, bur. St. Martin, Canterbury, 23 November 1593 [MF 15:3].

v ELIZABETH CHILTON, bp. St. Martin, Canterbury, 14 July 1594 [MF 15:3]; no further record.

vi JAMES CHILTON, bp. St. Martin, Canterbury, 22 August 1596 [MF 15:3]; d. by 11 September 1603.

vii INGLE CHILTON, bp. St. Paul, Canterbury, 29 April 1599 [MF 15:3]; m. (1) (as "Engeltgen Gilten") Leiden 27 August 1622 [NS] Robert Nelson [Leiden Pilgrims 198; Dexter 627]; m. (2) Leiden (banns) 26 March 1636 [NS] Daniel Pietersz; m. (3) Leiden 18 July 1637 [NS] Matthijs Tilligem.[1]

viii CHRISTIAN CHILTON (dau.), bp. St. Peter, Sandwich, Kent, 26 July 1601 [MF 15:3]; m. (1) Leiden (banns) 3 June 1635 [NS] Joris Abrahamsz; m. (2) Leiden (banns) 17 January 1636 [NS] Dionysius van Steenstraten.[2]

ix JAMES CHILTON, bp. St. Peter, Sandwich, 11 September 1603 [MF 15:3]; no further record.

x MARY CHILTON, bp. St. Peter, Sandwich, 31 May 1607 [MQ 75:137]; m. Plymouth by 22 May 1627 JOHN WINSLOW {1623, Plymouth} [PM 511].

---

[1] Leiden Church records marriages Nederlands Hervormd Ondertrouw (1575–1795), Part II, Period 1633–1637, Leiden, archive 1004, inventory 11, NH Ondertrouw L. augustus 1633–1637, folio L-168v (banns for Daniel Pietersz and Engeltgen Jacobsdr). Leiden Church records marriages Schepenhuwelijken (1592–1795), Part 199, Period 1633–1646, Leiden, archive 1004, inventory 199, July 18, 1637, Trouwen Gerecht C. juli 1633 – juli 1646, folio C-075 (marriage of Mathijs Tilligem and Engeltgen Jacobs). Unpublished research of Tamura Jones of Leiden.

[2] Leiden Church records marriages Dopen en Trouwen NH, Part 714, Period 1599–1646, Warmond, archive 0600, inventory 714, 3 June 1635, Doop en trouwboek NH 1599–1646, folio 42 (banns for Joris Abrahamsz and Christina Jacobsdr). Leiden Church records marriages Nederlands Hervormd Ondertrouw (1575–1795), Part II, Period 1633–1637, Leiden, archive 1004, inventory 11, NH Ondertrouw L. augustus 1633–1637, folio L-140v (banns for Dionysius van Steenstraten and Chrijstijntgen Jacobsdr). Unpublished research of Tamura Jones of Leiden.

PREMIGRATION BIOGRAPHY: James Chilton was born about 1556, probably at Canterbury, Kent, son of Lionel and Edith (_____) Chilton [MD 62:69–77]. In 1583 James Chilton, merchant tailor, was made a freeman of the city of Canterbury; during his years at Canterbury he took on at least two apprentices [NEA 8:2:40]. By 1584, he had married a woman whose name we do not know, first or last. Between 1587 and 1599, this couple had seven children born at Canterbury, four of them baptized at St. Paul parish and three at St. Martin. On 25 July 1598, "Alexander Bournley of Northgate within the liberty of the city of Canterbury, and James Chilton of the parish of St. Paul within the city of Canterbury in the aforesaid county, tailors," stood as sureties for Richard Allen of the parish of St. Paul on his application for a tavernkeeper's license [MQ 75:139–40]. Chilton's last appearance in the Canterbury records was in 1600 when he was fined for victualling without a license [NEA 8:2:40].

Within a year after this fine, James Chilton had left Canterbury and moved to nearby Sandwich, Kent. On 26 July 1601, daughter Christian Chilton, James's eighth child, was baptized at the parish of St. Peter, Sandwich, followed by son James in 1603 and daughter Mary in 1607. On 8 May 1609, the rector at St. Peter presented "Thomas Bartlet, [blank] the wife of James Chilton, Danyell Hooke and Mosses Flecher all of our said parish for privately burying a child of Andrewe Sharpe of St. Mary's parish ..., this they did the 25 or 24 of April last past, the lawfulness of which act some of them seem now since to dissent by calling into question the lawfullness of the king's constitutions in this and other behalfs, affirming these things to be popishly ceremonies and of no other force." On 12 June 1609, three of those presented, including James Chilton's wife, were excommunicated [NEHGR 153:407]. This was the last record for the Chiltons found in Sandwich, or anywhere else in England.

The earliest evidence for the presence of the Chiltons at Leiden was on 22 May 1615 [NS], when James Chilton's daughter Isabel was betrothed to Roger Wilson (also of Canterbury) [Leiden Pilgrims 142]. Only one record for James Chilton himself in Leiden has been found, but it is an important one, discovered by Jeremy Bangs. On 28 April 1619 [NS], while returning to his house on the Langebrug, James Chilton and his daughter were accosted by a group of boys who thought that Chilton was an Arminian and that he was hosting meetings of that sect at his house. In depositions taken after this attack, Chilton's age was given as sixty-three. The boys were mistaken, as Chilton was not an Arminian, but apparently they had a vague idea that he was involved with some sort of unconventional religious activity, perhaps confusing meetings of the Arminians with gatherings of the Pilgrim congregation. This episode occurred not long after a turbulent period during which the Arminian faction in Leiden had been in the ascendant, but had been subdued by town leaders associated with the Reformed Church. The attack on Chilton was one of the factors convincing the members of the Pilgrim congregation that the time had come to leave Leiden and seek a new place where they could practice their religion more peacefully. A little more than a year later James Chilton, his wife, and his daughter Mary joined those who sailed for the New World on the *Mayflower* [Strangers and Pilgrims 278–79].

COMMENTS: The death date for James Chilton is given variously as 6, 8, or 18 December 1620. The best evidence for the date is Prince, who cites a now-lost notebook kept by William Bradford [Prince 165]. (The date of 18 December presumably arose when someone corrected for the 1752 calendar change, an unnecessary confusion; a memorial stone with this date was erected at Provincetown.)

A longstanding tradition has held that Mary Chilton was the first of the *Mayflower* passengers to step onto Plymouth Rock. Charles Thornton Libby carried out a detailed examination of this story, published as *Mary Chilton's Title to Celebrity* (Boston 1926; rpt. Warwick, Rhode Island, 1978). He accepted the undocumented tradition as correct.

BIBLIOGRAPHIC NOTE: James Chilton has been treated in Volume Fifteen of the Five Generations Project of the General Society of Mayflower Descendants, published in 1997, prepared originally by Robert Moody Sherman and Verle D. Vincent and revised by Robert S. Wakefield [MF 15:1–150]. (This supersedes the version of this family published in Volume Two in 1978.)

RICHARD CLARKE

Moses Fletcher, John Goodman, Thomas Williams, Digory Priest, Edmund Margesson, Peter Browne, Richard Britteridge, Richard Clarke, Richard Gardiner, Gilbert Winslow.

Moses Fletcher, Thomas Williams, Digory Priest, John Goodman, Edmund Margesson, Richard Britteridge, Richard Clarke, all these died soon after arrival in the general sickness that befell. But Digory Priest had his wife and children sent hither afterwards, she being Mr. Allerton's sister. But the rest left no posterity here.

ORIGIN: Unknown.
MIGRATION: 1620 on the *Mayflower*.
FIRST RESIDENCE: Plymouth.

FREEMAN: On 11 November 1620, Richard Clarke signed the Mayflower Compact [Morton 26].

BIRTH: Born by 1599 (assuming he was twenty-one when he signed the Mayflower Compact).
DEATH: Early 1621 at Plymouth.
MARRIAGE: None known.
CHILDREN: None known.

FRANCIS COOKE

Francis Cooke and his son John, but his wife and other children came afterwards.

Francis Cooke is still living, a very old man, and hath seen his children's children have children. After his wife came over with other of his children; he hath three still living by her, all married and have five children, so their increase is eight. And his son John which came over with him is married, and hath four children living.

ORIGIN: Leiden.
PREVIOUS RESIDENCES: Norwich, Norfolk [NEHGR 143:197].
MIGRATION: 1620 on the *Mayflower.*
FIRST RESIDENCE: Plymouth.

OCCUPATION: Woolcomber (in 1603) [Leiden Pilgrims 152]. His inventory included several items that indicated that he was still a woolcomber at the time of his death: "1 pair of cards and one basket," "1 woolen wheel & scales," "3 pair of sheep shears," "three pair of old cards," "20 lb. of wool & 2 pair of old stockings," "16 sheep," and "5 lambs" [PCPR 2:2:1–2].
CHURCH MEMBERSHIP: In the first decade of the seventeenth century, Francis Cooke and his wife were members of the Walloon churches at Leiden and at Norwich [NEHGR 143:195–98]. Soon after 1611 they became members of John Robinson's Leiden congregation [Mayflower Passengers 122].

In his attempt to justify the structure and practice of the Plymouth church to an English audience, Edward Winslow included the following example:"Take notice of our practice at Leyden, viz: that one Samuel Terry was received from the French Church there, into communion with us; also the wife of Francis Cooke being a Walloon, [who] holds communion with the Church at Plymouth, as she came from the French, to this day, by virtue of communion of churches" [MD 27:64, from *Hypocrisie Unmasked*].
FREEMAN: On 11 November 1620, Francis Cooke signed the Mayflower Compact [Morton 26].

In the 1633 Plymouth list of freemen, ahead of those admitted on 1 January 1632/3 [PCR 1:3]; in the 7 March 1636/7 and 1639 lists of Plymouth freemen [PCR 1:52, 8:173]. In the Plymouth section of Plymouth Colony list of freemen of 1658 [PCR 8:197].

EDUCATION: His inventory included "1 great Bible & 4 old books"valued at 10s. [MD 2:26–27, citing PCPR 2:2:1–2; Plymouth Libraries 253].

OFFICES: Plymouth Colony committee to lay out the twenty-acre grants, 3 January 1627[/8] [PCR 12:14]. Committee to lay out land, 5 May 1640, 5 October 1640 [PCR 1:152, 163]. Committee to lay out highways, 1 October 1634, 2 May 1637, 1 February 1640/1, 10 June 1650 [PCR 1:31, 58, 2:7, 160]. Arbitrator in land dispute between Thomas Pope and William Shurtleff, 2 August 1659 [PCR 3:169].

Plymouth petit jury, 2 January 1637/8, 3 September 1639, 3 December 1639, 3 March 1639/40, 2 June 1640, 7 June 1642, 7 September 1642, 7 March 1642/3 [PCR 1:74, 7:7, 13, 14, 16, 31, 32, 34]. Grand jury, 5 June 1638, 2 June 1640, 7 March 1642/3, 6 June 1643 [PCR 1:87, 155, 2:53, 56]. Coroner's jury, 22 July 1648 [PCR 2:132].

Plymouth surveyor of highways 1 March 1641/2, 7 June 1642, 4 June 1645 [PCR 2:34, 40, 84].

In Plymouth section of 1643 Plymouth Colony list of men able to bear arms [PCR 8:187]. On 22 June 1644, Francis Cooke was in a list of seven men at Jones River who were to gather together in "case of alarm in time of war" [PTR 1:17]. His inventory included "2 old muskets" valued at 12s.

ESTATE: Appears on the diagram of "meersteads & garden plots of [those] which came first laid out 1620," between Isaac Allerton and Edward Winslow [PCR 12:3]. In 1623 Plymouth land division received two acres as passenger on *Mayflower,* plus four acres for the rest of his family who came on the *Anne* in 1623 [PCR 12:4, 5; MD 40:10]; some of this land had apparently been sold to William Bradford by 1639 [PCR 12:51]. In the 1627 Plymouth cattle division Francis Cooke, his wife Hester Cooke, John Cooke, Jacob Cooke, Jane Cooke, Hester Cooke, and Mary Cooke were the first seven persons in the first company [PCR 12:9].

Francis Cooke was one of the Purchasers, those who acquired the rights to land distributions in Plymouth Colony as a consequence of the agreement made between the London merchants and the Plymouth settlers in 1627 [Ford 282–88].

Assessed 18s. in the Plymouth tax list of 25 March 1633 and 9s. in the list of 27 March 1634 [PCR 1:10, 28].

On 3 December 1638, a small parcel of land that had been previously granted to Francis Cooke was instead granted to Thomas Prence [PCR 1:103]. On 4 February 1638/9, "a parcel of upland lying at the end of Goodman Shawe's land at Smilt River is granted to Francis Cooke" [PCR 1:112].

On 5 October 1640, Francis Cooke and John Cooke Jr. were granted a parcel of upland "provided it do not exceed two hundred acres of upland, and the meadow before it," along with a parcel of upland "containing about 10 or 12 acres" [PCR 1:163, 2:149, 164]. On 9 April 1650, Francis Cooke gave "his son Jacob Cook" all his right in one hundred acres at North River granted him 5 October 1640 [PCR 12:185]. On 17 October 1642, Francis Cooke was one of those who received six acres apiece "if it be there to be had" at North Meadow by Jones River [PCR 2:49].

In March 1651, Francis Cooke was included in a list of "those that have interest and properties in the town's land at Punckateeset over against Road Iland" [PTR 1:36, 66].

On 25 December 1655, the town of Plymouth granted to Francis Cooke "3 holes of meadow lying at the hither end of the great meadow called Jones River" [PTR 1:208]. On 5 July 1670, "[w]hereas it is evident to the Court, that a certain tract or parcel of land, called Old Cooke's Holes, lying at Jonses River meadow, was formerly granted unto Francis Cooke, of Plymouth, deceased, in the lieu of some land which is supposed would have fallen within his line at the Smelt Brooke, but is not fully settled on the said Cooke and his heirs and assigns, this Court doth by these presents fully and absolutely settle, ratify, assure and confirm the said grant of land or tract of land, being threescore acres ... unto the said Francis Cooke, his heirs and assigns forever, which said land was given by the said Francis Cooke unto Richard Wright and Thomas Michell, commonly called Old Cooke's Holes, and since his decease ratified and confirmed unto the said Richard Wright and Thomas Michell by John Cooke, the heir unto the said Francis Cooke" [PCR 5:44].

On 3 June 1662, Francis Cooke was included in the list of those who might "look out some accommodations of land, as being the first born children of this government" [PCR 4:19].

In his will, dated 7 December 1659 and proved 5 June 1663, Francis Cooke bequeathed to "my dear and loving wife" all moveables and cattle and to "Hester my wife ... my lands both upland and meadow lands which at present I possess during her life"; "my dear wife and my son John Cooke" to be joint executors [MD 2:24–25, citing PCPR 2:2:1].

The inventory of the estate of Francis Cooke, taken 1 May 1663, totaled £86 11s. 1d. "besides the housing and land," which was not included [MD 2:26–27, citing PCPR 2:2:1–2].

On 1 March 1663/4, the court "taking notice of such evidence as hath been produced for the clearing of a controversy between John Tompson, plaintiff, and Richard Wright, in reference to a parcel of land at Namassakett, do allow an agreement between the said parties, which was ordered here to be entered, as followeth, viz: that the said parties shall have equal share of the land allotted to Francis Cooke at Namaskett aforesaid, provided that they be equal in bearing the charge about the said land" [PCR 4:54].

On 8 June 1666, John Cooke, Jacob Cooke, Hester Wright the wife of Richard Wright, and Mary Tompson the wife of John Tompson, to prevent dispute over the intent of their father Francis Cooke in his will with regard to the land at Rocky Nook, agreed to divide it into five shares with John Cooke, the eldest son, getting two shares [PCLR 3:73].

BIRTH: England in or shortly after 1583 [MD 3:95–96, 8:49].
DEATH: Plymouth 7 April 1663 [PCR 8:23; MD 17:183; PVR 663].
MARRIAGE: Leiden 20 July 1603 [NS] or shortly thereafter Hester Mahieu [MD 27:145–55 (incorporating and correcting MD 8:48–50, 22:13–14); Plooij LXXIII], daughter of (Jacques?) and Jeanne Mahieu [NEHGR 143:195–99]. She died after 8 June 1666 [PCLR 3:73].
CHILDREN:

i JANE COOKE, b. say 1605; m. Plymouth in 1627 or soon after EXPERIENCE MITCHELL {1623, Plymouth} [NEHGR 127:94–95; TAG 59:28–31; PM 324; MD 66:5–9].

ii JOHN COOKE, bp. Walloon Church, Leiden, January-March 1607 [NS] [MD 27:153 (note that Bowman goes slightly astray in his comments on this baptism; NEHGS 143:197)]; in the Plymouth tax list of 27 March 1634 assessed 9s. [PCR 1:28]; m. Plymouth 28 March 1634 Sarah Warren [PCR 1:29], daughter of *RICHARD WARREN*.

iii Child COOKE, bur. Pieterskerk, Leiden, 20 May 1608 [NS] [NEHGR 143:197].

iv ELIZABETH COOKE, bp. Walloon Church, Leiden, 26 December 1611 [NS] [NEHGR 143:197]; no further record.

v JACOB COOKE, b. about 1618 (deposed 14 July 1674 "aged fifty-six years or thereabout" [MD 2:45–46, citing PLR 1:81]); m. (1) Plymouth shortly after 10 June 1646 (marriage contract) Damaris Hopkins [PCR 2:27; MD 2:27–28, citing PCLR 2:1:35], daughter of *STEPHEN HOPKINS*; m. (2) Plymouth 18 November 1669 Elizabeth (Lettice) Shurtleff [PVR 666], daughter of THOMAS LETTICE {1638, Plymouth} and widow of WILLIAM SHURTLEFF {1634, Plymouth} [GM 2:6:320–24].

vi HESTER COOKE, b. say 1624; m. Plymouth in 1644 RICHARD WRIGHT {1636, Plymouth} [PCR 2:79; see also TAG 59:165–70].

vii MARY COOKE, b. Plymouth say 1626; m. Plymouth 26 December 1645 John Tompson [PCR 12:94].

ASSOCIATIONS: PHILIP DELANO {1621, Plymouth} was nephew of Hester (Mahieu) Cooke, wife of Francis Cooke [NEHGR 143:198–99; PM 164–68].

PREMIGRATION BIOGRAPHY: Francis Cooke was born about 1583 in England. He was residing at Leiden as early as 1603 when he married Hester Mahieu, a member of the Walloon church at Leiden, where the marriage was presumably celebrated and where the couple had children baptized in 1607 and 1611. For some period between 1606 and 1608 the Cookes resided at Norwich, Norfolk, as members of the Walloon church there. On 1 January 1608 [NS], Francis and Hester were admitted to communion at the Leiden Walloon church by a letter of recommendation from the Norwich Walloon church. During their time in Norwich, the Cookes could well have become acquainted with Reverend John Robinson, who was residing there at the time, just before Robinson became associated with the Scrooby congregation [NEHGR 143:195–99; MQ 78:140–44]. The Cookes apparently joined John Robinson's Leiden congregation some time after 1611, and certainly by 1620.

COMMENTS: On 16 February 1620/1, an unnamed Plymouth resident was hunting in the woods near town when he observed a party of Indians without himself being observed. He was able to alert the townspeople of the approaching natives. "Captain Miles Standish and Francis Cook, being at work in the woods, coming home, left their tools behind them, but before they returned their tools were taken away by the savages" [Mourt 49]. The tools were returned a few days later [Mourt 53–54].

In the 1623 division of lands at Plymouth, the two acres granted to Francis Cooke as a passenger on the *Mayflower* were for himself and his son John, while the four acres granted to him as a passenger on the *Anne* were for his wife Hester, his daughters Jane and Hester, and his son Jacob [PCR 12:4–5; MD 40:10:58].

On 24 December 1636, John Harmon contracted to become the apprentice of Francis Cooke for seven years [PCR 1:46]. On 7 March 1636/7, Francis Cooke sued John Browne the elder and several others, and, on 7 June 1637, Francis Cooke, having sued Mr. John Browne, was granted an execution against him [PCR 1:60, 7:5].

BIBLIOGRAPHIC NOTE: The Five Generations Project of the General Society of Mayflower Descendants in 1996 published its account of the descendants of Francis Cooke as Volume Twelve in the series, compiled by Ralph Van Wood Jr.

In 1901 George E. Bowman prepared a genealogy of the family of Francis Cooke, in which he abstracted every record he could find for the immigrant and his wife and children [MD 3:95–105]. Lora A. W. Underhill, in her pursuit of the ancestry of Edward Small, published in 1934 an even more detailed study of the family [Small Gen 601–45]. Mary Walton Ferris also compiled a brief account of the family of Francis Cooke [Dawes-Gates 2:238–44]. In 1989 Jeremy Dupertuis Bangs published a number of records relating to Francis Cooke and his family in Leiden [NEHGR 143:195–98], in 2007 he presented the results of his research on the Mahieu family in Lille and vicinity [MD 56:150–62], and in 2012 he reported on Norwich records for the family [MQ 78:140–44].

HUMILITY COOPER

Edward Tilley and Ann his wife, and two children that were their cousins, Henry Sampson and Humility Cooper.

Edward Tilley and his wife both died soon after their arrival, and the girl Humility, their cousin, was sent for into England and died there.

ORIGIN: Leiden.
PREVIOUS RESIDENCES: Henlow, Bedfordshire.
MIGRATION: 1620 on the *Mayflower*.
FIRST RESIDENCE: Plymouth.
RETURN TRIPS: Returned permanently to England some time after 1627 and resided at the parish of Holy Trinity Minories, London.

CHURCH MEMBERSHIP: On 17 March 1638/9, "Humilitie," daughter of Robert Cooper, was baptized at Holy Trinity, Minories, London; she was born in Holland and was aged 19 years [TG 6:166].
ESTATE: In the 1623 Plymouth land division, "Humillitie Cooper" was granted one acre as a passenger on the *Mayflower* [PCR 12:4; MD 40:13]. In the 1627 Plymouth cattle division "Humillyty Cooper" was the last person in the fifth company [PCR 12:10].

BIRTH: Born Leiden by about 1619, daughter of Robert and Joan (Gresham) Cooper, formerly of Henlow, Bedfordshire [TG 6:166–86].
DEATH: Between 17 March 1638/9 (date of baptism in London) and 1651 (date of compilation of Bradford's list).
MARRIAGE: None known.
CHILDREN: None known.
ASSOCIATIONS: Humility Cooper was niece of Agnes (Cooper) Tilley, wife of *EDWARD TILLEY*, and first cousin of *HENRY SAMSON* [TAG 52:198–208].

COMMENTS: The adult baptism for Humility Cooper would mean that she was no more than a year old at the time the *Mayflower* sailed. She must have died in the twelve years between her baptism and Bradford's accounting of the *Mayflower* passengers; there is no evidence that she married or had children.

BIBLIOGRAPHIC NOTE: Caleb Johnson has published records from manorial courts in Henlow, Bedfordshire, and Arlesey, Bedfordshire, which document the ancestry of Robert Cooper, Humility Cooper's father [MQ 76:126–28; MD 61:70–75].

JOHN CRACKSTONE

John Crackston and his son John Crackston.

John Crackston died in the first mortality, and about some five or six years after his son died, having lost himself in the woods; his feet became frozen, which put him into a fever of which he died.

ORIGIN: Leiden.
PREVIOUS RESIDENCES: Colchester, Essex [Leiden Pilgrims 247].
MIGRATION: 1620 on the *Mayflower.*
FIRST RESIDENCE: Plymouth.

FREEMAN: On 11 November 1620, John Crackstone signed the Mayflower Compact [Morton 26].
ESTATE: In the 1623 Plymouth land division, John Crackstone received an unknown number of acres (perhaps two) as a passenger on the *Mayflower* [PCR 12:4; MD 40:12].

"Heirs of John Crackstone" were among the Purchasers, those who acquired the rights to land distributions in Plymouth Colony as a consequence of the agreement made between the London merchants and the Plymouth settlers in 1627 [Ford 282–88]. By 1652 this share of land had passed to William Bradford and William Bassett [MD 4:186; MQ 40:118]. On 7 March 1652[/3], a note on a deed relating to the Purchasers' land at Dartmouth reports that "the one half of John Crackstone's land which was Mr. Will[i]am Bradford Senior his land was passed over by the said Will[i]am Bradford to Mr. John Howland" [MD 4:185–86, citing PCLR 2:1:106–7].

BIRTH: England by about 1569 (based on date of marriage).
DEATH: Plymouth between 11 January 1620/1 and 10 April 1621 [Bradford 445; MD 2:116].
MARRIAGE: Stratford St. Mary, Suffolk, 9 May 1594 Katherine Bates [TAG 80:100]. She had probably died before 1620, and perhaps considerably earlier.

CHILDREN:

> i ANNA CRACKSTONE, b. say 1598; m. Leiden 22 December 1618 [NS] Thomas Smith [Dexter 634; Leiden Pilgrims 163].
>
> ii JOHN CRACKSTONE, b. say 1602; came to Plymouth in 1620; in 1623 Plymouth land division granted (probably) two acres (one for himself and one for his deceased father) [PCR 12:4; MQ 40:12]; in 1627 Plymouth cattle division listed as the thirteenth member of the second company [PCR 12:9]; d. Plymouth in 1627 or soon after [Bradford 445].

PREMIGRATION BIOGRAPHY: John Crackstone was born in England by about 1569. He first appeared in the records in 1594 when he married Katherine Bates at Stratford St. Mary, Suffolk. Stratford St. Mary is at the southern end of a group of Suffolk parishes that supported an active population of separatists in the 1590s and early 1600s [NEHGR 173:204]. The likelihood that Crackstone was associated with that group is supported by the inclusion of John Crackstone, the son of the deceased immigrant, in the company of Isaac Allerton in the 1627 division of cattle; Allerton was certainly part of the Suffolk separatist community [PCR 12:9]. At some point between his marriage and his removal to Leiden no later than 1616, John Crackstone and his family apparently lived in Colchester, Essex, or vicinity, as that town is given as his daughter Anna's origin when she married Thomas Smith at Leiden in 1618. (Colchester is about six miles southwest of Stratford St. Mary.)

COMMENTS: John Crackstone first appeared in Leiden records on 16 June 1616 [NS] when he witnessed the betrothal of Zachariah Barrow. On 22 December 1618, when the marriage banns for Thomas Smith and Anna Crackstone were entered at Leiden, the bride was described as "spinster, from Colchester in England" [MQ 40:117; Leiden Pilgrims 54, 96, 163, 247].

BIBLIOGRAPHIC NOTE: In 1974 Robert S. Wakefield gathered all the evidence then available on John Crackstone [MQ 40:117–19]. Wakefield noted that none of the baptismal records for children of a Thomas Smith in Leiden subsequent to 1618 appear to be for the Thomas Smith who married Anna Crackstone. In 2005 Caleb Johnson published the marriage record for John Crackstone [TAG 80:100].

EDWARD DOTY

Mr. Stephen Hopkins and Elizabeth his wife, and two children called Giles and Constanta, a daughter, both by a former wife. And two more by this wife called Damaris and Oceanus; the last was born at sea. And two servants called Edward Doty and Edward Lester.

Edward Doty and Edward Lester, the servants of Mr. Hopkins. Lester, after he was at liberty, went to Virginia and there died. But Edward Doty by a second wife hath seven children, and both he and they are living.

ORIGIN: London.
MIGRATION: 1620 on the *Mayflower.*
FIRST RESIDENCE: Plymouth.

OCCUPATION: Servant to *STEPHEN HOPKINS* (in 1620).
Planter [PCR 2:44, 69].
FREEMAN: On 11 November 1620, Edward Doty signed the Mayflower Compact [Morton 26].

In the 1633 Plymouth list of freemen, ahead of those admitted on 1 January 1632/3 [PCR 1:3], and in the list of 7 March 1636/7 [PCR 1:52]. In the Plymouth section of the Plymouth Colony list of 1639 [PCR 8:174].
EDUCATION: Signed his deeds by mark.
OFFICES: In the Plymouth section of 1643 Plymouth Colony list of men able to bear arms [PCR 8:187]. His inventory included "a matchcock musket" valued at 12s. and "a watch bill" valued at 3s. [PCPR 2:1:15–16].
ESTATE: In the 1623 Plymouth division of land there are two consecutive entries for "Edward [blank]," granted one acre; one of these must be for Edward Doty [PCR 12:4; MD 40:10]. In the 1627 Plymouth division of cattle "Edward Dolton" was the eleventh person in the fourth company [PCR 12:10].

Edward Doty was one of the Purchasers, those who acquired the rights to land distributions in Plymouth Colony as a consequence of the agreement made between the London merchants and the Plymouth settlers in 1627 [Ford 282–88].

Assessed £1 7s. in the Plymouth tax list of 25 March 1633 and 18s. in the list of 27 March 1634 [PCR 1:10, 27].

On 12 July 1637, "Edward Dotey" sold to Richard Derby "all those his messuages, houses and tenements at the High Cliff or Skeart Hill together with the four lots of lands and three other acres purchased of Josuah Pratt, Phineas Pratt and John Shawe," with the exclusion of an inner chamber in the "chief messuage ... wherein the said Edward Dotey layeth his corn"; Doty would keep possession of the other house and three lots until he received all the £150 and reaped the crop of corn. If Richard Derby failed to return from old England or failed to have the £150 paid by harvest time, Doty could sow another crop and reap it until Derby returned or paid [PCR 12:20–21]. Apparently Derby settled for the single lot and paid £22 [PCR 12:46].

On 16 September 1641, Edward Doty was granted a forty-acre parcel of upland at Lakenham [PCR 2:26]. On 7 May 1642, "Edward Dotey" purchased one acre of upland at High Cliff from Joshua Pratt [PCR 12:81]. On 5 May 1643, "Edward Dotey" sold two lots totaling forty acres of upland to Stephen Bryan and John Shaw Jr. [PCR 12:91].

In his will, dated 20 May 1655 and proved 5 March 1655/6, Edward Doty Senior of Plymouth "being sick" bequeathed "my purchase land lying at Coaksett unto my sons; my son Edward I give a double portion and to the rest of my sons equal alike," only to "my wife I leave a third during her life then after to return to my sons"; to "my loving wife ... my house and lands and meadows within the precincts of New Plymouth"; "my share of land at Punckquetest if it come to anything I give it unto my son Edward"; on 5 March 1655/6, "Faith the wife of Edward Dotten deceased" relinquished to her sons her right in lands at Coaksett [MD 3:87–88, citing PCPR 2:1:14].

The inventory of the estate of "Edward Dotten lately deceased," taken 21 November 1655, totaled £137 19s. 6d., of which £60 was real estate: "his dwelling house with his land adjoining," £25; "threescore acres of upland with the meadow adjoining to it lying in the woods," £10; "the land at Clarkes Iland," £5; and "the purchase land lying at Coaksett," £20 [MD 3:88–89, citing PCPR 2:1:15–16].

In her will, dated 12 December 1675 and proved 8 June 1676, "Faith Phillips the wife of John Phillipes" of Marshfield "though weak in body" bequeathed to "my daughter Mary" £9 in "my son John's hands"; to "my daughter Elizabeth £6"; to "my daughter Mary £3 due by bill of sale"; to "my daughter Desire £6 due by my bill of sale and a warming pan." On 4 November 1676, letters of administration were granted to "John Rouse Junior of Marshfield ... in the behalf of himself his wife and sisters: viz: Desire [torn] and Mary Doten" [MD 3:89–90, citing PCPR 3:2:12]. On 10 July 1677, "whereas there is about thirty shillings of the estate of Faith

Phillips deceased lying in the custody of John Phillips her husband, it is agreed by and between the sons of the said Faith Phillipes, and with their joint consent that the said sum shall be paid unto the daughters of the said Faith Phillipes, viz: Desire Sherman [*sic*], Elizabeth Rouse and Mary Doten in equal and alike proportions unless the two younger sisters shall see reason in respect of the low condition of the eldest to consider her in that respect" [MD 3:91, citing PCR 5:163].

BIRTH: By about 1599 (he was a servant on his arrival, but as he fought a duel within months of landing at Plymouth, he was more likely close to the end of his servitude rather than the beginning; he signed the Mayflower Compact, probably as an adult).
DEATH: Plymouth 23 August 1655 [PCR 8:17].
MARRIAGE: (1) Before 1635 _____ _____ (not seen in any record). Her existence is implied only by Bradford's comment in his 1651 list that Edward had "a second wife."
    (2) Plymouth 6 January 1634/5 "Fayth Clarke" [PCR 1:32], daughter of THURSTON CLARK {1634, Plymouth} [GM 2:2:99–101]. She married (2) Plymouth 14 March 1666[/7] John Phillips [PCR 4:163–64, 8:31; MD 18:56] and was buried at Marshfield on 21 December 1675 [MarVR 9].
CHILDREN:
    With second wife
        i EDWARD DOTY, b. say 1636 (eldest son in father's will); m. Plymouth 25 or 26 February 1662[/3] Sarah Faunce [MD 13:204; PCR 8:23], daughter of JOHN FAUNCE {1623, Plymouth} [PM 201].
        ii JOHN DOTY, b. say 1638; m. (1) by 1668 Elizabeth Cooke (eldest known child b. Plymouth 24 August 1668 [PVR 5]), daughter of Jacob Cooke and granddaughter of *FRANCIS COOKE* [MF 12:54, 81–82; PM 144]; m. (2) Plymouth 22 November 1694 Sarah Jones [PNQ 3:121], daughter of Joseph Jones and great-granddaughter of *RICHARD WARREN.*
        iii THOMAS DOTY, b. say 1640; m. by 1675 Mary Churchill (with whom he had had an illegitimate child in 1672), daughter of John Churchill. (Thomas Doty's widow Mary m. (2) 8 February 1687/8 Henry Churchill. In 1960 Florence Harlow Barclay studied the family of Thomas Doty and claimed that he married two women named Mary [TAG 36:1–7]. In 1996 Barbara Lambert Merrick

reexamined the problem and concluded that Thomas Doty had only one wife and that Henry Churchill was not a son of John Churchill [TAG 71:114–20]. We follow the latter article here.)

iv SAMUEL DOTY, b. say 1642; m. Piscataway, New Jersey, 13 November 1678 Jeane Harman [NJHSP 4:4:34] (by license dated 24 October 1678, bride and groom both of Piscataway, New Jersey [East Jersey Deeds 3:149; GMNJ 43:49]).

v DESIRE DOTY, b. about 1645 (d. Marshfield 22 January 1731, aged eighty-six years [MarVR 409]; see **COMMENTS**); m. (1) Marshfield 25 December 1667 William Sherman [MarVR 10], son of WILLIAM SHERMAN {1632, Plymouth} [PM 416]; m. (2) Marshfield 24 November 1681 Israel Holmes [MarVR 16], son of WILLIAM HOLMES {1635, Scituate} [GM 2:3:392–97; NEHGR 166:85–97]; m. (3) by 1689 as his second wife Alexander Standish, son of *MYLES STANDISH* [MD 12:48–52].

vi ELIZABETH DOTY, b. say 1646; m. (1) Marshfield 13 January 1674[/5] John Rowse [MarVR 8]; m. (2) Marshfield 28 January 1718/9 William Carver [MD 8:43; MarVR 35, 40].

vii ISAAC DOTY, b. Plymouth 8 February 1648/9 [MD 15:27; PCR 8:5]; m. by about 1673 Elizabeth England (in his will of 11 January 1684[/5], Hugh Parsons of Portsmouth, Rhode Island, who had married Elizabeth, the widow of William England, bequeathed to "my wife's two daughters, living on Long Island, viz: Susannah Carpenter and Elizabeth Doty" [Austin 144]).

viii JOSEPH DOTY, b. Plymouth 30 April 1651 [PCR 8:12]; on 27 October 1674, accused by Elizabeth Warren of fathering her child [PCR 5:156]; m. about summer 1674 Deborah Ellis (late enough to have conceived a child with her b. 22 February 1674/5 but not so soon as to have committed adultery to conceive a child with Elizabeth Warren still unborn 27 October 1674 [TAG 36:9–11]); m. (2) Rochester 5 March 1711/2 Sarah Edwards, widow [TAG 64:152–54].

ix MARY DOTY, b. say 1653; m. after 10 July 1677 Samuel
Hatch [PCR 5:239; MD 5:111–13, citing PCLR 4:345 and
PLR 25:120; TAG 36:7–8].

ASSOCIATIONS: Edward Doty had a complex financial relationship with
RICHARD DERBY {1637, Plymouth} but not one that necessarily implies
kinship.

PREMIGRATION BIOGRAPHY: Edward Doty was apparently an adult
when he arrived at Plymouth, and so born no later than 1599. He had
sailed to New England as a servant of Stephen Hopkins and is described
as being a London man when he set out on the exploratory journey in early December 1620. Being from London in these circumstances meant no
more than that he was one of the passengers who had joined the ships at
Southampton, rather than having come from Leiden.

COMMENTS: On 6 December 1620, "Edward Dotte" was one of "three
[men] of London" who, along with his master Stephen Hopkins and more
than a dozen others, set out on the voyage of discovery which selected
Plymouth as the place for their permanent settlement [Mourt 31–32].

Edward Doty is said to have been guilty of the "second offence" committed in Plymouth. As Bradford tells us, on 18 June 1621 "the first duel
[was] fought in New England, upon a challenge at single combat with
sword and dagger, between Edward Doty and Edward Leister, servants of
Mr. Hopkins. Both being wounded, the one in the hand, the other in the
thigh, they are adjudged by the whole company to have their head and feet
tied together, and so to lie for twenty-four hours, without meat or drink;
which is begun to be inflicted, but within an hour, because of their great
pains, at their own and their master's humble request, upon promise of
better carriage, they are released by the governor" [Prince 190–91, citing
Bradford's lost register].

This incident set the tone for the next twenty years in which Doty was
frequently in court for fighting, slandering, trespass, and debt. His dis-
ruptive behavior was consistent with his failure to hold any public offices during the three-and-a-half decades he resided at Plymouth. Edward
Doty was defendant in three civil suits at the court of 2 January 1632/3,
all involving hogs; he won one and lost two [PCR 1:6–7]. On 1 April 1633,
Doty was sued for slander by one of the winning plaintiffs and was fined
50s. [PCR 1:12].

Still he prospered, for he had an apprentice in 1633, although an unhap-
py one. On 2 January 1633/4, the court settled a dispute between Edward

Doty and his apprentice John Smith, reducing the time of the apprentice-ship from ten years to five [PCR 1:23]. On 31 August 1638, Doty received the assignment of seven years labor of William Snow from Snow's previous master, Richard Derby [PCR 1:94].

On 24 March 1633/4, Edward Doty was fined 10s. for breaking the peace and drawing blood from Josias Cooke [PCR 1:26]. On 28 March 1634, Edward Doty won a suit against Francis Sprague [PCR 1:29].

On 7 March 1636/7, Edward Doty was found guilty of a "deceitful bar-gain" over a lot of land, and restored the lot to George Clarke [PCR 7:5]. The controversy continued when George Clark won damages and costs from Doty on 2 October 1637, Clark charging him with denying liberty to hold land for the term he had taken it [PCR 7:6]. Things escalated, for that same day Clark also charged Doty for assault and battery, and Doty was further fined [PCR 7:6]. Doty was sued in less sanguinary encounters between 1638 and 1651 with Richard Derby, John Shaw, widow Bridget Fuller, and John Holmes over debt and trespass, and lost them all [PCR 7:10, 15, 16, 47, 48, 56]. On 7 December 1641, he successfully sued James Luxford for trespass [PCR 7:26].

On 1 February 1641/2, Thomas Symons charged "Edward Dotey" with carelessly allowing cattle put in his hands to "break into men's corn" endan-gering the cattle and other property, and Doty was ordered to put his cattle in a "keep" [PCR 2:33].

On 10 February 1643/4, "Edward Dotey" was one of six men directed by the town of Plymouth to build a wolftrap at Plain Dealing [PTR 1:16]. In March 1657 he was midway down the list of "those that have interest and proprieties in the town's land at Punckateeset over against Rhode Island" [PTR 1:37].

Edward Doty's daughter Desire, who married successively William Sherman, Isaac Holmes, and Alexander Standish, was said to have been eighty-six when she died in 1731, placing her birth about 1645. But her last child with Standish was born when she would have been forty-eight by this reckoning. She was probably a few years younger than her age at death shows, but it is hard to know just where to fit her into the sequence of children.

Savage stated that Edward Doty had children William and Faith in addition to the children listed above, but there is no evidence for such chil-dren. From the probate records for Edward Doty's widow we may be sure that no daughter by the name of Faith survived to adulthood. Savage also claims that Edward Doty removed to Yarmouth, but all records place him in Plymouth.

BIBLIOGRAPHIC NOTE: The Five Generations Project of the General Society of Mayflower Descendants has published its study of Edward Doty as Volume Eleven of the series, in three parts, compiled by Peter B. Hill. Part I, published in 1996 (and revised in 2009), covers the descendants of sons Edward and John. Part II, published in 1996, covers the descendants of sons Thomas and Samuel and daughters Desire and Elizabeth. Part III, published in 2000, covers the descendants of sons Isaac and Joseph and daughter Mary.

Writing in 1897 Ethan Allen Doty quoted many documents, including some that would be very helpful in refining our knowledge of this family, but which do not appear in the colony or town records. The most important of these were the receipts given by all the sons of the immigrant for their shares in his estate [*The Doty-Doten Family in America* (Brooklyn 1897), p. 28]. Perhaps these documents are privately held.

In 1988 Neil D. Thompson published a refutation of the false claim for the ancestry of Edward Doty made by Gustave Anjou [TAG 63:215].

FRANCIS EATON

Francis Eaton and Sarah his wife, and Samuel their son, a young child.

Francis Eaton his first wife died in the general sickness. And he married again and his second wife died, and he married the third and had by her three children. One of them is married and hath a child. The others are living but one of them is an idiot. He died about 16 years ago. His son Samuel who came over a sucking child, is also married and hath a child.

ORIGIN: Leiden [TAG 80:99].
MIGRATION: 1620 on the *Mayflower.*
FIRST RESIDENCE: Plymouth.

OCCUPATION: Carpenter. His inventory included "1 tool box" and a long list of carpenter's tools.
FREEMAN: On 11 November 1620, Francis Eaton signed the Mayflower Compact [Morton 26].

In the 1633 Plymouth list of freemen, ahead of those admitted on 1 January 1632/3 [PCR 1:3].
EDUCATION: Signed deed of 30 December 1631 [PCR 12:17].
OFFICES: Appointed arbiter in dispute between William Bennet and Edward Doty, 3 January 1632/3 [PCR 1:7].

His inventory included "1 pistol, one powder horn & one shot purse" valued at 9s. and "one piece" valued at £1 14s. [PCPR 1:17; MD 1:199].
ESTATE: In the 1623 Plymouth land division granted four acres as a passenger on the *Mayflower* [PCR 12:4]. (The four persons who earned this allotment were Francis Eaton, his deceased first wife, his second wife, and his son Samuel Eaton [MQ 40:13].) In the 1627 Plymouth cattle division, the first four members of the tenth company were Francis Eaton, Christian Eaton, Samuel Eaton, and Rachel Eaton [PCR 12:12].

Francis Eaton was one of the Purchasers, those who acquired the rights to land distributions in Plymouth Colony as a consequence of the agreement made between the London merchants and the Plymouth settlers in 1627 [Ford 282–88].

On 25 June 1631, Francis Eaton sold to Edward Winslow four acres in the North Field [PCR 12:16 (this was the land received in the 1623 division)]. On 30 December 1631, Francis Eaton sold to William Brewster "one share of land, containing twenty acres, lying at the place commonly called Nothingelse" in consideration of £21 12s., which would "pay his purchase for four shares"; Eaton also sold to William Brewster an additional twelve acres from the same lot [PCR 12:16]. On 8 January 1632/3, Francis Eaton sold to Kenelm and Josiah Winslow "the now dwelling house of the said Francis, with other appurtenances thereunto belonging" [PCR 1:8].

Francis Eaton was assessed 9s. in the Plymouth tax list of 25 March 1633 [PCR 1:10]. There is no entry for him or his widow in the 27 March 1634 list; her remarriage to Francis Billington may have been anticipated at the time this list was compiled, so that she would have been included in his household.

The inventory of the estate of "Fr[ancis] Eaton carpenter of Plymouth," taken 8 November 1633, totaled £64 8s. 7d., with no real estate included; to the inventory was appended a long list of debts owed by Francis Eaton [PCPR 1:17–18; MD 1:197–200]. On 25 November 1633, "whereas Franc[i]s Eaton, carpenter, late of Plymouth, deceased, died indebted far more than the estate of the said Franc[i]s would make good, insomuch as Christian, his late wife, durst not administer, it was ordered, that Mr. Thomas Prence & Mr. John Doane, in the behalf of the Court, should enter upon the estate, according to the inventory brought in upon oath the day of this present, that the creditors might have so far as the estate will make good, & the widow be freed & acquitted from any claim or demands of all or any his creditors whatsoever" [PCR 1:19–20].

As Caleb Johnson has observed, Francis Eaton's financial condition deteriorated in the early 1630s. Eaton sold off all his land and when he died was heavily indebted [Mayflower Passengers 139–40].

BIRTH: Baptized St. Thomas, Bristol, 11 September 1596, son of John and Dorothy (Smith) Eaton [TAG 72:303–4].
DEATH: Plymouth between 25 March 1633 (tax list) and 8 November 1633 (date of inventory). (In the allocation of mowing ground on 1 July 1633 Francis Eaton was not assigned a location, and there was granted to "Mr. Williams that which Fr[ancis] Eaton cut last year" [PCR 1:15], so Eaton may already have died by that date.)
MARRIAGE: (1) By 1619 Sarah _____, who came on the *Mayflower* and died early in 1621 [Bradford 446].

(2) About 1622 *DOROTHY* _____, who died soon after [TAG 72:304, 308–9]. (She was the unnamed maidservant of John Carver who "married and died a year or two after [1620], here in this place" [Bradford 444].)

(3) By about 1626 CHRISTIAN PENN {1623, Plymouth}; she married (2) in July 1634 Francis Billington [PCR 1:31], son of *JOHN BILLINGTON*.

CHILDREN:
> With first wife
>> i SAMUEL EATON, b. late 1619 or early 1620; apprenticed 13 August 1636 to John Cooke the younger for seven years [PCR 1:43]; m. (1) by 1646 Elizabeth _____, who died between 5 October 1652 and 10 January 1660[/1] [MF 9:5]; m. (2) Plymouth 10 January 1660[/1] Martha Billington [PCR 8:22].
>
> With third wife
>> ii RACHEL EATON, b. Plymouth about 1626 (deposed on 22 July 1648 "aged about 23 years" [PCR 2:132]; deposed on 5 October 1652 "aged twenty-six years or thereabouts" [PCR 3:18]); m. Plymouth 2 March 1645/6 Joseph Ramsden (or Ramsdell) [PCR 2:94; MD 36:187–89].
>> iii BENJAMIN EATON, b. Plymouth in March 1627/8; apprenticed 11 February 1635/6 to Bridget Fuller for fourteen years [PCR 1:36–37]; placed in service to John Winslow on 14 January 1642/3, "being about xv years in March next" [PTR 1:12]; m. Plymouth 4 December 1660 Sarah Hoskins [PCR 8:22], daughter of WILLIAM HOSKINS {1634, Plymouth} [GM 2:3:414–20].
>> iv Child EATON, b. Plymouth say 1630; "an idiot," living 1651 [Bradford 447].

PREMIGRATION BIOGRAPHY: Francis Eaton was born at Bristol in 1596, son of John and Dorothy (Smith) Eaton. Sometime in the first decade of the seventeenth century Eaton apparently served as an apprentice to a carpenter, as that is his occupation in all later records. He was still residing at Bristol as late as 1615 when he was renting a house there [TAG 72:302–3]. No records for Francis Eaton have been found in Leiden, but Caleb Johnson's analysis of William Bradford's list of *Mayflower* passengers indicates that Eaton was a member of the church there [TAG 80:99]. A year or two before the *Mayflower* sailed, he married a woman named Sarah and had with her a son named Samuel, born probably in late 1619 or early 1620.

BIBLIOGRAPHIC NOTE: In 1996 the General Society of Mayflower Descendants published an account of five generations of the descendants of Francis Eaton in the ninth volume of the Five Generations project. This volume was based on the research of Lee Douglas Van Antwerp, revised by Robert S. Wakefield [MF 9]. (This superseded an earlier treatment of Francis Eaton published as part of Volume One of the same series.)

In 1997 Neil D. Thompson published the information that confirmed earlier suggestions as to the English origin of Francis Eaton [TAG 72:301–4]. At the same time David L. Greene presented additional comments on the life and family of this immigrant [TAG 72:305–9].

_____ ELY

There were also other two seamen hired to stay a year here in the country, William Trevor, and one Ely. But when their time was out they both returned.

ORIGIN: England.
MIGRATION: 1620 on the *Mayflower.*
FIRST RESIDENCE: Plymouth.
RETURN TRIPS: Returned to England by 1623 (not in 1623 land division).

OCCUPATION: Seaman.

BIRTH: Born say 1600.
DEATH: After return to England.
MARRIAGE: None known.
CHILDREN: None known.

THOMAS ENGLISH

John Allerton and Thomas English were both hired, the latter to go master of a shallop here, and the other was reputed as one of the company but was to go back (being a seaman) for the help of others behind. But they both died here before the ship returned.

Thomas English and John Allerton died in the general sickness.

ORIGIN: Unknown (but see **COMMENTS**).
MIGRATION: 1620 on the *Mayflower*.
FIRST RESIDENCE: Plymouth.

OCCUPATION: Seaman.
FREEMAN: On 11 November 1620, Thomas English signed the Mayflower Compact [Morton 26].

BIRTH: By 1599 (assuming he was twenty-one when he signed the Mayflower Compact).
DEATH: Plymouth before 5 April 1621 (date of return of the *Mayflower* to England).
MARRIAGE: None known.
CHILDREN: None known.

COMMENTS: Thomas English was a member of the exploring party which left Provincetown Harbor on 6 December 1620 and selected Plymouth as the location for their permanent settlement [Mourt 32].

Dexter claimed that a Thomas England who witnessed a marriage at Leiden in 1613 was the same as this Thomas English, and he was followed in this by Banks [Dexter 614; English Homes 53]. Caleb Johnson also notes this record and observes further that the constant connection between Thomas English and John Allerton in the records suggests that English, like Allerton, had been at Leiden [Mayflower Passengers 141].

MOSES FLETCHER

Moses Fletcher, John Goodman, Thomas Williams, Digory Priest, Edmund Margesson, Peter Browne, Richard Britteridge, Richard Clarke, Richard Gardiner, Gilbert Winslow.

Moses Fletcher, Thomas Williams, Digory Priest, John Goodman, Edmund Margesson, Richard Britteridge, Richard Clarke, all these died soon after arrival in the general sickness that befell. But Digory Priest had his wife and children sent hither afterwards, she being Mr. Allerton's sister. But the rest left no posterity here.

ORIGIN: Leiden.
PREVIOUS RESIDENCES: Sandwich, Kent.
MIGRATION: 1620 on the *Mayflower.*
FIRST RESIDENCE: Plymouth.

OCCUPATION: Smith [Leiden Pilgrims 91].
FREEMAN: On 11 November 1620, Moses Fletcher signed the Mayflower Compact [Morton 26].

BIRTH: By about 1564 (based on date of first marriage).
DEATH: Early 1621 at Plymouth.
MARRIAGE: (1) St. Peter, Sandwich, Kent, 30 October 1589 Mary Evans [NEHGR 128:161]. She died between April 1609 (baptism of last known child) and December 1613 (remarriage of husband).
   (2) Leiden 21 December 1613 [NS] Sarah (____) Denby, widow of William Denby [Plooij XVII; Leiden Pilgrims 91; NEHGR 128:161]; no further record.
CHILDREN: (all baptisms from St. Peter, Sandwich [NEHGR 128:162]):
   With first wife
      i MARY FLETCHER, bp. 4 January 1589/90; no further record.
      ii JOHN FLETCHER, b. say 1592; m. Leiden 5 December 1618 [NS] Josina Sachariasdaughter [Leiden Pilgrims 91; NEHGR 128:163].
      iii CATHERINE FLETCHER, bp. 1 September 1594; no further record.

   iv RICHARD FLETCHER, bp. 2 January 1596/7; no further record.

   v PRISCILLA FLETCHER, bp. 24 March 1599/1600; m. (1) Leiden 4 April 1626 [NS] Thomas Coit [Leiden Pilgrims 91]; m. (2) Leiden 1 June 1637 [NS] Help/Solomon Terry [Leiden Pilgrims 92; NEHGR 128:162]; m. (3) Leiden 19 July 1652 [NS] Jan Jans Vermout [Leiden Pilgrims 92].

   vi MOSES FLETCHER, bp. 10 October 1602; bur. 21 April 1603.

   vii ELIZABETH FLETCHER, bp. 8 April 1604; m. (1) Casper Bamaart; m. (2) Leiden 21 May 1636 [NS] Michiel Voorchoren [Leiden Pilgrims 91; NEHGR 128:163].

   viii JANE FLETCHER, bp. 8 February 1606/7; no further record.

   ix MOSES FLETCHER, bp. 2 April 1609; no further record.

   x JUDITH FLETCHER, bur. 6 November 1609.

PREMIGRATION BIOGRAPHY: Moses Fletcher was born by about 1564 and is first of record in 1589 when he married Mary Evans at St. Peter, Sandwich, Kent, with whom he had ten children by 1609. Moses Fletcher was employed as sexton of St. Peter, Sandwich, for a number of years in the first decade of the seventeenth century. He was excommunicated from that church three times in 1609 and 1610. On two of these occasions the offense was the participation in an illegal burial, and on the second of these two occasions the person buried was Judith Fletcher, his daughter [NEHGR 153:407–10]. Not long after these events the Fletcher family made the move to Leiden where they joined John Robinson's congregation.

BIBLIOGRAPHIC NOTE: Robert S. Wakefield was the first to present in print information on the career of Moses Fletcher in Leiden [NEHGR 128:161–69; MQ 38:89, 41:45–47, 126–29]. Wakefield traced some lines of descent beyond the second generation and suggested the possibility of tracing living descendants.

    Tamura Jones built on Wakefield's work and has compiled a database of thousands of descendants of Moses Fletcher, all through his daughter Priscilla and her first husband Thomas Coit (or Koet) <https://www.tamurajones.net/TheMissingMayflowerPilgrim.xhtml>. Some descendants have been admitted to the Mayflower Society [MQ 53:289, 61:26–27].

    In 1999 Michael Paulick published his research in the records of Sandwich, Kent, relating to a number of families who eventually migrated to Leiden, including the Fletchers [NEHGR 153:407–10].

EDWARD FULLER

Edward Fuller and his wife, and Samuel their son.

Edward Fuller and his wife died soon after they came ashore, but their son Samuel is living and married and hath four children or more.

ORIGIN: Leiden.
PREVIOUS RESIDENCES: Redenhall, Norfolk.
MIGRATION: 1620 on the *Mayflower*.
FIRST RESIDENCE: Plymouth.

FREEMAN: On 11 November 1620, Edward Fuller signed the Mayflower Compact [Morton 26].
ESTATE: In the 1623 Plymouth division of land Samuel Fuller Junior [son of Edward Fuller] received three acres as a passenger on the *Mayflower* [PCR 12:4; MD 40:12]. (This allocation would be for himself, and for his mother and father who died at Plymouth during the first winter.)

BIRTH: Baptized Redenhall, Norfolk, 4 September 1575, son of Robert Fuller [NEHGR 55:192].
DEATH: Early 1621 at Plymouth.
MARRIAGE: By about 1605_____ _____ [MQ 86:34–35]. She died at Plymouth in early 1621.
CHILDREN:

> i MATTHEW FULLER, b. say 1605; m. by about 1630 Frances _____ [TAG 61:198–99; MF 4:5–6]. (Paul Prindle had prepared, prior to the demonstration that Matthew was son of Edward, an excellent account of Matthew Fuller and his family [*Ancestry of Elizabeth Barrett Gillespie...* (n.p. 1976), 157–62].)

> ii SAMUEL FULLER, b. about 1608; as "Samuell Fuller Junior" he is the third person in the eighth company (and in the household of his uncle Samuel Fuller) in the 1627 Plymouth division of cattle [PCR 12:11]; "Sammell Fowller" appears in the 1633 list of Plymouth freemen, just ahead of those admitted on 1 January 1634/5 [PCR 1:4]; assessed 9s. in the Plymouth tax list of 27 March 1634 [PCR 1:28]; m. Scituate 8 April 1635 Jane Lothrop,

daughter of Rev. JOHN LOTHROP {1635, Scituate}
[NEHGR 9:286; GM 2:4:345–51].

ASSOCIATIONS: Brother of *SAMUEL FULLER.*

PREMIGRATION BIOGRAPHY: Edward Fuller was born at Redenhall,
Norfolk, in 1575. Presumably his marriage and the births of his children took
place in England in the first decade of the seventeenth century. Although the
records of these events may have perished or may not yet have been discovered, the possibility exists that Edward Fuller was a member of a fully separatist
congregation in England, in which case the marriage and birth records would
not appear in the records of a Church of England parish. He was apparently
still residing in England when his father made his will in 1614 [MQ 86:33–
34]. Although no records have been found for Edward Fuller in Leiden, Caleb
Johnson's analysis of Bradford's list of *Mayflower* passengers places Fuller as a
member of John Robinson's Leiden congregation prior to 1620 [TAG 80:99].
(In 1985 Jeremy D. Bangs published a Leiden record that was thought to
pertain to Edward Fuller [MQ 51:58, citing "R.A. 79, L, folio 172 verso"]. In
2020 Donald G. Blauvelt demonstrated that this record was for an "Eduwaert
Fauwler, Englishman, living in The Hague," who was still of record in that city
in 1622, a year after the *Mayflower* passenger died [MQ 86:32–33].)

COMMENTS: The question of the paternity of Matthew Fuller was examined exhaustively by Bruce C. MacGunnigle, Robert M. Sherman, and
Robert S. Wakefield in 1986, and they came to the conclusion that Matthew
was a son of Edward Fuller [TAG 61:194–99]. Extensive data on the Fullers
of Redenhall and vicinity were published in 1901 by Francis H. Fuller
[NEHGR 55:192–96, 410–16].

In his third volume treating early settlers on the Penobscot, Philip
Howard Gray sets forth a completely new structure for the family of
Edward Fuller, including children not previously suspected [*Penobscot
Pioneers,* Volume 3 (Camden, Maine, 1993), pp. 62–66]. Gray employs a
style of logic and argumentation not normally found in the genealogical
literature, and his conclusions are not adopted here.

BIBLIOGRAPHIC NOTE: Bruce C. MacGunnigle compiled the treatment of Edward Fuller and his descendants in Volume Four of the Five
Generations Project of the General Society of Mayflower Descendants. The
third edition of this volume was published in 2006.

In 2020 Don Blauvelt presented evidence that Edward Fuller was not
in Leiden in 1612 and that he was probably still residing at Redenhall in
1614; he also noted that the given name of Edward's wife is not known
[MQ 86:32–35].

SAMUEL FULLER

Mr. Samuel Fuller and a servant called William Button. His wife was behind, and a child which came afterwards.

Mr. Fuller his servant died at sea; and after his wife came he had two children by her, which are living and grown up to years; but he died some fifteen years ago.

ORIGIN: Leiden.
PREVIOUS RESIDENCES: Redenhall, Norfolk.
MIGRATION: 1620 on the *Mayflower.*
FIRST RESIDENCE: Plymouth.

OCCUPATION: Surgeon. His inventory included "a surgeon's chest with the things belonging to it" valued at £5. Thomas Morton of Merrymount devoted a chapter to a scurrilous description of Fuller's medical skills, calling him "Dr. Noddy" [New English Canaan 297–99, 309].

Say-weaver (in Leiden) [Leiden Pilgrims 95, 96].
CHURCH MEMBERSHIP: Member and deacon of John Robinson's Leiden congregation (see **COMMENTS**).

Member and deacon of Plymouth church. In 1629 Samuel Fuller visited Salem, principally in his role as surgeon, but while there he consulted with Endicott about the organization and practices of the Plymouth church, a discussion that undoubtedly affected the founding of the Salem church in that year (and in the long term the development of Congregationalism in New England) [Bradford LB 46–48; Michael P. Winship, *Godly Republicanism: Puritans, Pilgrims, and a City on a Hill* (Cambridge, Massachusetts, 2012), Chapter Six, "Separatism at Salem?"]. He went on a similar mission to Massachusetts Bay in 1630 [Bradford LB 56–59]. In 1633 Bradford commented on the epidemic that took many of the Plymouth colonists, and specifically "in the end, after he had much helped others, Samuel Fuller who was their surgeon and physician and had been a great help and comfort unto them. As in his faculty, so otherwise being a deacon of the church, a man godly and forward to do good, being much missed after his death" [Bradford 260].
FREEMAN: On 11 November 1620, Samuel Fuller signed the Mayflower Compact [Morton 26].

"Samuel Fuller senior" appears early in the 1633 list of Plymouth freemen, before those admitted 1 January 1632/3 [PCR 1:3].

EDUCATION: Sufficient to act as a surgeon. He wrote three polished letters to Bradford in 1630 [Bradford LB 56–59]. His inventory included about thirty books valued at £3 2s. 6d.; they were mostly Bibles and other religious volumes, but there were also his "physic books," some dictionaries, and other practical publications [MD 2:8; Plymouth Libraries 24–30 (identifying and providing full titles for most of the volumes)].

OFFICES: Plymouth tax assessor for rate of 25 March 1633 [PCR 1:9].

His inventory included "2 fowling pieces & a musket" valued at £2 [MD 2:9].

ESTATE: In the 1623 Plymouth division of land Samuel Fuller received two acres as a passenger on the *Mayflower*, and his wife "Brigett Fuller" received one acre as a passenger on the *Anne* [PCR 12:4, 6; MD 40:10]. In the 1627 Plymouth division of cattle Samuel Fuller, his wife Bridget Fuller, and Samuel Fuller Junior were the first three persons in the eighth company [PCR 12:11]. (This "Samuel Fuller Junior" was not son of Samuel but of his brother Edward [MD 39:85].)

Samuel Fuller was one of the Purchasers, those who acquired the rights to land distributions in Plymouth Colony as a consequence of the agreement made between the London merchants and the Plymouth settlers in 1627 [Ford 282–88].

"Sam[uel] Fuller, Senior" was assessed 18s. in the 25 March 1633 Plymouth tax list, and "Widow Fuller" was assessed 9s. in the list of 27 March 1634 [PCR 1:9, 28].

"Mrs. Fuller" was allocated hay ground, 14 March 1635/6, 20 March 1636/7 [PCR 1:40, 56].

In his will, dated 30 July 1633 and proved 28 October 1633 [PCR 1:18], "Samuel Fullere the elder ... sick & weak" bequeathed "the education of my children to my brother Will[iam] Wright & his wife, only that my daughter Mercy be & remain with goodwife Wallen"; "if it shall please God to recover my wife out of her weak estate of sickness, then my children to be with her or disposed by her"; "there is a child committed to my charge called Sarah Converse, my wife dying as afore I desire my brother Wright may have the bringing up of her" and if he refuse then "I commend her to my loving neighbor & brother in Christ Thomas Prence," whosoever takes her to bring her up in the fear of God as their own "which was a charge laid upon me per her sick father when he freely bestowed her upon me"; "whereas Eliz[abeth] Cowles was committed to my education by her father & mother still living at Charles Towne" she to be conveniently apparelled and returned to her father or mother or either of them; "George Foster being placed with me upon the same terms by his parents still living at Sagos [Saugus]" he to be restored to his mother; to "Samuel my son my house & lands at the Smeltriver"; "my house & garden at town be sold & all my moveables there & at the Smeltriver (except my cattle) together with the present crop of corn ... except ... such as [my overseers] shall think meet in the present education of my two children Samuell & Mercy"; "two acres of land that fell unto me by lot ... to Samuell my son"; two acres of land "given me by Edward Bircher ... at Strawberry Hill if Mr. Roger Williams refuse to accept of them as formerly he hath done ... also one other acre by Mr. Heeks" to Samuel; "my cousin Samuell go freely away with his stock of cattle & swine without any further reckoning"; all the swine be sold "except my best hog which I would have killed this winter for the present comfort of my children"; whereas "I have disposed of my children to my Brother Will[iam] Wright & Prisilla his wife ... in case my wife die he enter upon my house & land at the Smelt River, & also my cattle not disposed on together with my two servants Thomas Symons & Rob[er]t Cowles for the remainder of their several terms to be employed for the good of my children"; in case "my said brother Will[iam] Wright or Prisilla his wife die, then my said children Samuell & Mercy together with the said joint charge committed to the said Will[iam] & Prisilla be void except my overseers or the survivor of them shall think meet"; a cow calf to the Church of God at Plymouth use to be determined by the Deacons; to "my sister Alice Bradford" 12s. for a pair of gloves; any debt due from Capt. Standish "I give unto his children"; a pair of 5s. gloves to "Mr. Joh. Winthrop, Govr. of the Massachusets"; to "my brother Wright" one cloth suit; the two pounds of beaver owed by Capt. John Endecott "I give it to his son"; when "my children come to age ... my overseers make a full valuation of that stock of cattle & the increase thereof & that it be equally divided between my children, and if any die in the meantime, the whole to go to the survivor or survivors," they to enjoy their portions at the age of discretion "not at any set time or appointment of years"; "my brother Wright" to have the refusal of the purchase of cattle; to "John Jenny & Joh. Wynslow" each a 5s. pair of gloves; to "Mrs. Heeks" 20s.; to "old Mr. William Brewster my best hat & band which I have never wore"; "if my children die, that then my stock be thus distributed: first that what care of pains or charge hath been by any about my children be fully recompensed"; next "as it may redound to the Governing Elder or Elders of this Church at Plymouth ... as my overseers shall think meet"; to "Rebecca Prence" 2s. 6d. for a pair of gloves; "my kinsman Sam[uel] Fuller now in the house with me enjoy whatsoever lands I am now possessed of except my dwelling house at town or whatsoever shall be due to me or them" if my children die before their full age, also "my rufflet cloak & my stuff suit I now wear"; "I institute my son Samuell my executor and because he is young & tender, I enjoin him to be wholly ordered by Edw[ard] Wynslow, Mr. Wil[liam] Bradford & Mr. Tho[mas] Prence" overseers, they to have 20s. each; to "Mercy my daughter one Bible with a black cover with Bezaes notes"; the rest of "my books to my son Samuel, which I desire my Brother Wright will safely preserve for him"; "when my daughter Mercy is fit to go to school ... Mrs. Heeks may teach her as well as my son"; whatsoever "Mr. Roger Williams is indebted to me upon my book for physic, I freely give him"; if "my wife" recover, she to have the education of the children; if the overseers die, then some other of the church be appointed; "whereas the widow Ring committed the oversight of her son Andrew to me at her death, my will is that Mr. Tho[mas] Prence one of my overseers, take the charge of him." The will was followed by a list of debts acknowledged by Samuel Fuller "upon his death bed" including "Henry Wood ... an old debt due at Leyden" and "an herbal belonging to Joh. Chew of Plymouth in old England" [MD 1:24–29, citing PCPR 1:1–3].

The inventory of the estate of "Samuel Fuller the elder" was presented at court 2 January 1633/4 and totaled £212 16s. 6d. "besides the books & the country house," with £25 in real estate: "a dwelling house &c. in the town," £15; and "the country house," £10 [MD 2:8–10, citing PCPR 1:22–24].

BIRTH: Baptized Redenhall, Norfolk, 20 February 1580[/1], son of Robert Fuller [MQ 86:35].

DEATH: Between 30 July 1633 (date of will) and 28 October 1633 (probate of will).

MARRIAGE: (1) Alice Glascock, who died by 1613 [Leiden Pilgrims 95].

(2) (as "Samuel Fuller, say-weaver, from London in England, widower of Alice Glascock") Leiden 24 April 1613 [NS] "Agnes Carpenter, single woman, from Wrington in England" [Plooij XIV; Leiden Pilgrims 95; MD 8:129–30], daughter of Alexander Carpenter (see PRISCILLA CARPENTER {1633, Plymouth} [PM 93]). She was buried at Pieterskerk, Leiden, on 3 July 1615 [NEA 3:2:49].

(3) (as "Samuel Fuller, say-weaver, from England, widower of Anna Carpenter") Leiden 27 May 1617 [NS] "Bridget Lee, single woman, also from England, accompanied by Josephine Lee, her mother" [Plooij XXX; Leiden Pilgrims 96; MD 8:129–30]. She died after 2 May 1667 [MD 39:86].

CHILDREN:
> With second wife
>> i Child FULLER, bur. Pieterskerk, Leiden, 29 June 1615 [NS] [Dexter 615; NEA 3:2:49].
>
> With third wife
>> ii (poss.) BRIDGET FULLER, b. say 1619; m. Plymouth 30 September 1641 Henry Sirkman [PCR 2:23]. (The temptation is strong to place Bridget in this family; we are told that Samuel Fuller had "a child which came afterwards," apparently meaning after both parents had arrived [Bradford 442]. Samuel did not, however, name her in his will [MF 10:6].)
>> iii MERCY FULLER, b. after 22 May 1627 (not in 1627 division of cattle); named in father's will; living at time of Bradford's accounting of 1651 [Bradford 445]; no further record.
>> iv SAMUEL FULLER, b. about 1629; m. (1) _____ _____; m. (2) between 11 April 1663 and 2 May 1667 Elizabeth (Nichols) Bowen, daughter of John Nichols and widow of Thomas Bowen [MD 39:86–87].

ASSOCIATIONS: Brother of *EDWARD FULLER*. Through his second wife, related to *WILLIAM BRADFORD*, WILLIAM WRIGHT {1621, Plymouth} [PM 524], and others (see sketch of PRISCILLA CARPENTER {1633, Plymouth} [PM 93–95]).

PREMIGRATION BIOGRAPHY: Samuel Fuller was born at Redenhall, Norfolk, in 1580. Given the quality of his surviving letters, he must have attended grammar school, but there is no record of him attending university. Somewhere in his education he learned the skills of a surgeon.

He is not seen again in English records until 19 May 1614, when his father, Robert Fuller, bequeathed him £10 at the same time that he gave much larger bequests to Samuel's brothers and sisters. Also, toward the end of the will, when listing the residuary legatees, Samuel is omitted [Archdeaconry Court of Norfolk, Registered Wills 1614, folio 259]. As Caleb Johnson remarks, "perhaps his father was not particularly happy with him" [Mayflower Passengers 146].

By the date of his father's will Samuel Fuller had already left England and resettled at Leiden. On 7 October 1611 [NS], Samuel Fuller witnessed the betrothal at Leiden of Degory Priest and Sarah (Allerton) Vincent [Leiden

Pilgrims 216]. In a pamphlet published in 1612, Christopher Lawne, a member of Francis Johnson's Ancient Church in Amsterdam, described at great length his own excommunication trial at that church on 28 July 1611. One of the elders of the Ancient Church was Daniel Studley, about whom Lawne said, "But if any would further know what this Dan[iel] Studley is, let them ask Samuel Fuller, a deacon of Master Robinson's church, and desire to see a copy of the letter which Daniel Studley sent unto him" [Christopher Lawne (and others), *The Prophane Schisme of the Brownists or Separatists With the Impietie, Dissensions, Lewd, and Abhominable Vices of That Impure Sect* (London 1612), 11].

By 1611, therefore, three years before his father's will, Samuel Fuller had declared himself a separatist and departed for Leiden. If his father were not of the same persuasion, the relatively small size of Samuel's legacy would be understandable. Furthermore, by choosing Samuel Fuller as a deacon so soon after they had established their church at Leiden, John Robinson and his congregation were demonstrating confidence in his commitment to their undertaking and must therefore have had strong evidence of his religious stance. This would further suggest that Samuel Fuller may already have been active as a separatist while still in England, and this could explain the failure to find any record of his first marriage in English parish registers, assuming that that marriage had taken place in England.

As members of the Leiden congregation began to make plans a few years later for their removal to the New World, Samuel Fuller was also active in those affairs. In a letter written from Leiden on 10 June 1620, Samuel Fuller, Edward Winslow, William Bradford, and Isaac Allerton wrote to John Carver and Robert Cushman, then in England, regarding some final details of the business arrangements for the voyage [Bradford 360–61].

BIBLIOGRAPHIC NOTE: Samuel Fuller has been treated in Volume Ten of the Five Generations Project of the General Society of Mayflower Descendants, published in 1996, prepared originally by Katharine Warner Radasch and Arthur Hitchcock Radasch and revised by Margaret Harris Stover and Robert S. Wakefield. (This supersedes the version of this family published in Volume One in 1975.)

RICHARD GARDINER

Moses Fletcher, John Goodman, Thomas Williams, Digory Priest, Edmund Margesson, Peter Browne, Richard Britteridge, Richard Clarke, Richard Gardiner, Gilbert Winslow.

Richard Gardiner became a seaman and died in England or at sea.

ORIGIN: Unknown.
MIGRATION: 1620 on the *Mayflower*.
FIRST RESIDENCE: Plymouth.
RETURN TRIPS: Returned to England after 1624.

OCCUPATION: Seaman. In a letter of May 1624 Emmanuel Altham, then at Plymouth, reported to James Sherley that Governor Bradford would "provide me a sufficient man for master, notwithstanding Richard Gardiner hath earnestly requested it, claiming it as his due by place, but some say not by sufficiency. I will say no more concerning him because I know you shall understand it by others; only thus much I must needs say: that so far as he could, he was willing to help us with the ship. And now he takes it somewhat unkindly that, seeing the Company have sent our ship's company assurance for their wages, that he is not intimated therein" [Three Visitors 47–48].
FREEMAN: On 11 November 1620, Richard Gardiner signed the Mayflower Compact [Morton 26].
ESTATE: In the 1623 Plymouth land division "Richard Gardener" was granted one acre [PCR 12:4; MD 40:10], but he does not appear in the 1627 cattle division.

BIRTH: Born by 1599 (assuming he was twenty-one when he signed the Mayflower Compact).
DEATH: After 1624, in England or at sea.
MARRIAGE: None known.
CHILDREN: None known.

COMMENTS: Caleb Johnson has found English records for two men named Richard Gardiner (or a close variant) who are plausible candidates to have been the *Mayflower* passenger, one from Harwich, Essex, and one from Guildford, Surrey [Mayflower Passengers 152–53; TAG 79:177].

JOHN GOODMAN

Moses Fletcher, John Goodman, Thomas Williams, Digory Priest, Edmund Margesson, Peter Browne, Richard Britteridge, Richard Clarke, Richard Gardiner, Gilbert Winslow.

Moses Fletcher, Thomas Williams, Digory Priest, John Goodman, Edmund Margesson, Richard Britteridge, Richard Clarke, all these died soon after arrival in the general sickness that befell. But Digory Priest had his wife and children sent hither afterwards, she being Mr. Allerton's sister. But the rest left no posterity here.

ORIGIN: Unknown (but see **COMMENTS**).
MIGRATION: 1620 on the *Mayflower*.
FIRST RESIDENCE: Plymouth.

FREEMAN: On 11 November 1620, John Goodman signed the Mayflower Compact [Morton 26].
ESTATE: In the 1623 Plymouth land division, John Goodman received a grant, presumably one acre, as a passenger on the *Mayflower* [PCR 12:4; MD 40:12].

BIRTH: By about 1600.
DEATH: After 19 January 1620/1 [Mourt 47 (but see **COMMENTS**)].
MARRIAGE: None known (but see **COMMENTS**).
CHILDREN: None known.

COMMENTS: On 12 January 1620/1, John Goodman and Peter Brown, while cutting thatch, became lost in the woods, spent a night in the open, and found their way back to the rest on the 13th. Goodman's feet were damaged, and "it was a long while after ere he was able to go," and on the 19th he "went abroad to use his lame feet" [Mourt 45–47].

For a man who generated so few records, John Goodman has left behind a remarkable number of unresolved problems. Dexter thought he was the "Jan Codmoer" who married at Leiden in 1619, but no evidence supports this conclusion [Dexter 615; Leiden Pilgrims 152].

Based on his structural analysis of Bradford's list of *Mayflower* passengers, Caleb Johnson concludes that Goodman was a member of the Leiden congregation, but Jeremy Bangs does not include him in his list of Leiden church members [TAG 80:99; Mayflower Passengers 154; Strangers and Pilgrims 706].

Bradford's statement that someone died in "the general sickness" should mean that the death occurred in early 1621, so there may be a simple clerical error in the 1623 compilation of land grants. In his analysis of the land grants, Robert S. Wakefield accepted Bradford's stated time of death for Goodman and suggested that "this share must be for money contributed" [MQ 40:12]. Another possibility (suggested by Wakefield in private correspondence) is that John Goodman was related to some other Plymouth resident who in 1623 made good a claim to Goodman's right to an acre of land. John Goodman had certainly died or departed by 1627, since he is not in the 1627 cattle division. (See Stratton 297 for discussion of attempts to identify John Goodman with other men of similar names.)

WILLIAM HOLBECK

Mr. William White and Susanna his wife and one son called Resolved, and one born a-shipboard called Peregrine, and two servants named William Holbeck and Edward Thompson.

Mr. White and his two servants died soon after their landing.

ORIGIN: Amsterdam (as servant of *WILLIAM WHITE*).
MIGRATION: 1620 on the *Mayflower.*
FIRST RESIDENCE: Plymouth.

OCCUPATION: Servant to *WILLIAM WHITE.*

BIRTH: Born say 1600.
DEATH: Early 1621 at Plymouth.
MARRIAGE: None.
CHILDREN: None.

COMMENTS: Various origins have been suggested for William Holbeck. Banks noted that the "name of Holbeck is found in St. Andrew's parish, Norwich, where the Rev. John Robinson had a curacy before his removal to Leyden. He is to be credited as one of the Leyden contingent" [English Homes 59]. Caleb Johnson has noticed occurrences of the name in Warwickshire and Lincolnshire [Mayflower Passengers 158]. The surname "Hollebeek" is found among Flemish refugees in Leiden [Strangers and Pilgrims 167, 175, 287, 727].

JOHN HOOKE

Mr. Isaac Allerton and Mary his wife, with three children, Bartholomew, Remember and Mary. And a servant boy John Hooke.

Mr. Allerton his wife died with the first, and his servant John Hooke.

ORIGIN: Leiden (as servant of *ISAAC ALLERTON*).
PREVIOUS RESIDENCES: Great Yarmouth, Norfolk.
MIGRATION: 1620 on the *Mayflower*.
FIRST RESIDENCE: Plymouth.

OCCUPATION: "Jan de Houck" was apprenticed to *ISAAC ALLERTON* at Leiden on 7 January 1619 [NS] [NEHGR 143:207–8].

BIRTH: Baptized Great Yarmouth, Norfolk, 18 January 1606/7 [NEHGR 173:204–5], son of John and Alice (Thompson) Hooke, who had been married at St. Peter Mancroft, Norwich, Norfolk, on 9 August 1605 [TAG 80:101].
DEATH: Early 1621 at Plymouth.
MARRIAGE: None.
CHILDREN: None.

BIBLIOGRAPHIC NOTE: In 1989 Jeremy D. Bangs published the apprenticeship record for John Hooke [NEHGR 143:207–8]. In 2005 Caleb Johnson published the marriage record for Hooke's parents [TAG 80:101] and in 2019 Sue Allan discovered John Hooke's baptismal record [NEHGR 173:204–5].

STEPHEN HOPKINS

Mr. Stephen Hopkins and Elizabeth his wife, and two children called Giles and Constanta, a daughter, both by a former wife. And two more by this wife called Damaris and Oceanus; the last was born at sea. And two servants called Edward Doty and Edward Lester.

Mr. Hopkins and his wife are now both dead, but they lived above twenty years in this place and had one son and four daughters born here. Their son became a seaman and died at Barbadoes, one daughter died here and two are married; one of them hath two children, and one is yet to marry. So their increase which still survive are five. But his son Giles is married and hath four children. His daughter Constanta is also married and hath twelve children, all of them living and one of them married.

ORIGIN: London.
PREVIOUS RESIDENCES: Upper Clatford, Hampshire; Winchester, Hampshire; Hursley, Hampshire; Bermuda; Jamestown.
MIGRATION: 1620 on the *Mayflower.*
FIRST RESIDENCE: Plymouth.

OCCUPATION: Merchant.
FREEMAN: On 11 November 1620, Stephen Hopkins signed the Mayflower Compact [Morton 26].

In the 1633 list of Plymouth freemen Stephen Hopkins is included among the assistants [PCR 1:3]. In the list of Plymouth Colony freemen of 7 March 1636/7 (as "Steephen Hopkins, gen.") [PCR 1:52]. In the Plymouth section of the 1639 Plymouth Colony list of freemen (as "Mr. Steephen Hopkins," later annotated "dead") [PCR 8:173].
EDUCATION: He signed his will. His inventory included "diverse books" valued at 12s. [PCPR 1:63; Plymouth Libraries 178].
OFFICES: Assistant, 1633–36 [PCR 1:5, 21, 32, 36].

Volunteered for service in the Pequot War, 1637 [PCR 1:61].
ESTATE: In the 1623 Plymouth division of land "Steven Hobkins" received six acres as a passenger on the *Mayflower* [PCR 12:4; MD 40:10]. In the 1627 Plymouth division of cattle Stephen Hopkins, his wife Elizabeth

Hopkins, Gyles Hopkins, Caleb Hopkins, and Deborah Hopkins are the first five persons in the seventh company, and Damaris Hopkins is the thirteenth person in the eighth company [PCR 12:11, 12].

Stephen Hopkins was one of the Purchasers, those who acquired the rights to land distributions in Plymouth Colony as a consequence of the agreement made between the London merchants and the Plymouth settlers in 1627 [Ford 282–88].

In the Plymouth tax list of 25 March 1634 Stephen Hopkins was assessed £1 7s. and in the list of 27 March 1634 £1 10s. [PCR 1:9, 27].

On 1 July 1633, "Mr. Hopkins" was ordered to mow where he had mowed the year before [PCR 1:15], followed by similar orders on 14 March 1635/6 and 20 March 1636/7 [PCR 1:41, 57].

On 5 February 1637/8, "Mr. Stephen Hopkins requesteth a grant of lands towards the Six Mile Brook" [PCR 1:76]. On 7 August 1638, "[l]iberty is granted to Mr. Steephen Hopkins to erect a house at Mattacheese, and cut hay there this year to winter his cattle, provided that it be not to withdraw him from the town of Plymouth" [PCR 1:93].

On 17 July 1637, "Steephen Hopkins of Plymouth, gent.," sold to George Boare [Bower] of Scituate, yeoman, "all that his messuage, houses, tenements, outhouses lying and being at the Broken Wharfe towards the Eele River together with the six shares of lands thereunto belonging containing six acres" [PCR 12:21]. On 30 November 1638, "Mr. Steephen Hopkins" sold to Josias Cooke "all those his six acres of land lying on the south side of the Town Brook of Plymouth" [PCR 12:39]. On 8 June 1642, William Chase mortgaged to "Mr. Stephen Hopkins ... all that his house and lands in Yarmouth containing eight acres of upland and six acres more lying at the Stony Cove" [PCR 12:83].

On 1 June 1640, "Mr. Hopkins" was granted twelve acres of meadow [PCR 1:154, 166].

In his will, dated 6 June 1644 and proved 20 August 1644, Stephen Hopkins "of Plymouth ... weak yet in good and perfect memory" directed that he be buried "as near as conveniently may be to my wife, deceased," and bequeathed to "son Giles Hopkins" the great bull now in the hands of Mrs. Warren; to "Steven Hopkins my son Giles his son" 20s. in Mrs. Warren's hands; to "daughter Constanc[e] Snow, wife of Nicholas ... my mare"; to "daughter Deborah Hopkins" cows; to "daughter Damaris Hopkins" cows; to "daughter Ruth" cows; to "daughter Elizabeth" cows; to "four daughters Deborah, Damaris, Ruth and Elizabeth Hopkins" all the moveable goods; if any of the daughters die, their share to be divided equally among the survivors; to "son Caleb heir apparent" house and lands at Plymouth, one pair of oxen and hire of them and all the debts "now owing unto me"; daughters to have free recourse to use of the house in Plymouth while single; "son Caleb" executor; Caleb and Captain Standish joint supervisors [PCPR 1:61].

The inventory of the estate of Stephen Hopkins, taken 17 July 1644, was untotaled, with no real estate included [PCPR 1:62–63].

On 28 October 1644, "Caleb Hopkins son and heir unto Mr. Steephen Hopkins of Plymouth deceased" deeded to "Gyles Hopkins of Yarmouth, planter, one hundred acres of those lands taken up for the Purchasers of Satuckquett which said lands do accrue unto the said Steephen as a Purchaser" [PCR 12:104].

BIRTH: Baptized Upper Clatford, Hampshire, 30 April 1581, son of John and Elizabeth (Williams) Hopkins [TAG 79:243].

DEATH: Plymouth between 6 June 1644 (date of will) and 17 July 1644 (probate of will).

MARRIAGE: (1) By 1604 Mary Kent *alias* Back, b. say 1583, daughter of Robert and Joan (Machell) Kent *alias* Back [MD 61:38–59, 134–54, 64:40–41; MQ 78:122–39, 79:52–78]. She was buried at Hursley, Hampshire, 9 May 1613 [TAG 73:169].

(2) St. Mary Matfelon, Whitechapel, Middlesex, 19 February 1617/8 Elizabeth Fisher. She died at Plymouth sometime in the early 1640s before her husband, who desired to be buried near her; Bradford indicated that both she and her husband had lived in Plymouth above twenty years. (The conclusion that this marriage record pertains to the *Mayflower* passenger is plausible, but not fully proved [MQ 78:122–23].)

CHILDREN:
With first wife

i ELIZABETH HOPKINS, bp. Hursley, Hampshire, 13 March 1604/5 [private correspondence with Caleb Johnson]; living on 12 May 1613 [TAG 73:165]; no further record.

ii CONSTANCE HOPKINS, bp. Hursley, Hampshire, 11 May 1606 [TAG 73:170]; m. Plymouth by 1627 NICHOLAS SNOW {1623, Plymouth} [PM 428] (in the 1627 Plymouth division of cattle "Nickolas Snow" and "Constance Snow" were the sixth and seventh persons in the seventh company, which was headed by Stephen Hopkins [PCR 12:11]).

iii GILES HOPKINS, bp. Hursley, Hampshire, 30 January 1607/8 [TAG 73:170]; m. Plymouth 9 October 1639 Catherine Whelden [PCR 1:134; TAG 48:5].

With second wife

    iv DAMARIS HOPKINS, b. say 1618; probably d. at Plymouth
        before the birth of her younger sister of the same name.

    v   OCEANUS HOPKINS, b. at sea between 16 September and
        11 November 1620; died by 1627.

    vi CALEB HOPKINS, b. Plymouth say 1624; "became a
        seaman & died at Barbadoes" between 1644 and 1651
        [Bradford 445].

    vii DEBORAH HOPKINS, b. Plymouth say 1626; m. Plymouth
        23 April 1646 as his first wife Andrew Ring [PCR 2:98;
        TAG 42:202–5], son of widow MARY RING {1629 or
        1630, Plymouth} [PM 389].

    viii DAMARIS HOPKINS, b. Plymouth say 1628; m. Plymouth
        shortly after 10 June 1646 Jacob Cooke [MD 2:27–8], son
        of *FRANCIS COOKE*. (Since this Damaris was still bear-
        ing children in the early 1670s, she cannot be the same as
        the Damaris who came on the *Mayflower*.)

    ix RUTH HOPKINS, b. Plymouth say 1630; d. after 30
        November 1644 and by spring 1651 [Bradford 445]; unm.

    x   ELIZABETH HOPKINS, b. Plymouth say 1632; believed
        to have died by 6 October 1659 when her property was
        appraised "in case Elizabeth Hopkins do come no more"
        [MD 4:114–19]; unm.

PREMIGRATION BIOGRAPHY: Stephen Hopkins was born in Upper
Clatford, Hampshire, in 1581. By 1586 the family had removed to the parish
of St. Thomas, Winchester, where Stephen's father died in 1593. We next find
Stephen Hopkins at Hursley, Hampshire, apparently having married recently;
between 1604 and 1608 this couple had three children baptized there.

In 1609 Stephen Hopkins decided to sail for Virginia on the *Sea
Venture*. The ship encountered a hurricane and shipwrecked on Bermuda,
where the survivors were stranded for a year. Hopkins led a rebellion
against the leaders of the expedition and was convicted and sentenced to
death, but was soon pardoned. In 1610 they managed to get to Virginia,
where Hopkins remained for several years. In 1613, while he was still in
Virginia, Stephen's wife died back in Hursley, thinking he was dead and
she was a widow. By early 1618 he was back in England, where he is likely
the man who married Elizabeth Fisher at St. Mary Matfelon, Whitechapel
[Mayflower Passengers 160–65].

COMMENTS: Caleb Johnson's discovery [TAG 73:161–71] of the family of Stephen Hopkins in Hursley, Hampshire, at last definitively eliminates the suggestion that Stephen Hopkins was son of Stephen Hopkins, a clothier, of Wortley, Wotton under Edge, Gloucestershire [MF 6:3, citing "[t]he Wortley historian"].

Johnson's discovery also strengthens the argument that this was the same Stephen Hopkins who was the minister's clerk on the vessel *Sea Venture*, which met with a hurricane in 1609 while on a voyage to Virginia [TAG 73:165–66]. One of one hundred and fifty survivors marooned on Bermuda, he fomented a mutiny and was sentenced to death, but "so penitent he was and made so much moan, alleging the ruin of his wife and children in this his trespass," that his friends procured a pardon from the Governor [MF 6:3, citing William Strachey's account]. (This episode is one of the underlying sources for Shakespeare's *The Tempest* [Hobson Woodward, *A Brave Vessel: The True Tale of the Castaways Who Rescued Jamestown and Inspired Shakespeare's* The Tempest (New York 2009)]).

A brief docket item in official English records raises tantalizing possibilities. On 20 September 1614, a letter was sent "to Sir Thomas Dale Marshall of the Colony in Virginia, to send home by the next return of ships from thence Eliezer Hopkins" [*Calendar of State Papers, Domestic Series, of the Reign of James I, 1611–1618* (London 1858), p. 253; *Calendar of State Papers, Colonial Series, 1574–1660* (London 1860), p. 17]. However, examination of the original of this record by Michael J. Wood verifies that "Eliezer" is the correct reading of the calendar entry (but may have resulted from a contemporaneous misreading of the original letter, which is now lost).

Stephen Hopkins was a member of the party that explored the Outer Cape from 15 to 17 November 1620 [Mourt 19]. He was also a member of the exploratory party that left Provincetown Harbor on 6 December 1620 and selected the site for the town of Plymouth [Mourt 32].

In June 1621 Steven Hopkins and Edward Winslow were chosen by the governor to approach Massasoit, and Hopkins repeated this duty as emissary frequently thereafter [Mourt 60; Bradford 87].

Despite his social standing and his early public service, Stephen Hopkins managed to run afoul of the authorities several times in the late 1630s. On 7 June 1636, while an Assistant, he was fined for battery of John Tisdale, whom he "dangerously wounded" [PCR 1:41–42]. On 2 October 1637, he was fined for allowing drinking on the Lord's Day and the playing of "shovell board" [PCR 1:68] and, on 2 January 1637/8, he was "presented for suffering excessive drinking in his house" [PCR 1:75]. On 5 June 1638, he was "presented for selling beer for 2d. the quart, not worth 1d. a quart"

[PCR 1:87]; for this and other similar infractions he was on 4 September 1638 fined £5 [PCR 1:97]. He dealt harshly with his pregnant servant Dorothy Temple and only the intercession of John Holmes freed him from being held in contempt of court [PCR 1:111–13]. On 3 December 1639, he was presented for selling a looking glass for 16d. when a similar glass could be bought in the Bay for 9d. [PCR 1:137].

BIBLIOGRAPHIC NOTE: John D. Austin compiled the account of Stephen Hopkins and his descendants as the sixth volume in the Five Generations Project of the General Society of Mayflower Descendants, now in its third edition (2001).

In 1998 Caleb Johnson published his discovery of the baptismal place of the children of Stephen Hopkins and his first wife [TAG 73:161–71]. In 2007 Johnson published a biography of Stephen Hopkins called *Here Shall I Die Ashore – Stephen Hopkins: Bermuda Castaway, Jamestown Survivor, and Mayflower Pilgrim.*

In 2004 Ernest Martin Christensen published data on the parentage and baptism of Stephen Hopkins [TAG 79:241–49]. In 2012 Simon Neal published extensive research into the identity of both wives of Stephen Hopkins [MQ 78:122–39, 79:134–54; MD 61:38–59, 134–54].

JOHN HOWLAND

Mr. John Carver, Katherine his wife, Desire Minter, and two manservants, John Howland, Roger Wilder. William Latham, a boy, and a maidservant and a child that was put to him, Jasper More.

His servant John Howland married the daughter of John Tilley, Elizabeth, and they are both now living and have ten children, now all living, and their eldest daughter hath four children; and their second daughter one, all living, and other of their children marriageable. So 15 are come of them.

ORIGIN: Leiden (as servant of *JOHN CARVER*).
PREVIOUS RESIDENCES: Fenstanton, Huntingdonshire.
MIGRATION: 1620 on the *Mayflower*.
FIRST RESIDENCE: Plymouth.

OCCUPATION: Servant to *JOHN CARVER*.
FREEMAN: On 11 November 1620, John Howland signed the Mayflower Compact [Morton 26].

In the 1633 list of Plymouth freemen John Howland is near the head of the list, among the Assistants [PCR 1:3]. In the 6 March 1636/7 list of Plymouth Colony freemen [PCR 1:52]. In the Plymouth sections of the 1639, 1658, and 29 May 1670 lists of Plymouth Colony freemen [PCR 5:274, 8:173, 197].

EDUCATION: His inventory included "1 great Bible and Annotations on the 5 Books of Moses" valued at £1 and "Mr. Tindall's Works, Mr. Wilson's Works, 7 more books" valued at £1 [MD 2:73–77, citing PCPR 3:1:51–54; Plymouth Libraries 285–86].

In 2018 David L. Greene carefully analyzed a frequently published signature of John Howland the authenticity of which had long been debated and deemed it to be genuine [TAG 90:184–88].

OFFICES: Plymouth Colony Assistant, 1 January 1632/3, 1 January 1633/4, 1 January 1634/5 [PCR 1:5, 21, 32].

Deputy for Plymouth to Plymouth Colony General Court, 1 June 1641, 28 October 1645, 1 June 1647, 7 June 1648, 8 June 1649, 4 June 1650, 5 June 1651, 3 June 1652, 7 June 1653, 7 March 1653/4, 6 June 1654, 1 August 1654, 8 June 1655, 3 June 1656, 1 June 1658, 4 June 1661, 1 June 1663,

1 June 1666, 5 June 1667 [PCR 2:16, 94, 117, 123, 144, 154, 167, 3:8, 31, 44, 49, 63, 79, 99, 135, 214, 4:37, 122, 148].

In charge of the fur trading post at Kennebec, 1634 [MD 2:10–11]. Committee on the fur trade, 3 October 1659 [PCR 3:170].

In the Plymouth section of the 1643 Plymouth Colony list of men able to bear arms (as "John Howland Sen.") [PCR 8:187].

ESTATE: In the 1623 Plymouth division of land John Howland received four acres as a passenger on the *Mayflower* [PCR 12:4; MD 40:10]. In the 1627 Plymouth division of cattle John Howland, his wife Elizabeth Howland, John Howland Junior, and Desire Howland were the first four persons in the fourth company [PCR 12:10].

John Howland was one of the Purchasers, those who acquired the rights to land distributions in Plymouth Colony as a consequence of the agreement made between the London merchants and the Plymouth settlers in 1627 [Ford 282–88].

In the Plymouth tax list of 25 March 1633 John Howland was assessed 18s. and in the list of 27 March 1634 £1 4s. [PCR 1:9, 27].

On 4 December 1637, "forty acres of land are granted to Mr. John Howland, lying at the Island Creeke Pond at the western end thereof, with the marsh ground that he useth to mow there" [PCR 1:70]. On 5 November 1638, the "island called Spectacle, lying upon Green's Harbor, is granted to Mr. John Howland" [PCR 1:102, 110, 168]. Granted six acres of meadow "at the North Meadow by Jones River," 17 October 1642 [PCR 2:49].

In his will, dated 29 May 1672 and proved 6 March 1672/3, "John Howland Seni[o]r of the town of New Plymouth ... being now grown aged, having many infirmities of body upon me," bequeathed to "John Howland my eldest son besides what lands I have already given him, all my right and interest to that one hundred acres of land granted me by the court lying on the eastern side of Taunton River"; to "my son Jabez Howland all those my upland and meadow that I now possess at Satuckett and Paomett"; to "my son Jabez Howland all that my one piece of land that I have lying on the south side of the mill brook"; to "Isaac Howland my youngest son all those my uplands and meadows ... in the town of Middlebery and in a tract of land called the Major's Purchase near Namassakett Ponds which I have bought and purchased of William White of Marshfield"; to "my said son Isacke Howland the one half of my twelve acre lot of meadow that I now have at Winnatucsett River"; to "my dear and loving wife Elizabeth Howland the use and benefit of my now dwelling house in Rockey Nooke in the township of Plymouth ... with the outhousing lands ... uplands and meadow lands ... in the town of Plymouth ... excepting what meadow and upland I have before given to my sons Jabez and Isacke Howland during her natural life"; to "my son Joseph Howland after the decease of my loving wife Elizabeth Howland my aforesaid dwelling house at Rockey Nooke"; to "my daughter Desire Gorum 20s."; to "my daughter Hope Chipman 20s."; to "my daughter Elizabeth Dickenson 20s."; to "my daughter Lydia Browne 20s."; to "my daughter Hannah Bosworth 20s."; to "my daughter Ruth Cushman 20s."; to "my grandchild Elizabeth Howland the daughter of my son John Howland 20s."; "these legacies given to my daughters [to] be paid by my executrix"; to "my loving wife Elizabeth Howland my debts and legacies being first paid, my whole estate," she to be executrix [MD 2:70–73, citing PCPR 3:1:49–50].

The inventory of "Mr. John Howland lately deceased," taken 3 March 1672/3, totaled £157 8s. 8d. [MD 2:73–77, citing PCPR 3:1:51–54]. After the inventory, the appraisers noted that "the testator died possessed of these several parcels of land following": "his dwelling house with the out-housing, uplands and meadow belonging thereunto lying at Rockey Nooke in the town of New Plymouth," "a parcel of meadow at Jones River mead-ow," "the one half of a house and a parcel of meadow and upland belong-ing thereunto lying and being at Colchester in the aforesaid township," "a parcel of meadow and upland belonging thereunto lying near Jones River bridge in the town of Duxburrow," "one house and 2 shares of a tract of land and meadow that lyeth in the town of Middleberry that was pur-chased by Captain Thomas Southworth of and from the Indian Sachem Josias Wampatucke," and "2 shares of a tract of land called the Major's Purchase lying near Namassakett ponds" [MD 2:77, citing PCPR 3:1:54]. (See also PCR 5:108, 110, 127.)

In her will, dated 17 December 1686 and proved 10 January 1687/8, "Elizabeth Howland of Swanzey ... being seventy nine years of age" bequeathed to "my eldest son John Howland the sum of £5 ... and my book called *Mr. Tindale's Works* and also one pair of sheets & one pair of pil-lowbeers and one pair of bed blankets"; to "my son Joseph Howland my stilliards [scales] and also one pair of sheets and one pair of pillowbeers"; to "my son Jabez Howland my featherbed & bolster that is in his custody & also one rug & two blankets that belongeth to the said bed & also my great iron pot & pothooks"; to "my son Isaack Howland my book called *Willson on the Romanes* & one pair of sheets & one pair of pillowbeers & also my great brass kettle already in his possession"; to "my son-inlaw Mr. James Browne my great Bible"; to "my daughter Lidia Browne my best featherbed & bolster two pillows & three blankets & a green rug & my small cupboard one pair of andirons & my lesser brass kettle & my small Bible & my book of Mr. Robbinson's Works called *Observations Divine & Moral* & also my finest pair of sheets & my holland pillowbeers"; to "my daughter Elisabeth

Dickenson one pair of sheets & one pair of pillowbeers & one chest"; to "my daughter Hannah Bosworth one pair of sheets & one pair of pillowbeers"; to "my granddaughter Elizabeth Bursley one pair of sheets and one pair of pillowbeers"; to "my grandson Nathanael Howland (the son of Joseph Howland) ... my lot of land with the meadow thereto adjoining ... in the township of Duxbury near Jones River Bridge"; to "my grandson James Browne one iron bar and one iron trammell now in his possession"; to "my grandson Jabez Browne one chest"; to "my granddaughter Dorothy Browne my best chest & my warming pan"; to "my granddaughter Desire Cushman four sheep"; "my wearing clothes linen and woolen" and the residue to "my three daughters Elisabeth Dickenson, Lidia Browne and Hannah Bosworth to be equally divided amongst them"; "my loving son-in-law James Browne and my loving son Jabez Howland" executors [MD 3:54–57, citing BrPR 1:13–14].

BIRTH: By 1599, son of Henry and Margaret (_____) Howland of Fenstanton, Huntingdonshire.
DEATH: Plymouth 23 February 1672/3 "above eighty years" [PCR 8:34]. (This age at death is almost certainly exaggerated [Mayflower Passengers 287 (footnote 188)].)
MARRIAGE: Plymouth by about 1624 Elizabeth Tilley, baptized Henlow, Bedfordshire, 30 August 1607, daughter of *JOHN TILLEY*. She died at Swansea 22 December 1687, aged eighty [SwVR 27].
CHILDREN:

  i DESIRE HOWLAND, b. say 1624; m. by 1644 John Gorham (eldest known child b. Plymouth 2 April 1644 [MD 5:72]).
  ii JOHN HOWLAND, b. Plymouth 24 February 1626[/7] [Sewall 463]; m. Plymouth 26 October 1651 Mary Lee [PCR 8:13].
  iii HOPE HOWLAND, b. say 1629; m. by 1647 John Chipman (eldest known child b. Plymouth 24 June 1647 [PCR 8:4]) [*The Howland Quarterly* 60:2:8–13].
  iv ELIZABETH HOWLAND, b. say 1631; m. (1) Plymouth 13 September 1649 Ephraim Hicks [PCR 8:8], son of ROBERT HICKS {1621, Plymouth} [PM 243]; m. (2) Plymouth 10 July 1651 John Dickerson [PCR 8:13; *The Howland Quarterly* 60:3:13–19].
  v LYDIA HOWLAND, b. say 1633; m. by about 1655 James Brown, son of JOHN BROWN {1635, Plymouth} [GM 2:1:420–29].

vi HANNAH HOWLAND, b. say 1637; m. Swansea 6 July 1661 Jonathan Bosworth [SwVR 23], son of JONATHAN BOSWORTH {1633, Cambridge} [GMB 1:187–91].

vii JOSEPH HOWLAND, b. say 1640; m. Plymouth 7 December 1664 Elizabeth Southworth [PCR 8:25], daughter of THOMAS SOUTHWORTH {1628, Plymouth} [PM 437].

viii JABEZ HOWLAND, b. about 1644 (deposed on 19 July 1680 aged 36 years [SJC #1915]); m. by 1669 Bethiah Thacher, daughter of ANTHONY THACHER {1635, Newbury} [GM 2:7:14–22] (eldest known child b. Plymouth 15 November 1669 [PVR 668; NYGBR 42:154]).

ix RUTH HOWLAND, b. say 1646; m. Plymouth 17 November 1664 Thomas Cushman [PCR 8:25], son of Thomas Cushman.

x ISAAC HOWLAND, b. Plymouth 15 November 1649; m. by 1677 Elizabeth Vaughn, daughter of George Vaughn [TAG 23:24–26].

ASSOCIATIONS: Brother of HENRY HOWLAND {1632, Plymouth} [PM 275] and Arthur Howland [NGSQ 71:84].

John Howland sailed on the *Mayflower* as a servant of *JOHN CARVER*. John Carver's wife, Catherine (White) (Leggatt) Carver, had a sister Jane White who married Ranulph (or Randall) Thickens of Leiden. Ranulph Thickens had a brother Ralph Thickens of London, who was associated with John Howland, citizen and salter of London. No genealogical connection has yet been discovered between John Howland of the *Mayflower* and John Howland of London, but this web of relationships may explain how the former came to be part of the Carver household in 1620 [Caleb Johnson and Simon Neal, "A 1623 Indenture That References John Howland, Citizen and Salter of London," MD 63:225–31].

COMMENTS: During a particularly bad storm on the crossing, John Howland (characterized by Bradford as "a lusty young man") went above deck and was swept overboard, "but it pleased God that he caught hold of the topsail halyards which hung overboard and ran out at length. Yet he held his hold (though he was sundry fathoms under water) till he was hauled up by the same rope to the brim of the water, and then with a boat hook and other means got into the ship again and his life saved. And though he was something ill with it, yet he lived many years after and became a profitable member both in church and commonwealth" [Bradford 59].

On 6 December 1620, John Howland was a member of the exploratory party which eventually chose the settlement site which would become the town of Plymouth [Morton 32].

In 1627, pursuant to the renegotiation of the financial agreement between the London merchants and the Plymouth settlers, John Howland became one of the eight Undertakers who agreed to oversee the liquidation of Plymouth Colony's debts [Bradford 194–96; Bradford LB 38–40].

In an undated deposition we learn that in April 1634 John Hocking sailed to Kennebec and challenged the rights of the Plymouth men to their exclusive trade in that place. Mr. John Howland, in charge of the trading post, went out in their bark with several other men and warned Hocking off, but was taunted and defied. Howland "bid three of his men go cut his cable [Hocking's anchor]," but the flow of the stream was too strong and Howland called them back. He added Moses Talbot to the crew. Hocking, seeing that their intent was to cut the cable, "presently put his piece almost to Moyses Talbott's head, which Mr. Howland seeing called to him desiring him not to shoot his man but take himself for his mark saying his men did but that which he commanded them and therefore desired him not to hurt any of them, if any wrong was done it was himself that did it and therefore called again to him to take him for his mark saying he stood very fair, but Hocking would not hear nor look towards our bark, but presently shooteth Moyses in the head, and presently took up his pistol in his hand but the Lord stayed him from doing any further hurt by a shot from our bark himself was presently struck dead being shot near the same place in the head where he had murderously shot Moyses" [MD 2:10–11].

BIBLIOGRAPHIC NOTE: Between 1990 and 2008 Elizabeth Pearson White prepared four volumes covering the first five generations of the descendants of John Howland through his four eldest children: Desire (1990), John (1993), Hope (2008), and Elizabeth (2008). These were published by Picton Press, independently of the Five Generations Project. (These volumes should be used with caution [MD 42:15–16, 58:97–98].)

The Five Generations Project of the General Society of Mayflower Descendants has continued the treatment of the descendants of John Howland in three volumes compiled by Ann Smith Lainhart. The first part of Volume Twenty-six covers the first four generations of descent from John Howland's six younger children: Lydia, Hannah, Joseph, Jabez, Ruth, and Isaac [MF 26:1 (2006)]. The second part treats the fifth-generation descendants of Lydia and Hannah [MF 26:2 (2010)], while the third part covers the fifth- and sixth-generation descendants of Joseph and Jabez [MF 26:3 (2012)]. The fifth-generation descendants of Ruth and Isaac remain to be published.

JOHN LANGMORE

Mr. Christopher Martin and his wife and two servants, Solomon Prower and John Langmore.

Mr. Martin, he and all his died in the first infection, not long after the arrival.

ORIGIN: England (see **COMMENTS**).
MIGRATION: 1620 on the *Mayflower.*
FIRST RESIDENCE: Plymouth.

OCCUPATION: Servant to CHRISTOPHER MARTIN.

BIRTH: Born say 1600.
DEATH: Early 1621 at Plymouth.
MARRIAGE: None.
CHILDREN: None.

COMMENTS: As a servant of Christopher Martin, John Langmore may also have been from Billericay, Essex. Caleb Johnson notes, however, that the Langmore surname does not appear in Essex and presents evidence of the appearance of the surname in other English counties [Mayflower Passengers 176].

WILLIAM LATHAM

Mr. John Carver, Katherine his wife, Desire Minter, and two manservants, John Howland, Roger Wilder. William Latham, a boy, and a maidservant and a child that was put to him, Jasper More.

His servant boy Latham, after more than 20 years' stay in the country, went into England and from thence to the Bahama Islands in the West Indies, and there with some others was starved for want of food.

ORIGIN: Leiden (as servant of *JOHN CARVER*).
MIGRATION: 1620 on the *Mayflower*.
FIRST RESIDENCE: Plymouth.
REMOVES: Duxbury, Marblehead, Marshfield.
RETURN TRIPS: In or after 1645 Latham returned to England, and then soon moved on to the Bahamas.

OCCUPATION: Servant to *JOHN CARVER* (in 1620).
  Planter [Lechford 421]. Yeoman [PCR 1:101, 105].
OFFICES: In the Marshfield section of the 1643 Plymouth Colony list of men able to bear arms [PCR 8:196].
ESTATE: In the 1627 Plymouth division of cattle William Latham was the seventh person in the eleventh company [PCR 12:12].
  In the Plymouth tax list of 25 March 1633 William Latham was assessed 9s. and the same amount on 27 March 1634 [PCR 1:11, 28].
  On 1 July 1633, Myles Standish was to "mow the ends of the grounds belonging to Edward Bumpasse and Will[iam] Latham" [PCR 1:14]. On 14 March 1635/6, Standish was to mow "at the ends of the lands of William Latham and John Washburne" [PCR 1:40].
  On 26 December 1639, "Will[ia]m Lathame of Duxborrow, planter," sold to "Mr. Ralph Partrich [Partridge] of the same" his dwelling house, twenty acres of land, and one acre of meadow [PCR 12:54].

BIRTH: About 1609 (deposed about 8 July 1641 "aged 32 years" [Lechford 421]).
DEATH: Late 1647 or early 1648 on Eleuthera Island in the Bahamas.

MARRIAGE: By 1643 Mary _____. She was born about 1625 and was hanged at Boston on 21 March 1643/4 [MQ 75:49–53] (see *COMMENTS*).
CHILDREN: None known.

COMMENTS: William Latham's name does not appear in the 1623 Plymouth division of land. Robert S. Wakefield suggested that he may have been included in the household of William Brewster [MQ 40:9], but Caleb Johnson pointed out Latham was more likely included in the household of William Bradford. Both Brewster and Bradford had been granted a share beyond the immediate members of their families, but in the 1627 division of cattle, Latham was included in the company of William Bradford [MQ 75:49].

In the inventory of Francis Eaton, dated 8 November 1633, "Will[i]am Lathan" appeared as a creditor, being owed £1 8s. [MD 1:200]. On 5 June 1638, "William Lathame" was fined 40s. "for entertaining of John Phillips into his house contrary to the act of the Court" [PCR 1:87, 106]. He had a crop of Indian corn with John Phillips of Duxbury, as seen in a 6 July 1638 deed [PCR 12:31].

On 5 November 1638, "William Latham of Duxborrow, yeoman," posted bond to appear at court "concerning his drunkenness at Plymouth & Duxborrow" [PCR 1:101]. On 4 December 1638, "William Lathame, of Duxborrow, yeoman," posted bond to appear at court for an unstated reason [PCR 1:105].

In a deposition of about 8 July 1641, "William Latham of Duxbury planter aged 32 years" gave evidence in a case involving John Moses and Thomas Keyser [Lechford 421].

On 24 February 1643/4, Edward Winslow wrote to the constables of a number of towns between Plymouth and Boston to inform them that he had in his custody "Mary the wife of William Latham late of Marblehead but now at Marshfield for adultery committed upon the body of the said Mary by one James Brittaine of Weymouth" and to ask them to transport Mary to Boston for trial [WP 4:445–46]. Latham's wife Mary was "a proper young woman about 18 years of age, whose father was a godly man and had brought her up well." Having been jilted by a local suitor, she vowed to "marry the next that came to her," and that turned out to be William Latham. She soon began to associate with "diverse young men [who] solicited her chastity," one of whom was James Britton of Weymouth. James and Mary were convicted of adultery by the Massachusetts Bay Court of Assistants and were hanged at Boston on 21 March 1643/4 [WJ 2:190–91; LENE 10–11; MQ 75:49–53].

On 28 October 1645, "Roger Cooke and William Lathame" complained against John Barker and Ann, his wife, charging the latter with accidentally burning their house [PCR 7:41]. (Note that this occurred after the execution of Latham's wife. Roger Cooke apparently never married, so this was an instance of two unmarried men living together, a domestic arrangement not generally approved of by the colony authorities.)

Soon after William Latham returned to old England and joined a company that was planning to establish a colony in the Bahamas. These settlers left England in 1647, made a brief stop in Bermuda, and then sailed on to the Bahamas. A shipboard revolt led to the party splitting into two groups, with Latham adhering to that group that landed on the island of Eleuthera, where most of them, including Latham, starved to death in late 1647 or early 1648 [Hubbard 522–24; MQ 75:49–53].

BIBLIOGRAPHIC NOTE: In 2009 Caleb Johnson unearthed the story of William Latham's wife Mary and Latham's subsequent departure from New England [MQ 75:49–53]. In his article, Johnson noted the baptism of a William Latham at Eccleston by Chorley, Lancashire, on 4 February 1608/9 as a possible candidate for the *Mayflower* passenger.

EDWARD LEISTER

Mr. Stephen Hopkins and Elizabeth his wife, and two children called Giles and Constanta, a daughter, both by a former wife. And two more by this wife called Damaris and Oceanus; the last was born at sea. And two servants called Edward Doty and Edward Lester.

Edward Doty and Edward Lester, the servants of Mr. Hopkins. Lester, after he was at liberty, went to Virginia and there died. But Edward Doty by a second wife hath seven children, and both he and they are living.

ORIGIN: England.
MIGRATION: 1620 on the *Mayflower*.
FIRST RESIDENCE: Plymouth.
REMOVES: Virginia soon after 1623.

OCCUPATION: Servant to *STEPHEN HOPKINS*.
FREEMAN: On 11 November 1620, Edward Leister signed the Mayflower Compact [Morton 26].
ESTATE: In the 1623 Plymouth land division granted one acre as a passenger on the *Mayflower* [PCR 12:2; MQ 40:10].

BIRTH: By 1599 (based on signing the Mayflower Compact).
DEATH: In Virginia after 1623.
MARRIAGE: None known.
CHILDREN: None known.

COMMENTS: Edward Leister is said to have been guilty of the "second offence" committed in Plymouth. As Bradford tells us, on 18 June 1621 "the first duel [was] fought in New England, upon a challenge at single combat with sword and dagger, between Edward Doty and Edward Leister, servants of Mr. Hopkins. Both being wounded, the one in the hand, the other in the thigh, they are adjudged by the whole company to have their head and feet tied together, and so to lie for twenty-four hours, without meat or drink; which is begun to be inflicted, but within an hour, because of their great pains, at their own and their master's humble request, upon promise of better carriage, they are released by the governor" [Prince 190–91, citing Bradford's lost register].

Following Stephen Hopkins in the 1623 division of land are two men with first name Edward but without surnames; these must be his two servants, Edward Doty and Edward Leister [MQ 40:10]. But Leister is not in the 1627 division of cattle, so he must have left for Virginia between those two dates. He does not appear in the February 1623/4 list of those in Virginia living and dead, or in the February 1624/5 Virginia muster of inhabitants.

EDMUND MARGESSON

Moses Fletcher, John Goodman, Thomas Williams, Digory Priest, Edmund Margesson, Peter Browne, Richard Britteridge, Richard Clarke, Richard Gardiner, Gilbert Winslow.

Moses Fletcher, Thomas Williams, Digory Priest, John Goodman, Edmund Margesson, Richard Britteridge, Richard Clarke, all these died soon after arrival in the general sickness that befell. But Digory Priest had his wife and children sent hither afterwards, she being Mr. Allerton's sister. But the rest left no posterity here.

ORIGIN: England.
MIGRATION: 1620 on the *Mayflower*.
FIRST RESIDENCE: Plymouth.

FREEMAN: On 11 November 1620, Edmund Margesson signed the Mayflower Compact [Morton 26].

BIRTH: Born by 1599 (assuming he was twenty-one when he signed the Mayflower Compact).
DEATH: Early 1621 at Plymouth.
MARRIAGE: None known.
CHILDREN: None known.

COMMENTS: Caleb Johnson notes that the name "Edmund Margetson" appears in various parishes in Norfolk [Mayflower Passengers 182].

CHRISTOPHER MARTIN

Mr. Christopher Martin and his wife and two servants, Solomon Prower and John Langmore.

Mr. Martin, he and all his died in the first infection, not long after the arrival.

ORIGIN: Billericay, Great Burstead, Essex.
MIGRATION: 1620 on the *Mayflower.*
FIRST RESIDENCE: Plymouth.

OCCUPATION: Merchant.
CHURCH MEMBERSHIP: Christopher Martin refused to kneel at holy communion at Easter, 1612 [Martin Bio 10]. On 3 March 1619/20, Christopher Martin of Billericay was cited for "suffering his son to answer me ... that his father gave him his name" [NEHGR 21:77, citing Archdeaconry Court of Chelmsford].
FREEMAN: On 11 November 1620, Christopher Martin signed the Mayflower Compact [Morton 26].
EDUCATION: Signed his name as witness to a will [MQ 76:209].
ESTATE: Christopher Martin owned multiple properties in Billericay [Martin Bio 5–6].

BIRTH: England by about 1582 (based on date of marriage).
DEATH: Plymouth 8 January 1620/1 ("Saturday the 6th of January [1620/1] Master Marten was very sick, and, to our judgment, no hope of life. So Master Carver was sent for to come aboard to speak with him about his accounts; who came the next morning" [Mourt 43–44]; "January 8 this day dies Mr. Christopher Martin" [Prince 182]).
MARRIAGE: Great Burstead, Essex, 26 February 1606/7 Mary (____) Prower, widow of Edward Prower [Martin Bio 3 and plate facing 10; MQ 76:242–46]. She died in Plymouth the first winter.
CHILD:

> i NATHANIEL MARTIN, bp. Great Burstead 26 February 1609[/10] [Martin Bio 3]; apparently alive at Great Burstead in 1620 [Martin Bio 7].

ASSOCIATIONS: Christopher Martin was stepfather of *SOLOMON PROWER.*

PREMIGRATION BIOGRAPHY: Christopher Martin was born in England by about 1582. In early 1607 he married the widow Mary Prower at the town of Billericay in the parish of Great Burstead, Essex. In the same year, Christopher Martin, mercer, was charged at the Quarter Sessions with unlawful trading. In 1611 he was chosen as one of the Great Burstead churchwardens. Toward the end of his year's term as churchwarden, Martin and his wife refused to kneel at communion, indicating that they held puritan beliefs. He also failed to submit his accounts at the end of this year of parochial service [Martin Bio 3–5].

During these years Martin's business must have been successful, for in 1613 manorial court records show that he had acquired three tenements in the town of Billericay. Martin disposed of one of his properties on 22 June 1617 and then on 8 June 1620 he sold what was apparently the last of his properties in town, probably in preparation for his departure on the *Mayflower* [Martin Bio 7, 10].

As the members of the Leiden congregation were making their preparations for the voyage to New England, they needed someone in England who could help them with the financial and logistical aspects of the venture. As a merchant in a town only twenty-five miles from London, Martin undoubtedly had connections in the metropolis. We first learn of Martin's involvement from Bradford:

> Besides these things there fell out a difference among those three men that received the moneys, and made the provisions in England; for besides these two formerly mentioned sent from Leyden for this end, viz: Mr. Carver and Robert Cushman, there was one chosen in England to be joined with them to make the provisions for the voyage. His name was Mr. Martin, he came from Billerica in Essex, from which parts came sundry others to go with them, as also from London and other places. And therefore it was thought meet and convenient by them in Holland that these strangers that were to go with them should appoint one thus to be joined with them, not so much for any great need of their help as to avoid all suspicion or jealousy of any partiality.

The point in dispute which triggered this passage in Bradford's account was detailed in a letter of 10 June 1620 from Robert Cushman to John Carver relating that Martin had failed to follow instructions on the manner of provisioning the *Mayflower* [Bradford 44–46]. Further disputes ensued, about both provisioning and payments, including Martin's refusal to render financial accounts to the Leiden contingent, echoing his failure some years earlier to deliver in his accounts as Great Burstead churchwarden [Bradford 49–56].

COMMENTS: The Mr. Christopher Martin who was active in the early settlement of Virginia must have been a different man, as he was still of record in Virginia two years after the *Mayflower* man had died [TAG 80:246].

BIBLIOGRAPHIC NOTE: In 1982 R. J. Carpenter published a pamphlet that thoroughly traces what was known at the time of Christopher Martin in English court and ecclesiastical records [*Christopher Martin, Great Burstead and The Mayflower* (Chelmsford, Essex, 1982), cited above as Martin Bio].

In 2010 Caleb H. Johnson published two articles providing more information on this passenger: "Solomon Prower: New Information on a Little-known *Mayflower* Passenger" and "Mary (Prower) Martin: A New *Mayflower* ancestor?" [MQ 76:242–46].

DESIRE MINTER

Mr. John Carver, Katherine his wife, Desire Minter, and two manservants, John Howland, Roger Wilder. William Latham, a boy, and a maidservant and a child that was put to him, Jasper More.

Desire Minter returned to her friend and proved not very well and died in England.

ORIGIN: Leiden.
MIGRATION: 1620 on the *Mayflower*.
FIRST RESIDENCE: Plymouth.
RETURN TRIPS: Returned permanently to England before 1623.

ESTATE: Desire Minter's father William Minter had died by 1618 when his widow Sarah remarried to Roger Simons (or Simonson). Roger died within a few years and by 1622 Sarah had married a third time, to Roger Eastman. By this time Desire may already have returned to England. On 10 May 1622, Roger and Sarah (Willett) (Minter) (Simons) Eastman "made an agreement with Thomas Brewer ... that he would pay out annually 120 guilders for the benefit and support of Sarah's child born of her marriage to William Minter. This was the interest on a capital sum of 1,900 guilders apparently given to Brewer to be invested. Payment was to continue until the child reached the age of twenty-one." In 1623 "Sarah and Roger Eastman appeared before a notary again, to authorize [John] Kebel and [William] Jepson to act as their agents in collecting the money." Roger and Sarah were about to move away from Leiden [NEHGR 143:209].

BIRTH: Born say 1610, daughter of William and Sarah (Willett) Minter [NEHGR 143:209].
DEATH: England after 10 May 1622 (assuming Desire was still alive on that date when her mother made an agreement regarding Desire's support).
MARRIAGE: None known.
CHILDREN: None known.
ASSOCIATIONS: Although the precise connection is not yet clear, Desire Minter was related to *JOHN CARVER* in some way [NEHGR 174:5–20], thus placing her in the Southeast Suffolk Separatist cluster of immigrants to Leiden.

Desire Minter's mother Sarah Willett was sister of THOMAS WILLETT {1630, Penobscot} [PM 497–503].

COMMENTS: Desire Minter's father was admitted citizen of Leiden on 3 May 1613 [NS] [Leiden Pilgrims 190].

Bradford says that "Desire Minter returned to her friend." The OED indicates that "friend" could at this time mean relation or kinsman, citing Shakespeare: "But she I mean is promised by her friends, Unto a youthful gentleman of worth" (*The Two Gentlemen of Verona* III.1.106–7). See the sketch of JOYCE BRADWICK {1632, Boston} for the same usage [GMB 1:215]; perhaps the word at this time also had the meaning of "guardian."

ELLEN MORE

Mr. Edward Winslow, Elizabeth his wife and two men-servants called George Soule and Elias Story; also a little girl was put to him called Ellen, the sister of Richard More.

Mr. Edward Winslow his wife died the first winter, and he married with the widow of Mr. White and hath two children living by her, marriageable, besides sundry that are dead. One of his servants died, as also the little girl, soon after the ship's arrival. But his man, George Soule, is still living and hath eight children.

ORIGIN: Shipton, Shropshire.
MIGRATION: 1620 on the *Mayflower*.
FIRST RESIDENCE: Plymouth.

BIRTH: Baptized 24 May 1612, Shipton, Shropshire, the repudiated daughter of Samuel and Catherine (More) More.
DEATH: Early 1621 at Plymouth.

COMMENTS: Four siblings, children of Samuel and Catherine (More) More of Shipton, Shropshire, sailed on the *Mayflower*, sons Jasper and Richard and daughters Ellen and Mary. Their story is unlike that of any of the other passengers.

In 1959 Anthony Wagner came upon a document that told an interesting tale about these children. In 1610 Samuel More married Catherine More, his third cousin, and Wagner noted that "it looks as if the marriage was arranged to keep Larden [an estate in Shipton] in the More family." After some years Samuel discovered that his wife had maintained an adulterous relation with one Jacob Blakeway, who was the father of some if not all of the children. After considerable difficulty, Samuel More managed to divorce Catherine, and, wanting to start a family of his own, he arranged for Catherine's four children to be put in the care of John Carver and Robert Cushman, who would transport them into Virginia, maintain them for seven years, and then provide them with fifty acres of land. Carver and Cushman placed these children with various of the families sailing on the *Mayflower* and so the four young Mores ended up in New England rather than Virginia [NEHGR 114:163–68]. (Wagner also published an outline of various royal descents for the More children [NEHGR 124:85–87].)

BIBLIOGRAPHIC NOTE: Sir Anthony Richard Wagner provided us with the most accurate account of the English background of Richard More and his siblings [NEHGR 114:163–68 and 124:86–87]. More recently Donald Harris has presented much of this same material, placing it in historical context [MD 43:123–132, 44:11–20, 109–118].

JASPER MORE

Mr. John Carver, Katherine his wife, Desire Minter, and two manservants, John Howland, Roger Wilder. William Latham, a boy, and a maidservant and a child that was put to him, Jasper More.

Mr. Carver and his wife died the first year, he in the spring, she in the summer. Also, his man Roger and the little boy Jasper died before either of them, of the common infection.

ORIGIN: Shipton, Shropshire.
MIGRATION: 1620 on the *Mayflower*.
FIRST RESIDENCE: Plymouth.

BIRTH: Baptized 8 August 1613, Shipton, Shropshire, the repudiated son of Samuel and Catherine (More) More.
DEATH: Early 1621 at Plymouth.

COMMENTS: Four siblings, children of Samuel and Catherine (More) More of Shipton, Shropshire, sailed on the *Mayflower*, sons Jasper and Richard and daughters Ellen and Mary. Their story is unlike that of any of the other passengers.

In 1959 Anthony Wagner came upon a document that told an interesting tale about these children. In 1610 Samuel More married Catherine More, his third cousin, and Wagner noted that "it looks as if the marriage was arranged to keep Larden [an estate in Shipton] in the More family." After some years Samuel discovered that his wife had maintained an adulterous relation with one Jacob Blakeway, who was the father of some if not all of the children. After considerable difficulty, Samuel More managed to divorce Catherine, and, wanting to start a family of his own, he arranged for Catherine's four children to be put in the care of John Carver and Robert Cushman, who would transport them into Virginia, maintain them for seven years, and then provide them with fifty acres of land. Carver and Cushman placed these children with various of the families sailing on the *Mayflower* and so the four young Mores ended up in New England rather than Virginia [NEHGR 114:163–68]. (Wagner also published an outline of various royal descents for the More children [NEHGR 124:85–87].)

BIBLIOGRAPHIC NOTE: Sir Anthony Richard Wagner provided us with the most accurate account of the English background of Richard More and his siblings [NEHGR 114:163–68, 124:86–87]. More recently Donald Harris has presented much of this same material, placing it in historical context [MD 43:123–132, 44:11–20, 109–118].

MARY MORE

Mr. William Brewster, Mary, his wife, with two sons, whose names were Love and Wrestling. And a boy was put to him called Richard More, and another of his brothers. The rest of his children were left behind and came over afterwards.

Richard More's brother died the first winter, but he is married and hath four or five children, all living.

ORIGIN: Shipton, Shropshire.
MIGRATION: 1620 on the *Mayflower.*
FIRST RESIDENCE: Plymouth.

BIRTH: Baptized 16 April 1616, Shipton, Shropshire, the repudiated daughter of Samuel and Catherine (More) More.
DEATH: Early 1621 at Plymouth.

COMMENTS: Four siblings, children of Samuel and Catherine (More) More of Shipton, Shropshire, sailed on the *Mayflower*, sons Jasper and Richard and daughters Ellen and Mary. Their story is unlike that of any of the other passengers.

In 1959 Anthony Wagner came upon a document that told an interesting story about these children. In 1610 Samuel More married Catherine More, his third cousin, and Wagner noted that "it looks as if the marriage was arranged to keep Larden [an estate in Shipton] in the More family." After some years Samuel discovered that his wife had maintained an adulterous relation with one Jacob Blakeway, who was the father of some if not all of the children. After considerable difficulty, Samuel More managed to divorce Catherine, and, wanting to start a family of his own, he arranged for Catherine's four children to be put in the care of John Carver and Robert Cushman, who would transport them into Virginia, maintain them for seven years, and then provide them with fifty acres of land. Carver and Cushman placed these children with various of the families sailing on the *Mayflower* and so the four young Mores ended up in New England rather than Virginia [NEHGR 114:163–68]. (Wagner also published an outline of various royal descents for the More children [NEHGR 124:85–87].)

The document printed by Wagner refers to "the four children of the petitioner Katharine More," and in the baptismal records are two boys and two girls. The list prepared by Bradford explicitly names Ellinor (Helen), Jasper, and Richard, and refers to the fourth child only as Richard's brother, which implies three boys and one girl. The most parsimonious resolution to this discrepancy is that after the passage of three decades Bradford's memory had erred, and the fourth More child on the *Mayflower*, referred to by Bradford as "another of [Richard's] brothers," was in fact Mary, the last child, baptized in 1616. Less likely, Catherine More may have had a fifth child, a boy, not recorded at Shipton. This would of course require that the daughter Mary had died by July 1620. The close spacing between births of the first three children implies that the More family was employing a wet nurse, and so another child might have been born in 1615. Nevertheless, we have adopted here the former of these two explanations.

BIBLIOGRAPHIC NOTE: Sir Anthony Richard Wagner has provided us with the most accurate account of the English background of Richard More and his siblings [NEHGR 114:163–68 and 124:86–87]. More recently Donald Harris has presented much of this same material, placing it in historical context [MD 43:123–132, 44:11–20, 109–118].

RICHARD MORE

Mr. William Brewster, Mary, his wife, with two sons, whose names were Love and Wrestling. And a boy was put to him called Richard More, and another of his brothers. The rest of his children were left behind and came over afterwards.

Richard More's brother died the first winter, but he is married and hath four or five children, all living.

ORIGIN: Shipton, Shropshire.
MIGRATION: 1620 on the *Mayflower*.
FIRST RESIDENCE: Plymouth.
REMOVES: Duxbury, Salem 1637.
RETURN TRIPS: To England after 1627 and returned June or July 1635 on the *Blessing*. Traveled to Virginia and Maryland frequently [NGSQ 62:168].

OCCUPATION: Mariner. In June 1661 when William Shakkerley, master of the bark *Hopewell*, complained that the vessel was insufficient for a voyage to Newfoundland, the court commissioned Richard More, master, and others to examine it [EQC 2:313]. On 26 November 1674, Thomas Smith "deposed that about the beginning of August last, he was on board the ship *Friendship* of Salem, Richard Moore, master" [EQC 5:444].

Tavernkeeper. On 29 September 1674, "Capt. Richard More was licensed to keep an ordinary and to sell beer and cider, but not wine or liquors, for a year" [EQC 5:400].
CHURCH MEMBERSHIP: Admitted to Salem church on 27 February 1642/3 [SChR 11].
FREEMAN: Massachusetts Bay 28 February 1642/3 [EQC 1:50].
EDUCATION: He signed his name to deeds but his wife Christian made her mark.
OFFICES: Perhaps some of the considerable petit jury and grand jury service in Essex County pertained to this Richard More, although there was another man of this name in Lynn contemporaneously [EQC 3:154, 4:292].
ESTATE: In the 1623 land division Richard More is presumably included in the household of William Brewster [MQ 40:9]. In the 1627 Plymouth division of cattle Richard More was the fourth person in the fifth company headed by William Brewster [PCR 12:10].

On 1 November 1637, "Richard Moore of Ducksborrow, yeoman," sold all his property in Duxbury to Abraham Blush [PCR 12:22–23].

On 3 October [1649], James Hyndes of Salem sold to Richard More one dwelling house on the south river side with three-quarters of an acre adjoining and ten acres of upland in the south field [ELR 1:16]. On 20 September 1659, Richard More of Salem, mariner, mortgaged to Henry Shrimpton of Boston one dwelling house with three-quarters of an acre, with the yard, warehouse, and stable in Salem [ELR 1:69]. On 13 September 1655, John Horne of Salem sold to Richard More of Salem one dwelling house and an acre of land [ELR 2:82A].

On 7 July 1662, "Mr. Richard Moore and Mary Chichester, wife of William, came into court and acknowledged their free act and deed in exchanging a piece of land of about seven poles that lay on the north side of said Marie's ground for so much lying on the east side of said ground, as the fence now stands" [EQC 2:432].

On 11 July 1664, Henry Bartholomew of Salem, with the consent of his wife Eliza[beth], sold to Richard More of Salem a dwelling house and an acre of land in Salem [ELR 2:82A]. On 20 January 1667[/8], Richard More of Salem, mariner, sold to Edward Grove of Salem, sailmaker, half an acre "which More has by an execution against John Prescott" [ELR 3:27]. On 10 January 1670[/1], Richard More of Salem, mariner, and Christian his wife, sold to Thomas Pitman of Marblehead, husbandman, ten acres in Marblehead [ELR 3:107]. On 21 September 1658, Richard Moore of Salem, mariner, sold to William Flint of Salem, husbandman, ten acres in the south field [ELR 3:127]. On 27 September 1671, Richard Moore Sr. of Salem, mariner, sold to William Browne Jr. of Salem, half an acre in Salem [ELR 3:127 (and re-recorded 3:174)].

On 30 August 1673, "Richard More of Salem, mariner," with the consent of Christian his wife, sold his rights as a purchaser at Swansea to Samuel Shrimpton of Boston [PCLR 3:303].

On 10 June 1675, Richard More of Salem for "natural affection" deeded to "Caleb More & Richard More my sons and my daughters Susanna & Christian More ... my dwelling house in Salem where I now live with all out houses etc. and all movables quick and dead" [ELR 4:114].

On 4 June 1684, Richard More Sr. of Salem deeded for natural affection and "more especially for & in consideration of marriage betwixt him the said Samuel Dutch and my daughter Susannah his now wife" land in Salem where Samuel Dutch's house then stood and a quarter of an acre where a highway ran through part of More's orchard [ELR 6:123].

On 9 October 1687, Richard More Sr. of Salem, mariner, sold to John Higginson Jr. of Salem, merchant, a parcel of flats and wharf land in Salem south of "my now dwelling house" [ELR 8:9]. On 17 December 1687, Richard More of Salem, mariner, mortgaged to Mr. Phillip Cromwell of Salem, slaughterer, a small parcel of land in Salem containing the out kitchen and lean-to [ELR 8:15]. On 15 May 1688, Richard More Sr. of Salem, mariner, sold to William Browne Esq. and Mr. Benjamin Browne, both of Salem, "my homestead which I am now possessed of ... in Salem ... excepting the piece of land I mortgaged to Philip Cromwell" [ELR 8:85]. On 10 May 1690, Richard More of Salem deeded the land he had mortgaged in 1687 to Philip Cromwell, slaughterer [ELR 8:150].

On 10 July 1688, Richard More Sr. of Salem, mariner, deeded to "my son Richard More Jr." part of "my dwelling house called by new room or long room with the garden enclosed and the cellar under it" [ELR 8:95]. On 14 August 1688, Richard More Sr. and Richard More Jr., both of Salem, mariners, sold to Peter Osgood of Salem, tanner, sixty poles of ground in Salem, part of the houselot [ELR 8:93].

BIRTH: Baptized Shipton, Shropshire, 13 November 1614, the repudiated son of Samuel and Catherine (More) More of Shipton.
DEATH: Salem between 19 March 1693/4 and 20 April 1696 [MD 22:49, 78], "aged 84 years" [MD 4:198, 22:49].
MARRIAGE: (1) Plymouth 20 October 1636 Christian Hunter [PCR 1:45], daughter of Thomas and Susan (Gentleman) Hunter [TAG 78:241–44]. She was born about 1615 and died Salem 18 March 1676, "aged 60 years" [MD 3:198]. She was twenty years old when she came on the *Blessing* in 1635 [TAG 40:77].

(2) By 1678 Jane (_____) Crumpton, widow of Samuel Crumpton who was slain at Muddy Brook Bridge on 18 September 1675, in the company of THOMAS LOTHROP {1633, Salem} [Bodge 137; GMB 2:1201–6]. On 23 May 1678, "Richard More, as husband of the relict of Samuel Crumpton," sued Christopher Lattimore for debt [EQC 7:111]. Jane died at Salem on 8 October 1686, "aged 55 years" [MD 3:198].
CHILDREN:
With first wife
> i SAMUEL MORE, bp. Salem 6 March 1641/2 [SChR 18]; living 1651 [Bradford 444] but no further record.
> ii THOMAS MORE, bp. Salem 6 March 1641/2 [SChR 18]; living 1651 [Bradford 444] but no further record.

    iii CALEB MORE, bp. Salem 31 March 1644 [SChR 20]; d. Salem 4 January 1678/9, "aged 34 years" [MD 3:199]; unm.

    iv JOSHUA MORE, bp. Salem 3 May 1646 [SChR 21]; living 1651 [Bradford 444] but no further record.

    v RICHARD MORE, bp. Salem 2 January 1647/8 [SChR 21]; m. by 1673 Sarah _____ [MD 3:199].

    vi SUSANNA MORE, bp. Salem 12 May 1650 [SChR 22]; m. (1) say 1675 Samuel Dutch (her father witnessed her bond as administratrix of Samuel's estate 19 March 1693/4 [EPR Case #8420]); m. (2) by 1696 Richard Hutton [EPR Case #8426]; m. (3) (int.) Wenham 11 April 1714 John Knowlton. (The best account of the Dutch family was published by Walter Goodwin Davis in 1947 [Phoebe Tilton Anc 87–107].)

    vii CHRISTIAN MORE, bp. Salem 5 September 1652 [SChR 23]; m. Salem 31 August 1676 Joshua Conant.

COMMENTS: Four siblings, children of Samuel and Catherine (More) More of Shipton, Shropshire, sailed on the *Mayflower*, sons Jasper and Richard and daughters Ellen and Mary. Their story is unlike that of any of the other passengers.

In 1959 Anthony Wagner came upon a document that told an interesting story about these children. In 1610 Samuel More married Catherine More, his third cousin, and Wagner noted that "it looks as if the marriage was arranged to keep Larden [an estate in Shipton] in the More family." After some years Samuel discovered that his wife had maintained an adulterous relation with one Jacob Blakeway, who was the father of some if not all of the children. After considerable difficulty, Samuel More managed to divorce Catherine, and, wanting to start a family of his own, he arranged for Catherine's four children to be put in the care of John Carver and Robert Cushman, who would transport them into Virginia, maintain them for seven years, and then provide them with fifty acres of land. Carver and Cushman placed these children with various of the families sailing on the *Mayflower* and so the four young Mores ended up in New England rather than Virginia [NEHGR 114:163–68].

A "Richard More of Salem in New England" married on 23 October 1645 at St. Dunstan, Stepney, Middlesex, at a time when Richard More of Salem was certainly married. Unless there were two Richard Mores in Salem at this time, then Captain Richard More must have been a bigamist.

Evidence that Richard More might have been capable of bigamy appears years later in the Salem church records. In July 1688, "Old Captain More having been for many years under suspicion and a common fame of lasciviousness, and some degree at least of incontinency and therefore was at several times spoken to, by sundry brethren and also by the Elders in a private way, because for want of proof we could go no further ... he was convicted before justices of the peace by three witnesses of gross unchastity with another man's wife and was censured by them" [SChR 166].

The bell taken at Port Royal, Nova Scotia, in 1654 was brought to Salem "in Capt. Moor's ketch" [EQC 7:310–12].

On 25 January 1641/2, John Stacy sued Richard More for killing his swine [EQC 1:30]. On 1 January 1645/6, Thomas Tuck testified that Richard Moore "made a well upon the common for his own use the last summer, being very dry and water scarce upon the neck. Tuck hired a cow, which came to drink at the well, and the water being very low the cow broke her neck" [EQC 1:93].

On 29 June 1654, the administrators of the estate of Richard Hollingsworth acknowledged a judgment to Capt. Traske and another to Rich[ard] More [EQC 1:359].

On 30 September 1665, Robert Starr deeded to Capt. Richard More and Mr. Philip Cromwell as guardians to "my three children Robert, Richard and Susanna" a house "given to me by my father-in-law Richard Hollingsworth as a portion with my wife ... for the use and benefit of my three children" [ELR 3:139].

For the 27 June 1665 court, Richard More, aged "about fifty years," deposed in a case between Symond Crosby and Henry Roads [EQC 3:256]. On 15 January 1665[/6], Bartholomew Roes Jr. at "Charlestown in Carolina" authorized payment to "Capt. Richard Moore" of 673 pounds of "good Muschovadee Sugar" [ELR 3:101]. On 24 January 1666[/7], Richard More executed a bill of lading for the ship *Swan* carrying tobacco on account of Col. Augustine Warner of Virginia [ELR 3:5]. On 3 March 1668/9, Richard More deposed regarding the law and customs for the entry of vessels into Maryland [SJC #907].

BIBLIOGRAPHIC NOTE: In 1997 the General Society of Mayflower Descendants published a revised version of the family and descendants of Richard More in Volume Fifteen of the Five Generations Project, compiled by Robert Moody Sherman, Robert S. Wakefield, and Lydia Dow Finlay [MF 15:151–87]. (This superseded an earlier treatment of the family in Volume Two of the series, published in 1978.)

In 1901 George Ernest Bowman published several depositions given by Richard More late in his life regarding events that had happened in his early New England years; this article also included photographs and transcriptions of a number of early More family tombstones [MD 3:193–201].

The English origin for Richard More and his siblings was first published in 1905 by Edwin A. Hill. He found the baptisms at Shipton, Shropshire, of the four *Mayflower* siblings and the marriage of their parents, Samuel More and his third cousin Catherine More. He was stymied in his further research as he was not aware of the domestic difficulties and divorce of Samuel and Catherine [MD 5:256; NYGBR 36:213–19, 291–301]. The next advance was made by Anthony R. Wagner in 1959, when he was shown a privately held record which documented the divorce of Catherine and Samuel and the "disposing of the four children of Catherine More" described above [NEHGR 114:163–68]. Wagner also published an outline of various royal descents for the More children [NEHGR 124:85–87]. More recently Donald Harris has presented much of this same material, placing it in historical context, but adding little about Richard More himself [MD 43:123–132, 44:11–20, 109–118].

In 2002 David Lindsay published *Mayflower Bastard: A Stranger Among the Pilgrims* (New York 2002), a biography of Richard More which takes great liberties with the available evidence [TAG 77:318–19].

WILLIAM MULLINS

Mr. William Mullins and his wife and two children, Joseph and Priscilla, and a servant, Robert Carter.

Mr. Mullins and his wife, his son and his servant died the first winter. Only his daughter Priscilla survived, and married with John Alden; who are both living and have eleven children. And their eldest daughter is married and hath five children.

ORIGIN: Dorking, Surrey.
PREVIOUS RESIDENCES: Stoke-next-Guildford, Surrey; Holy Trinity, Guildford, Surrey.
MIGRATION: 1620 on the *Mayflower*.
FIRST RESIDENCE: Plymouth.

OCCUPATION: Shoemaker [MD 61:223]. (The will of William Mullins mentions "twenty-one dozen of shoes and thirteen pair of boots which I give into the Company's hands.")
FREEMAN: On 11 November 1620, William Mullins signed the Mayflower Compact [Morton 26].
EDUCATION: On 30 March 1612, William Mullins witnessed the will of John Wood of Dorking by making his mark [MD 61:22–23].
ESTATE: For most of the decade prior to his migration, William Mullins owned and resided at a substantial house in Dorking which is still standing at 58–61 West Street, just off the High Street [MD 62:78–87]. Mullins probably operated his shoemaking business on the ground floor of this building and rented portions of the building to tenants.

On 23 July 1621, administration on the estate of William Mullins was granted to "Sare Blunden *alias* Mullins filie naturali et legitime dicti defuncti" [Sara Blunden *alias* Mullins, natural and legitimate daughter of the said deceased] [MQ 34:10; Waters 254–55; MD 1:230–32 (all citing PCC 68 Dale)].

In his nuncupative will, drafted 2 April 1621 and proved July 1621, William Mullins directed that from the £40 in the hand of Goodman Woodes "I give my wife £10, my son Joseph £10, my daughter Priscilla £10, and my eldest son £10, also I give to my eldest son all my debts, bonds, bills (only that £40 excepted in the hands of Goodman Wood) ... with all the stock in his own hands"; to "my eldest daughter I give 10s. to be paid out of my son's stock"; "the goods I have in Virginia as followeth, to my wife Alice half my goods & to Joseph and Priscilla the other half equally divided"; "I have twenty-one dozen of shoes and thirteen pair of boots which I give into the Company's hands for £40 at seven years ... or as my overseers shall think good"; "and if they like them at that rate at the divident I shall have nine shares whereof I give as followeth, two to my wife, two to my son William, two to my son Joseph, two to my daughter Priscilla, and one to the Company"; "if my son William will come to Virginia I give him my share of land"; to "my two overseers Mr. John Carver and Mr. Williamson, 20s. apiece to see this my will performed desiring them that he would have an eye over my wife and children to be as fathers and friends to them, also to have a special eye to my man Robert which hath not so approved himself as I would he should have done" [MQ 34:9–10; Waters 254–55; MD 1:230–32; MHSP 2:5:33–37 (all citing PCC 68 Dale)].

In the 1623 Plymouth land division, the deceased William Mullins and his wife were presumably accounted for in the household of John Alden [MQ 40:13].

BIRTH: By about 1572 (based on marriage date of parents), son of John and Joan (Bridger) Mullins of Dorking [MF 16:1:16; MD 61:26–27].
DEATH: Plymouth 21 February 1620/1 ("February 21. Die Mr. William White, Mr. William Mullins, with two more" [Prince 184]. "Amongst others in the time fore named, died Mr. William Mullins, a man pious and well deserving, endowed also with a considerable outward estate; and had it been the will of God that he had survived, might have proved an useful instrument in his place, with several others who deceased in this great and common affliction, whom I might take notice of to the like effect" [Morton 37]).
MARRIAGE: By 1593 Alice _____ (assuming she is the mother of all the children). She died at Plymouth in the first winter. (In 2012 Caleb Johnson undertook an extensive investigation into Alice's parentage, arriving at the speculative hypothesis that William Mullins had two wives, first Elizabeth Wood, daughter of John and Joan (Taylor) Wood of Dorking, and second Alice (_____) Brown, widow of either William Brown or Thomas Brown of Dorking [MQ 78:44–57].)
CHILDREN:

> i WILLIAM MULLINS, b. say 1593; m. (1) by 1618 _____
> _____ [MQ 39:83]; m. (2) Boston 7 May 1656 Ann
> (_____) Bell [BVR 56], widow of Thomas Bell. (William
> Mullins was in Duxbury by 1637, died apparently early
> in 1674, and had a daughter who married three times but
> had no children [MD 7:37–48, 179–83].)

ii ELIZABETH MULLINS, bp. Holy Trinity, Guildford, Surrey, 11 November 1598 [MQ 78:45]; no further record.

iii SARAH MULLINS, b. say 1600; m. by 1621 _____ Blunden [PCC 68 Dale].

iv PRISCILLA MULLINS, b. say 1602; m. by about 1623 *JOHN ALDEN.*

v JOSEPH MULLINS, b. say 1604; d. Plymouth in early 1621.

ASSOCIATIONS: Caleb Johnson has thoroughly researched the association of William Mullins with several other Dorking families, showing potential relationships with *PETER BROWN* and with others who later came to New England [TAG 79:161–78; MQ 78:44–57; MD 61:17–27, 64:37–39 (with Simon Neal)].

PREMIGRATION BIOGRAPHY: William Mullins was born in England by about 1572, perhaps at Dorking, Surrey. He probably served an apprenticeship as a shoemaker during the late 1580s [MD 61:19]. William Mullins first appeared in the Dorking records at a manorial court of 4 October 1595 when he was living in Chippingborough, the central market area of the town [MD 61:19].

Shortly thereafter William removed about ten miles to the west to Stoke-next-Guildford, Surrey, where he is included in the militia list of 1596 [MD 61:19–20]. In 1598 he had a child baptized in the immediately neighboring parish of Holy Trinity, Guildford [MQ 61:20].

By 1604 William Mullins had returned to Dorking, where he appeared on 5 October of that year as tithingman of the Eastborough section of the town [MD 61:20–21]. On 12 December 1612, William Mullins purchased from John Jettor the property on West Street in the tithing of Chippingborough in Dorking, where he resided for the remainder of the decade. In one record this property is described as "a messuage divided into several tenements," so for these years Mullins presumably rented out parts of the building, as well as operating his shoemaking business out of the ground floor. In May 1619, possibly in preparation for migration, Mullins sold this property to Ephraim Bothell [MD 61:24–25, 62:78–87].

On 3 August 1620, the leaders of the Pilgrim party that were in Southampton, preparing for their departure to New England, wrote to the merchants in London that were supporting them regarding some changes in the business agreement made between the various parties. The principal point was "concerning the dividing or holding of house and lands." The letter states that a copy of a document stating the position of the migrants on this issue "we have sent unto you, with some additions then added by us;

which being liked on both sides, and a day set for the payment of moneys, those of Holland paid in theirs. After that, Robert Cushman, Mr. Peirce, and Mr. Martin, brought them into a better form and writ them in a book now extant; and upon Robert's showing them and delivering Mr. Mullins a copy thereof under his hand (which we have) he paid in his money" [Bradford 49–50]. In his will, Mullins left a portion of his estate to "the Company," which must have been intended to honor some portion of this agreement that he had signed.

BIBLIOGRAPHIC NOTE: A summary of what is known about the English background of William Mullins and about his family is incorporated in the Five Generations Project volume on John Alden [MF 16:1:14–19]. In 2004 Caleb Johnson published some records from Dorking, Surrey, for this immigrant [TAG 79:161].

DEGORY PRIEST

Moses Fletcher, John Goodman, Thomas Williams, Digory Priest, Edmund Margesson, Peter Browne, Richard Britteridge, Richard Clarke, Richard Gardiner, Gilbert Winslow.

Moses Fletcher, Thomas Williams, Digory Priest, John Goodman, Edmund Margesson, Richard Britteridge, Richard Clarke, all these died soon after arrival in the general sickness that befell. But Digory Priest had his wife and children sent hither afterwards, she being Mr. Allerton's sister. But the rest left no posterity here.

ORIGIN: Leiden.
PREVIOUS RESIDENCES: London.
MIGRATION: 1620 on the *Mayflower*. His wife and two daughters came to Plymouth on the *Anne* in 1623.
FIRST RESIDENCE: Plymouth.

OCCUPATION: Hatter (when admitted as a citizen of Leiden) [Leiden Pilgrims 216].
CHURCH MEMBERSHIP: Degory and Sarah (Allerton) (Vincent) Priest were members of the Leiden separatist congregation [Strangers and Pilgrims 709].
FREEMAN: On 16 November 1615 [NS], "Diggore Pryst," of England, hatter, was admitted as a citizen of Leiden; his guarantors were Roger Wilson and Isaac Allerton [Leiden Pilgrims 216].

On 11 November 1620, Degory Priest signed the Mayflower Compact [Morton 26].
ESTATE: In the 1623 Plymouth land division "Cudbart Cudbartsone" received six acres as a passenger on the *Anne* in 1623 [PCR 12:6]; four of these six shares would be for the deceased Degory Priest, his widow Sarah, and his two daughters [MQ 40:10]. In the 1627 Plymouth cattle division "Marra Priest" and "Sarah Priest" were the tenth and eleventh persons in the second company, just after their mother and stepfather [Godbert Godbertson] [PCR 12:9].

BIRTH: About 1579 (aged about forty in April 1619 [Strangers and Pilgrims 425; TAG 80:243]).

DEATH: Plymouth 1 January 1620/1 [Prince 182].

MARRIAGE: Leiden 4 November 1611 [NS] "Sara Vincent, widow of Jan Vincent" [Plooij IX; MD 7:129–30; Leiden Pilgrims 216]; Priest is said to be of London. She was sister of *ISAAC ALLERTON* and married (3) Leiden 13 November 1621 or soon after (betrothed 25 October 1621 [NS]) GODBERT GODBERTSON {1623, Plymouth} [Plooij XLVII; Leiden Pilgrims 101; PM 226].

CHILDREN:

> i MARY PRIEST, b. say 1612; m. by about 1630 PHINEAS PRATT {1622, Weymouth} [PM 369].
>
> ii SARAH PRIEST, b. say 1614; m. by about 1632 JOHN COOMBS {1630, Plymouth} [PM 153].

PREMIGRATION BIOGRAPHY: Degory Priest was born about 1579. He may have been born in Hartland, Devon, or vicinity, but in his 1611 marriage record at Leiden he was said to be of London (which may only indicate that he was from somewhere in the vicinity of the English metropolis). He first appeared at Leiden in 1611 records when he married Sarah (Allerton) Vincent, sister of Isaac Allerton, and presumably also joined John Robinson's congregation. The couple's two children were born in Leiden in the years immediately after their marriage. Over the next nine years Degory Priest was an active member of the English community in Leiden [TAG 80:241–60].

COMMENTS: In 1957 John G. Hunt published the 1582 baptism for a "Digorius Prust" in Hartland, Devon [NEHGR 111:320]. In 2005 Patricia Law Hatcher analyzed this record and many others and concluded that this baptism could not be confidently connected to the *Mayflower* passenger. She did observe that the distribution of the given name Degory was highly concentrated in Hartland, Devon, and adjacent parts of Devon and Cornwall and that the surname Priest and its variants were also common in that same region. Although she could not place the *Mayflower* passenger in any of the Priest family groups of Hartland and vicinity, Hatcher believes that Degory Priest's origin will ultimately be found in that part of England [TAG 80:241–60].

Degory Priest and his wife were active in the affairs of the English community in Leiden. Sarah (Allerton) (Vincent) Priest witnessed the 1612 marriage of William White and Ann Fuller and the 1613 marriage of Moses Fletcher and Sarah Denby [Leiden Pilgrims 91, 291].

In 1617 Priest became entangled in the affairs of John Cripps, defending himself against a charge of assault and then a day later accusing Cripps of adultery [Mayflower Passengers 197; TAG 80:243]. In 1618 and 1619 Priest witnessed several depositions [TAG 80:243–44]. In April 1619, he attested to the character of Nicholas Claverly, who resided with Priest [Strangers and Pilgrims 425; TAG 80:243]. In a deposition of 3 September 1619, John Wallace reported that Degory Priest had a house on the Levendaal, a canal in the southeast quadrant of Leiden, within the city walls [TAG 80:243].

BIBLIOGRAPHIC NOTE: In 1994 Degory Priest and his descendants were treated in the second edition of Volume Eight of the Five Generations project of the General Society of Mayflower Descendants, compiled by Mrs. Charles Delmar Townsend, Robert S. Wakefield, and Margaret Harris Stover.

SOLOMON PROWER

Mr. Christopher Martin and his wife and two servants, Solomon Prower and John Langmore.

Mr. Martin, he and all his died in the first infection, not long after the arrival.

ORIGIN: Billericay, Great Burstead, Essex.
MIGRATION: 1620 on the *Mayflower.*
FIRST RESIDENCE: Plymouth.

OCCUPATION: Servant to his stepfather, *CHRISTOPHER MARTIN.*
CHURCH MEMBERSHIP: On 14 March 1619/20, Solomon Prower was presented to the Archdeaconry Court of Chelmsford by his vicar for "refusing to answer me at all unless I would ask him some questions in some catechism" [NEHGR 21:77; MQ 76:243, citing ERO D/AEA 31 f. 266d]. On 11 April 1620, Prower deposed that he "did answer Mr. Pease the vicar when he asked him who gave him his name: he answered him he did not know because his father was dead and he did not know his godfathers" [MQ 76:243, citing ERO D/AEA 31 f. 279d]. (As Caleb Johnson comments, "These presentments before the Archdeaconry in early 1620 clearly illustrate that Christopher Martin and Solomon Prower were refusing to participate in some of the rituals and ceremonies of the Church of England" [MQ 76:243].)

BIRTH: Great Burstead, Essex, about 1597, son of Edward and Mary (_____) Prower [MQ 76:243–46]. (On 15 September 1619, "Solomon Prower, singleman," was on night watch duty at Billericay, indicating he was at least twenty-one years old at the time [MQ 76:242, citing ERO Quarter Sessions Records, Q/SR 227/73, 110].)
DEATH: Plymouth 24 December 1620 ("December 24, this day dies Solomon Martin *[sic]*, the sixth and last who dies this month" [Prince 168, from lost Bradford manuscript].
MARRIAGE: None.
CHILDREN: None.
ASSOCIATIONS: Stepson of *CHRISTOPHER MARTIN.*

BIBLIOGRAPHIC NOTE: In 2010 Caleb H. Johnson published two articles providing more information on this passenger: "Solomon Prower: New Information on a Little-known *Mayflower* Passenger" and "Mary (Prower) Martin: A New *Mayflower* ancestor?" [MQ 76:242–46].

JOHN RIGDALE

John Rigdale and Alice his wife.

And so did John Rigdale and his wife [die in the first sickness].

ORIGIN: Leiden.
MIGRATION: 1620 on the *Mayflower.*
FIRST RESIDENCE: Plymouth.

FREEMAN: On 11 November 1620, John Rigdale signed the Mayflower Compact [Morton 26].

BIRTH: Born by about 1595 (but possibly much earlier).
DEATH: Early 1621 at Plymouth.
MARRIAGE: By 1620 Alice _____. She also died at Plymouth in early 1621.
CHILDREN: None.

COMMENTS: Based on his analysis of Bradford's list, Caleb Johnson suggests the Rigdales may have come from Leiden [TAG 80:99; Mayflower Passengers 200], but Jeremy Bangs does not include them in his synthetic list of members of the Leiden congregation [Strangers and Pilgrims 709].

Caleb Johnson reports the marriage of John Rigsdale and Alice Gallard at Weston, Lincolnshire, on 17 November 1577 [Mayflower Passengers 200]. Although this could possibly be the *Mayflower* couple, they would be quite old to undertake such a voyage.

Pope, with his usual orthographic indifference, notes an Alice Rickdall who joined the church at Dorchester about 1639, and on this slight basis suggests a possible (but highly unlikely) relationship.

THOMAS ROGERS

Thomas Rogers and Joseph his son; his other children came afterwards.

Thomas Rogers died in the first sickness but his son Joseph is still living and is married and hath six children. The rest of Thomas Rogers' came over and are married and have many children.

ORIGIN: Leiden.
PREVIOUS RESIDENCES: Watford, Northamptonshire.
MIGRATION: 1620 on the *Mayflower.*
FIRST RESIDENCE: Plymouth.

OCCUPATION: Draper [Leiden Pilgrims 231].
FREEMAN: On 25 Jun 1618 [NS], Thomas Rogers, "grein-draper," was admitted as a citizen of Leiden, guaranteed by Roger Wilson and William Jepson [Leiden Pilgrims 231].

On 11 November 1620, Thomas Rogers signed the Mayflower Compact [Morton 26].

ESTATE: On 22 February 1617 [NS], Thomas Rogers purchased from Jan Blomsaet a one-room house on the Barbarasteeg (in the southeast quadrant of Leiden, within the city walls). On 22 February 1619 [NS], Rogers successfully sued Blomsaet in order to free this property from a lien (presumably preparatory to selling the property prior to leaving for New England). On 1 April 1620 [NS], Thomas Rogers sold the Barbarasteeg house to Mordecheus Colven [NEHGR 143:207; Strangers and Pilgrims 323–24].

In the 1623 Plymouth land division Joseph Rogers was granted two acres as a passenger on the *Mayflower* (for himself and his deceased father) [PCR 12:4; MQ 40:10]. In the 1627 Plymouth cattle division Joseph Rogers was the fifth person in the eleventh company [PCR 12:12].

Sons Joseph and John were each assessed the minimum 9s. in the 25 March 1633 Plymouth tax list [PCR 1:11]. On 6 April 1640, "Joseph Rogers and John Rogers, his brother," were granted fifty acres of upland each at the North River [PCR 1:144].

BIRTH: By about 1572 (based on date of marriage), son of William and Eleanor (_____) Rogers of Watford, Northamptonshire [TG 10:143].

DEATH: Early 1621 at Plymouth.

MARRIAGE: Watford, Northamptonshire, 24 October 1597 Alice Cosford, daughter of George Cosford [TG 10:140].

CHILDREN: (baptized Watford, Northamptonshire [TG 10:140]):

    i THOMAS ROGERS, bp. 24 March 1598/9; bur. 27 May 1599.

    ii (possibly) RICHARD ROGERS, bp. 12 March 1599/1600; bur. 4 April 1600.

    iii JOSEPH ROGERS, bp. 23 January 1602/3; m. by 1633 Hannah _____ (assuming she was his only wife; eldest known child of Joseph Rogers b. 6 August 1633 [MD 16:238]); appears in 1633 list of Plymouth freemen in vicinity of others admitted on 1 January 1632/3 [PCR 1:4]; assessed 9s. in the Plymouth tax lists of 25 March 1633 and 27 March 1634 [PCR 1:11, 28].

    iv JOHN ROGERS, bp. 6 April 1606; assessed 9s. in the Plymouth tax list of 25 March 1633 [PCR 1:11]; m. Plymouth 16 April 1639 Anna Churchman [PCR 1:120].

    v ELIZABETH ROGERS, bp. 26 December 1609; living at Leiden in 1622; perhaps came later to New England and married there [TAG 52:110–13; Bradford 446].

    vi MARGARET ROGERS, bp. 30 May 1613; living at Leiden in 1622; perhaps came later to New England and married there [TAG 52:110–13; Bradford 446].

PREMIGRATION BIOGRAPHY: Thomas Rogers was born about 1572 at Watford, Northamptonshire, son of William and Eleanor (_____) Rogers. William Rogers was a husbandman who owned several parcels of land at Watford. In 1597 Thomas Rogers married Alice Cosford, daughter of George Cosford, also a Watford husbandman. Thomas and Alice had six children born at Watford between 1599 and 1613. By 1617 the family was residing at Leiden where Rogers purchased a house on the Barbarasteeg. At some point he had entered the cloth trade, as he called himself a draper when he was admitted as a Leiden citizen in 1618. When Thomas and his son Joseph sailed for New England in 1620, his wife and other children remained behind. In 1622 Thomas's widow was listed in a Leiden census along with her son John and daughters Elizabeth and Margaret. No further record has been found for the widow or the daughters, but son John came to Plymouth in 1629 or 1630.

COMMENTS: Robert S. Wakefield and Jeremy D. Bangs have discussed the 1622 poll tax for Leiden which revealed Thomas Rogers's widow and children living in the Over't Hoff quarter of Leiden in the household of Anthony Clement [TAG 52:110–13; NEHGR 154:432–33]. Since the widow, son John, and daughters of Thomas Rogers were not in the land division of 1623 or the cattle division of 1627, they presumably came to Plymouth with the last of the Leiden contingent in 1629 or 1630.

BIBLIOGRAPHIC NOTE: In 2013 the General Society of Mayflower Descendants published a revised edition of the Thomas Rogers volume as the first part of Volume Nineteen of the Five Generations Project, originally compiled by Alice A. W. Westgate and revised by Ann T. Reeves and Peggy M. Baker [MF 19:1]. (This supersedes an earlier version published in 1978 as part of Volume Two of the series.) The second part of Volume Nineteen, published in 2019 and compiled by Peggy M. Baker, begins the treatment of the sixth generation.

In 1998 Clifford Stott discovered the English origin of Thomas Rogers [TG 10:138–49].

HENRY SAMSON

Edward Tilley and Ann his wife, and two children that were their cousins, Henry Sampson and Humility Cooper.

Edward Tilley and his wife both died soon after their arrival, and the girl Humility, their cousin, was sent for into England and died there. But the youth Henry Sampson is still living and is married and hath seven children.

ORIGIN: Leiden.
PREVIOUS RESIDENCES: Henlow, Bedfordshire.
MIGRATION: 1620 on the *Mayflower.*
FIRST RESIDENCE: Plymouth.
REMOVES: Duxbury.

FREEMAN: In the 1633 Plymouth list of freemen Henry Samson appears immediately after two men admitted on 5 January 1635/6, and before a man admitted on 2 March 1635/6 [PCR 1:4]. (This list was begun in 1633 and added to for the next three or four years, explaining the presence of 1636 records among records for 1633 [GMN 5:17].) In the 7 March 1636/7 list of freemen [PCR 1:53]. In the Duxbury sections of the Plymouth Colony lists of 1639, 1658, and 29 May 1670 [PCR 5:275, 8:175, 198].
EDUCATION: He signed his will and his deeds by mark. His inventory included "arms, wearing clothes and library" valued at £4 10s. [MD 2:143].
OFFICES: Plymouth grand jury, 1 June 1641, 6 June 1649, 4 June 1650, 2 October 1650, 7 June 1659, 1 June 1663 [PCR 2:16, 140, 155, 162, 3:162, 4:37]. Petit jury, 5 November 1644, 4 June 1645, 7 July 1646, 7 June 1649, 7 October 1651, 2 March 1651/2, 5 October 1652, 7 March 1653/4, 4 October 1655, 3 March 1662/3, 25 October 1668, 29 October 1670 [PCR 7:38, 41, 42, 46, 56, 58, 62, 70, 75, 108, 150, 163]. Coroner's jury, 8 December 1669 [PCR 5:29].

Duxbury constable, 4 June 1661 [PCR 3:215]. Tax collector, 5 June 1667, 3 June 1668 [PCR 4:150, 183]. Arbiter, 2 May 1648, 4 October 1648 [PCR 2:122, 135–36]. Surveyor, 29 October 1649, 10 June 1650 [PCR 2:147, 160].

On 7 June 1637, he volunteered for the Pequot War [PCR 1:61]. In the Duxbury section of the 1643 Plymouth Colony list of men able to bear arms [PCR 8:189]. His inventory included "arms, wearing clothes and library" valued at £4 10s. [MD 2:143].

ESTATE: In the 1623 Plymouth division of land "Henerie Samson" received one acre as a passenger on the *Mayflower* [PCR 12:4; MQ 40:13]. In the 1627 Plymouth division of cattle "Henri Samson" is the fifth person in the fifth company [PCR 12:10].

Henry Samson was one of the Purchasers, those who acquired the rights to land distributions in Plymouth Colony as a consequence of the agreement made between the London merchants and the Plymouth settlers in 1627 [Ford 282–88].

On 1 January 1637/8, Henry Samson received a grant of the "overplus on the south side of the lands besides Henry Rowland's three shares" [PCR 1:72]. On 6 April 1640, he was granted the common lying at the head of his lot [PCR 1:144]. On 2 November 1640, Henry Samson received fifty acres with some meadow at the North River [PCR 1:165].

Prior to 26 October 1647, Kenelm Winslow had sold some land to "Henry Sampson" [PCR 2:119]. On 27 October 1647, Ephraim Tinkham and Mary his wife sold to "Henry Sampson of Duxborough" one-third part of a lot that had belonged to Peter Browne in Duxbury [PCR 12:146].

On 3 October 1662 and on 8 June 1664, he was one of the men allowed to look for lands [PCR 4:27, 67]. On 7 June 1665, he was on the list of those with lands granted to them on the westerly side of Namasskett River "for his children" [PCR 4:94, 5:5]. On 2 July 1667, Henry Samson was granted liberty to "look out land to accommodate his children" [PCR 4:160].

On 24 December 1668, "Henery Samson" of Duxbury sold to Edward Gray of Plymouth Lot #19 at Namassakett [PCLR 3:237]. On 17 April 1682, Henry Samson of Duxbury, yeoman, sold to Seth Pope of Dartmouth, cooper, "all that my seven acres of meadowland which was my interest in the undivided meadows at Cokesett" in Dartmouth [PCLR 5:207]. On 18 December 1684, Henry Samson of Duxbury, yeoman, sold to Joseph Russell of Dartmouth, husbandman, "all that my fifty acres of upland" in Dartmouth, with four acres and a half of meadow adjoining, with "one-eighth part of one whole share of undivided land excepting 25 acres and one-thirtieth part of undivided land already sold out of the said eighth part of undivided lands" [PCLR 5:292].

In his will, dated 24 December 1684 and proved 5 March 1684/5, "Henery Sampson of Duxburrow" bequeathed to "my son Stephen one-third part of my whole purchase of land lying and being in the township of Dartmouth"; to "my son John one-third of my whole purchase of lands lying and being within the township of Dartmouth"; to "my son James the remaining part of the other third of my land lying within the township of Dartmouth" (part of this third having been sold to Joseph Russell, the proceeds of which went to James); to "my son James one shilling"; to "my son Caleb one shilling"; to "my daughter now the wife of Roberd Sprout one shilling"; to "my daughter Hannah now the wife of Josias Holmes one shilling"; to "my daughter now the wife of John Hanmore ten shillings"; to "Mary my daughter now the wife of John Summers one shilling"; to "my daughter Dorcas now the wife of Thomas Bony one shilling"; son Stephen to be executor; "my trusty and honored friend Mr. Wiswall" to be overseer [MD 2:142–43, citing PCPR 4:2:94–95].

The inventory of the "estate of the late deceased Henery Sampson of Duxberrow," taken 24 February 1684/5, totaled £106 14s., of which £70 was real estate: "land in Dartmouth," £70 [MD 2:143–44, citing PCPR 4:2:95].

BIRTH: Baptized Henlow, Bedfordshire, 15 January 1603/4, son of James and Martha (Cooper) Samson [TAG 52:207].

DEATH: Duxbury between 24 December 1684 (date of will) and 24 February 1684/5 (date of inventory).

MARRIAGE: Plymouth 6 February 1635/6 ANNE PLUMMER {1635, Plymouth} [PCR 1:36]. She died after 24 December 1668 [PCLR 3:237] and before 24 December 1684 (date of husband's will).

CHILDREN:

    i STEPHEN SAMSON, b. say 1637; m. by 1686 Elizabeth _____ (eldest known child, son Benjamin, d. Kingston 19 April 1758 in 72nd year) [MF 20:1:8–9, 27].

    ii JOHN SAMSON, b. say 1639; d. between 1702 and 1718, unm. [TAG 28:5].

    iii ELIZABETH SAMSON, b. say 1641; m. by 1662 Robert Sprout (eldest known child b. Scituate 15 July 1662).

    iv JAMES SAMSON, b. say 1643; m. by 1679 Hannah (_____) Wait, widow of Samuel Wait [MF 20:1:7–8].

    v HANNAH SAMSON, b. say 1645; m. Duxbury 20 March 1665[/6?] Josiah Holmes.

    vi Daughter SAMSON, b. say 1647; m. by 1682 (but probably some years earlier) John Hanmore [MF 20:1:5].

    vii MARY SAMSON, b. say 1649; m. by 1684 (but probably some years earlier) John Summers [MF 20:1:5–6].

viii DORCAS SAMSON, b. say 1651; m. by 1684 (but probably some years earlier) Thomas Bonney [MF 20:1:6–7], son of THOMAS BONNEY {1635, Charlestown} [GM 2:1:340–43].

ix CALEB SAMSON, b. say 1653; m. (1) by about 1686 Mercy Standish, daughter of Alexander Standish (eldest known child b. about 1686 [MF 20:1:33]; in his will of 21 February 1701/2, Alexander Standish made a bequest to "Mercy Samson the wife of Caleb Samson" [MD 12:101, citing PPR 1:362]); m. (2) Duxbury 30 January 1728/9 Rebecca (Bartlett) (Bradford) Stanford, daughter of Benjamin Bartlett and widow of William Bradford and Robert Stanford [MF 20:1:9–10].

ASSOCIATIONS: Henry Samson was nephew of Agnes (Cooper) Tilley, wife of *EDWARD TILLEY*, and first cousin of *HUMILITY COOPER* [TAG 52:198–208].

PREMIGRATION BIOGRAPHY: Henry Samson was born at Henlow, Bedfordshire, in 1604 and presumably removed to Leiden with his aunt and uncle Tilley in or before 1618.

COMMENTS: There are few chronological clues to help us in arranging the children of Henry Samson. There were nine children, and we know from Bradford that seven of them were born by 1651. The first daughter known to be married was Elizabeth who had a child born in 1662, and Hannah was married just a few years later. As Elizabeth and Hannah are listed first and second among the daughters in their father's will, it may be that he named them in birth order. In the absence of other guideposts, we will make the same assumption about the sons. Thus, the birth order of the children presented above derives from these assumptions, placing the children at approximately two-year intervals after the marriage of Henry Samson. This is certainly not the only possible arrangement, but it is consistent with the available evidence.

On 5 January 1640/1, Henry Samson was assigned the remainder of Phillip Davis's indenture from John Cooke. Davis's "indenture bears the date 20th of April, 1638, & is to serve for eleven years & two months from the first day of his arrival in New England" [PCR 2:6].

BIBLIOGRAPHIC NOTE: Volume Twenty of the Five Generations Project of the General Society of Mayflower Descendants covering the descendants of Henry Samson has been published in three parts. The first part, issued in 2000, treats the first four generations of descendants, compiled by Robert Moody Sherman and Ruth Wilder Sherman and edited by Robert S. Wakefield [MF 20:1]. Parts two and three, published in 2005 and 2006, cover the fifth-generation descendants; these volumes were prepared by Jane Fletcher Fiske, Robert Moody Sherman, and Ruth Wilder Sherman [MF 20:2 and MF 20:3].

In 1952 Florence Barclay studied the family of Henry Samson and arrived at some useful conclusions, with special emphasis on his son Caleb [TAG 28:5–8]. In 1976 Robert Leigh Ward published records that demonstrate the parentage of Henry Samson and his connection with Edward Tilley [TAG 52:198–208]. In 1980 Ward added to Samson's ancestry by identifying his grandfather [TAG 56:141–43], and in 1985 he further extended the ancestry of this group of immigrants [TG 6:166–86].

GEORGE SOULE

Mr. Edward Winslow, Elizabeth his wife and two men-servants called George Soule and Elias Story; also a little girl was put to him called Ellen, the sister of Richard More.

Mr. Edward Winslow his wife died the first winter, and he married with the widow of Mr. White and hath two children living by her, marriageable, besides sundry that are dead. One of his servants died, as also the little girl, soon after the ship's arrival. But his man, George Soule, is still living and hath eight children.

ORIGIN: Leiden (as servant of *EDWARD WINSLOW*).
MIGRATION: 1620 on the *Mayflower*.
FIRST RESIDENCE: Plymouth.
REMOVES: Duxbury.

OCCUPATION: Servant to *EDWARD WINSLOW* (in 1620).
Planter [PCLR 3:126]. Husbandman [PCLR 10:2:327].
FREEMAN: On 11 November 1620, George Soule signed the Mayflower Compact [Morton 26].

In the 1633 Plymouth list of freemen, ahead of those admitted on 1 January 1632/3 [PCR 1:4]. In the list of 7 March 1636/7 freemen [PCR 1:52]. In the Duxbury sections of the 1639, 1658, and 29 May 1670 Plymouth Colony lists of freemen [PCR 5:275, 8:175, 198].
EDUCATION: Signed his name as witness to the will of John Barnes of Plymouth, 6 March 1667/8 [MD 4:98, citing Scrapbook 56]. Signed his will. His inventory included "books" valued at £1 [MD 2:83; Plymouth Libraries 349].
OFFICES: Deputy for Duxbury to Plymouth Colony General Court, 27 September 1642, 28 October 1645, 3 March 1645/6, 7 July 1646, 4 June 1650, 5 June 1651, 7 June 1653, 7 March 1653/4, 6 June 1654 [PCR 2:46, 3:31, 44, 49, 94, 95, 104, 154, 167].

Plymouth grand jury, 7 March 1642/3, 6 June 1643 [PCR 2:53, 56]. Jury, 3 June 1656, 3 March 1662/3 [PCR 3:102, 7:108]. Petit jury, 1 June 1647 [PCR 2:117].

Committee to grant land, 5 May 1640, 4 June 1645 [PCR 1:151, 2:88]. Committee to "draw up an order concerning disorderly drinking of tobacco," 20 October 1646 [PCR 2:108]. Committee on magistrates and deputies, [blank] October 1650 [PCR 11:155]. Committee on boundaries, 1 June 1658 [PCR 3:138].

Volunteered for Pequot War, 7 June 1637 [PCR 1:60]. His inventory included "a gun" valued at 15s. [MD 2:83].

ESTATE: In the 1623 Plymouth division of land received one acre as a passenger on the *Mayflower* [PCR 12:4; MQ 40:10]. In the 1627 Plymouth division of cattle George Soule, Mary Soule, and Zakariah Soule were the eleventh, twelfth, and thirteenth persons in the ninth company [PCR 12:12].

George Soule was one of the Purchasers, those who acquired the rights to land distributions in Plymouth Colony as a consequence of the agreement made between the London merchants and the Plymouth settlers in 1627 [Ford 282–88].

Assessed 9s. in the Plymouth tax lists of 25 March 1633 and 27 March 1634 [PCR 1:10, 27].

On 1 July 1633, he was permitted to "mow for a cow near his dwelling house" [PCR 1:15]. On 20 March 1636/7, he was allowed the hay ground where he got hay the year before [PCR 1:56]. On 4 December 1637, George Soule was granted a garden place "on Ducksborrow side" [PCR 1:69]. On 7 May 1638, one acre of land was granted to George Soule "at the watering place" in lieu of another acre that was taken from him for other use, and also two acres of stony marsh at Powder Point were granted to him [PCR 1:83]. On 13 July 1639, George Soule sold to Robert Hicks two acres at the watering place on the south side of Plymouth [PCR 12:45]. On 2 November 1640, George Soule was granted "the meadow he desires" at Green's Harbor [PCR 1:165].

On 4 May 1658, George Soule was granted five acres of meadow [PCR 3:134]. On 22 January 1658 and 17 July 1668, George Soule gave his Dartmouth propriety to his sons Nathaniel and George as a single undivided share [PCLR 3:123, 245]. On 3 June 1662, "Gorg Soule" was on a list of freemen desiring to look for additional land "being the first born children of this government" [PCR 4:19].

On 23 July 1668, "G[e]orge Soule Senior of Duxburrow ..., planter, ... with the consent of Mary my wife," deeded to "Francis Walker husband to my daughter Elizabeth half my whole share of lands at Namassakett both upland and meadow" [MD 27:39–40, citing PCLR 3:126]. On 26 January 1668[/9], "G[e]orge Soule of Duxburrow" deeded to "Patience Haskall his true and natural daughter and unto John Haskall her husband all that his half share of land at Namassakett both upland and meadow ... having given the other half share formerly unto Francis Walker" [MD 27:40, citing

PCLR 3:153]. On 12 March 1668[/9], "George Soul of Duxburro ..., husbandman," deeded to "my daughter Elizabeth wife unto Francis Walker ... the moiety or half share of all my purchase or purchases lying and being as before expressed in the place commonly called Namascutt"; "wife Mary Soul" relinquished her dower rights [MD 27: 40–41, citing PLR 10:2:327].

In his will, dated 11 August 1677 and proved 5 March 1679/80, "G[e]orge Soule Senior of Duxberry ... being aged and weak of body" confirmed that he had formerly given by deeds "unto my two sons Nathaniel and G[e]orge all my lands in the township of Dartmouth ... [and] I have formerly given unto my daughters Elizabeth and Patience all my lands in the township of Middlebery"; to "my daughters Sussannah and Mary," 12d. apiece; "forasmuch as my eldest son John Soule and his family hath in my extreme old age and weakness been tender and careful of me and very helpful to me, and is likely so to be while it shall please God to continue my life here, therefore I give and bequeath unto my said son John Soule all the remainder of my housing and lands whatsoever"; to "my son John Soule all my goods and chattels whatsoever"; "my son John Soule to be my sole executor." In a codicil dated 20 September 1677, "G[e]orge Soule" indicated that if "my son John Soule" were to disturb "my daughter Patience or her heirs ... in the peaceable possession or enjoyment of lands I have given her at Namassakett *alias* Middleberry," then "my gift to my son John Soule shall be void" and "my daughter Patience shall have all my lands at Duxburrey and she shall be my sole executrix ... and enter into my housing lands and meadows at Duxburrow" [MD 2:81–83, citing PCPR 4:1:50].

The inventory of the estate of George Soule of Duxbury, taken 22 January 1679[/80], totaled £40 19s., of which £25 was real estate: "dwelling house, orchard, barn and upland," £20; and "meadow land," £5. John Soule appended a long list of charges against the estate, including an item "for diet and tendance since my mother died which was three year the last December" [MD 2:83–84, citing PCPR 4:1:51].

BIRTH: By 1599 (assuming he was twenty-one when he signed the Mayflower Compact).
DEATH: Between 20 September 1677 (codicil to will) and 22 January 1679[/80] (date of inventory), and probably closer to the latter date.
MARRIAGE: By 1627 MARY BUCKETT {1623, Plymouth} [PM 85] (in the 1627 Plymouth division of cattle George Soule had wife Mary and son Zachariah; Mary has been identified by many writers as Mary Buckett of the 1623 land division on the basis that no other Mary was available in the

limited Plymouth population of the earliest years). She died in or about December 1676 (son John Soule indicated in an account of 22 January 1679/80 that "my mother died which was three year the last December" [MD 2:83–84]).

CHILDREN:

    i ZACHARIAH SOULE, b. by 1627; m. by 1663 Margaret _____ [Scrapbook 20].

    ii JOHN SOULE, b. about 1632 (deposed 6 July 1685 "aged fifty-four years or thereabouts" [MD 60:134–35]; deposed 8 March 1705/6 aged "about seventy-four years" [MD 5:46, citing PLR 7:35]); m. by about 1656 Rebecca Simonson (eldest known child, Rebecca (Soule) Weston, d. Plympton 18 November 1732 "in her 76th year"), daughter of MOSES SIMONSON {1621, Plymouth} [PM 419]; m. (2) by 1679 Esther (Delano) Samson, daughter of PHILIP DELANO {1621, Plymouth} [PM 164] and widow of Samuel Samson [TAG 15:165–67; TG 1:233; MF 3:7].

    iii NATHANIEL SOULE, b. between say 1634 and 1646 (adult by 1667/8 [PCR 3:178]); before 4 March 1673/4 fathered a child with an unnamed Indian woman and ordered to pay ten bushels of corn to her for the keeping of the child [PCR 5:163]; m. by 1681 Rose _____ (eldest known child b. Dartmouth 12 January 1681[/2]).

    iv GEORGE SOULE, b. about 1639 (deposed 1 March 1672/3 "aged 34 years or thereabouts" [RICT 3:28]); m. by about 1664 Deborah _____ (eldest known child b. by early 1665 [MFIP Soule 5]).

    v SUSANNA SOULE, b. say 1641; m. by about 1662 Francis West (eldest known child b. by about 1662 [MFIP Soule 6]).

    vi MARY SOULE, b. about 1643 (in 1653 bound out for seven years or eight if she did not marry [MD 1:214]); m. by about 1665 John Peterson (eldest known child b. by about 1665 [MFIP Soule 6]).

    vii ELIZABETH SOULE, b. say 1645 (fined for committing fornication 3 March 1662/3 [PCR 5:34]; sued Nathaniel Church 5 October 1663 for refusing to marry her [PCR 7:111]; ordered whipped 2 July 1667 for committing fornication a second time [PCR 5:162]); m. by 23 July 1668 Francis Walker [MD 27:39–40, citing PCLR 3:126].

   viii PATIENCE SOULE, b. say 1647; m. Middleborough January 1666[/7] John Haskell [MiddleVR 1:1].

   ix BENJAMIN SOULE, b. say 1649; fell with Capt. Pierce 26 March 1676 during King Philip's War [Bodge 350]; unm.

COMMENTS: In 2009 Caleb Johnson published a thorough survey of English records for men named George Soule, finding more than a dozen men of that name of the appropriate time period. He was able to eliminate most of these candidates, leaving only a small handful who deserve further research [MQ 75:245–61].

On 3 January 1636/7, George Soule and Nathaniel Thomas sued and countersued each other over two heifers [PCR 7:4]. On 5 March 1667/8, George Soule Sr. stood surety with his son John for the good behavior of his son Nathaniel Soule who had verbally abused Mr. John Holmes, teacher of the church at Duxburrow [PCR 4:178].

BIBLIOGRAPHIC NOTE: In 1980 the General Society of Mayflower Descendants published a genealogy of five generations of descent from George Soule as the third volume of the Five Generations Project, compiled by John E. Soule and Milton E. Terry and compiled by Anne Borden Harding. This is a seriously flawed volume which should not be relied upon. George E. McCracken and Neil D. Thompson published lengthy reviews pointing out some of the problems [TG 1:225–58; TAG 57:57–58]. Between 2000 and 2008 the General Society of Mayflower Descendants replaced the 1980 volume with a series of five volumes in its *Mayflower Families in Progress* series, prepared by Louise Walsh Throop. The first of these five volumes contained the first four generations of descent and began the fifth generation, while the remaining four volumes completed the revision of the fifth generation. In 2015 Throop prepared an expanded and updated treatment of the first four generations.

MYLES STANDISH

Captain Myles Standish and Rose his wife.

Captain Standish his wife died in the first sickness and he married again and hath four sons living and some are dead.

ORIGIN: Leiden.
PREVIOUS RESIDENCES: Isle of Man (but see *BIBLIOGRAPHIC NOTE*).
MIGRATION: 1620 on the *Mayflower.*
FIRST RESIDENCE: Plymouth.
REMOVES: Duxbury.
RETURN TRIPS: Sent to London in late 1625 and returned early 1626.

OCCUPATION: Soldier.
CHURCH MEMBERSHIP: Myles Standish was a member of John Robinson's Leiden congregation [Strangers and Pilgrims 709].
FREEMAN: On 11 November 1620, Myles Standish signed the Mayflower Compact [Morton 26].

In the 1633 Plymouth list of freemen "Capt[ain] Myles Standish" is first among the Assistants, immediately after the governor [PCR 1:3]. In the 7 March 1636/7 list of freemen [PCR 1:52]. In the 1639 list of freemen, among Assistants and in Duxbury section [PCR 8:173, 174].

EDUCATION: He signed several documents sent to Massachusetts Bay and must have been conversant with figures to be colony treasurer. His inventory included several dozen books, valued at £9 3s., among which there were three Bibles and a number of other theological volumes, as well as such titles as Homer's *Iliad* and Caesar's *Commentaries* [MD 3:155; Plymouth Libraries 203–15 (identifying and providing full titles for most of the volumes)].

OFFICES: Plymouth Acting Governor, 3 May 1653 [PCR 3:27]. Assistant, 1 January 1632/3, 1 January 1634/5, 14 January 1636/7, 6 March 1637/8, 5 March 1638/9, 3 March 1639/40, 2 March 1640/1, 4 June 1645, 2 June 1646, 1 June 1647, 7 June 1648, 6 June 1649, 4 June 1650, 5 June 1651, 3 June 1652, 7 June 1653, 6 June 1654, 8 June 1655, 3 June 1656 [PCR 1:5, 32, 48, 79, 116, 140, 2:8, 83, 100, 115, 123, 139, 153, 166, 3:7, 30, 48, 77, 99]. Treasurer, 20 August 1644, 2 June 1646, 1 June 1647, 7 June 1648, 6 June 1649, 5 June 1651, 3 June 1652, 7 June 1653, 6 June 1654, 8 June 1655 [PCR

2:76, 101, 115, 123, 139, 166, 3:7, 30, 48, 77]. Council of War, 27 September 1642, 10 October 1643, 6 April 1653 [PCR 2:47, 64, 100, 3:26, 28].

"Capt. Standish" is in the Duxbury section of the 1643 Plymouth Colony list of men able to bear arms [PCR 8:190].

Captain, 1620–56 [PCR 1:52, 59, 80, 82, 84, 90–92, 98, 100].

Commander of forces [PCR 2:47, 146]. Captain of troops raised for Dutch war [PCR 3:29, 55]. His inventory included "one fowling piece, 3 muskets, 4 carbines, 2 small guns, one old barrel" valued at £8 1s. and "one sword, one cutlass, 3 belts" valued at £2 7s. [MD 3:155].

ESTATE: In the 1623 Plymouth division of land "Captain Myles Standish" received two acres as a passenger on the *Mayflower* [for himself and his first wife, Rose], and "Mrs. Standish" [his second wife, Barbara] received one acre as a passenger on the *Anne* in 1623 [PCR 12:4, 6; MQ 40:13]. In the 1627 Plymouth division of cattle Captain Standish, Barbara Standish, Charles Standish, Alexander Standish, and John Standish are the first five persons in the third company [PCR 12:10].

Myles Standish was one of the Purchasers, those who acquired the rights to land distributions in Plymouth Colony as a consequence of the agreement made between the London merchants and the Plymouth settlers in 1627 [Ford 282–88].

In 1631 "Captain Myles Standish of Plymouth" sold to Edward Winslow of Plymouth "two acres of land lying in the north field" [PCR 12:16].

In the Plymouth tax lists of 25 March 1633 and 27 March 1634 "Capt[ain] Myles Standish" was assessed 18s. [PCR 1:9, 27].

From 1633 to 1637, Captain Standish was allowed to mow land he had formerly mowed [PCR 1:14, 40, 56]. On 4 December 1637, "Captain Myles Standish" was granted the surplusage of land on "Ducksborrow side" in consideration of the "want of lands he should have had to his proportion" [PCR 1:70]. On 2 July 1638, "Captain Myles Standish" received three hundred acres of uplands [PCR 1:91]. On 1 October 1638, he was granted a garden place on "Duxborrow side," which was formerly laid forth for him [PCR 1:99].

On 4 March 1650/1, "whereas Captain Miles Standish hath been at much trouble and pains, and hath gone sundry journeys into Yarmouth aforesaid in the said town's business, and likely to have more in that behalf, in respect whereunto the Court have granted unto the said Captain Standish" about forty or fifty acres [PCR 2:164]. On 5 October 1658, confirmation was made of a sale by "Capt. Myles Standish" (with consent of his wife Barbara) to Mr. Thomas Howes of Yarmouth of "a certain farm lying in the liberties of Yarmouth," which had been granted to Standish by the court on 4 March 1650 [MD 13:142–43, citing PCLR 2:2:11].

On 9 May 1654, "Capt. Myles Standish" sold to Capt. Thomas Willett of Plymouth his purchaser's right at Sowamsett, Mattapoisett, and places adjacent; "Mrs. Barberye Standish wife of the said Capt. Standish" consented to his deed [MD 6:246–47, citing PCLR 2:1:111].

On 3 June 1656, the General Court granted to "Captain Myles Standish" "three hundred acres of upland ... with a competency of meadow to such a proportion of upland lying and being at Satuckquett Pond, provided it come not within the court's grant of Bridgwater" [PCR 3:101, 107].

In his will, dated 7 March 1655[/6] and proved 4 May 1657, "Myles Standish Senior of Duxburrow" asked that "if I die at Duxburrow my body to be laid as near as conveniently may be to my two daughters Lora Standish my daughter and Mary Standish my daughter-in-law" and bequeathed to "my dear and loving wife Barbara Standish" one-third of his estate after all debts are paid; to "my son Josias Standish upon his marriage" cattle to the value of £40 (if possible); "that every one of my four sons viz: Allexander Standish, Myles Standish, Josias Standish and Charles Standish may have forty pounds apiece"; to "my eldest son Allexander ... a double share in land"; "so long as they [i.e., the four sons listed above] live single that the whole [of the land] be in partnership betwixt them"; "my dearly beloved wife Barbara Standish, Allexander Standish, Myles Standish and Josias Standish" to be joint executors; "my loving friends Mr. Timothy Hatherley and Capt. James Cudworth" to be supervisors; to "Marcye Robinson whom I tenderly love for her grandfather's sake" £3; to "my servant John Irish Jr." 40s. beyond what is due him by covenant; and to "my son & heir apparent Allexander Standish all my lands as heir apparent by lawful descent in Ormistick, Borsconge, Wrightington, Maudsley, Newburrow, Crawston and the Isle of Man and given to me as right heir by lawful descent but surruptuously [*sic*] detained from me my great-grandfather being a second or younger brother from the house of Standish of Standish" [MD 3:153–55, citing PCPR 2:1:37–38].

The inventory of the estate of "Captain Miles Standish gent.," taken 2 December 1656, totaled £358 7s., of which £140 was real estate: "one dwelling house and outhouses with the land thereunto belonging," £140 [MD 3:155–56, citing PCPR 2:1:39–40].

On 4 May 1657, "Mr. Allexander Standish and Mr. Josias Standish do accept of being executors with Mrs. Barbery Standish, their mother, on the estate of Captain Myles Standish, deceased" [PCR 3:114].

BIRTH: By the early 1580s (assuming he was a soldier in the Low Countries in the first decade of the seventeenth century, but see **BIBLIOGRAPHIC NOTE**).

DEATH: Duxbury 3 October 1656 [MD 1:12–13 (and especially footnote on page 12); NEHGR 87:152].

MARRIAGE: (1) By about 1618 Rose _____. She died Plymouth 29 January 1620/1 ("January 29 [1620/1]. Dies Rose, the wife of Captain Standish" [Prince 184]).

(2) By 1624 Barbara _____. She died after 6 October 1659 [MD 4:119].

CHILDREN:

With second wife

    i CHARLES STANDISH, b. say 1624 (included in 1627 Plymouth division of cattle); living 1627; d. by about 1635.

    ii ALEXANDER STANDISH, b. say 1626 (died 6 July 1702 "being about 76 years of age" [NEHGR 87:153]); m. (1) by about 1660 Sarah Alden, daughter of *JOHN ALDEN*; m. (2) by 1689 Desire (Doty) (Sherman) Holmes, daughter of *EDWARD DOTY*.

    iii JOHN STANDISH, b. say 1627 (included in 1627 Plymouth division of cattle); no further record.

    iv MYLES STANDISH, b. say 1629; m. Boston 19 July 1660 Sarah Winslow, daughter of JOHN WINSLOW {1621, Plymouth} [PM 511; BVR 76].

    v LORA STANDISH, b. say 1631; d. by 7 March 1655[/6], unm. (from father's will).

    vi JOSIAS STANDISH, b. say 1633; m. (1) Marshfield 19 December 1654 Mary Dingley [MarVR 1]; m. (2) after 1655 Sarah Allen, daughter of Samuel Allen (in his will of 2 August 1669 Samuel Allen bequeathed to "my son-in-law Josiah Standish" [SPR 6:27]).

    vii CHARLES STANDISH, b. say 1635 [NEHGR 87:152–53]; living 7 March 1655[/6] (named last among the sons in father's will); no further record.

PREMIGRATION BIOGRAPHY: Myles Standish was born in Lancashire (or perhaps on the Isle of Man) in the early 1580s. Nathaniel Morton eulogized him as

> a gentleman, born in Lancashire, and was heir apparent unto a great estate of lands and livings, surreptitiously detained from him, his greatgrandfather being a second or younger brother from the house of Standish. In his younger time he went over into the low countries, and was a soldier there, and came

acquainted with the church at Leyden, and came over into New England, with such of them as at the first set out for the planting of the plantation of New Plimouth, and bare a deep share of their first difficulties, and was always very faithful to their interest [Morton 170].

The first sentence in this brief biography is taken directly from Standish's will. The remainder may have been obtained directly from Standish, as Morton was about forty-four years old when the Captain died.

Jeremy Bangs reconstructs the military service of Myles Standish in the Netherlands under the assumption that he served under Colonel Horatio Vere, who "recruited for the Dutch wars on the Isle of Man and in Lancashire." During this service Standish would have been an ordinary soldier and not an officer. A 1601 Leiden hospital record of recuperating soldiers includes the name "Myls Stansen," which could be a bilingual corruption of the name Myles Standish [NEHGR 143:201–3].

In a letter from Leiden dated 19 December 1623 [NS], Rev. John Robinson exhorted William Bradford "to consider of your disposition of your Captain, whom I love, and am persuaded the Lord in great mercy and for much good hath sent you him, if you use him aright. He is a man humble and meek amongst you, and towards all in ordinary course" [Bradford 375]. Although this was written in the context of the possible need to relieve Standish of his duties pursuant to the killing of several Indians, the character assessment nevertheless shows that Robinson had come to know Standish well, which could only have happened at Leiden.

COMMENTS: Myles Standish was a member of the party that explored the Outer Cape from 15 to 17 November 1620 [Mourt 19]. He was also a member of the exploratory party that left Provincetown Harbor on 6 December 1620 and selected the site for the town of Plymouth [Mourt 32]. On 22 March 1620/1, Captain Standish and Master Williamson [probably William Brewster] met Massasoit at the brook and began negotiations, soon joined by the governor, John Carver [Mourt 55–57].

Although THOMAS MORTON {1622, Merrymount} [GMB 1299–1300] has left us with a description of Standish as "Captain Shrimp," Bradford described him in gentler terms during the first great sickness:

[S]o as there died sometimes two or three of a day ... that of one hundred & odd persons, scarce fifty remained. And of these in the time of most distress, there was but six or seven sound persons, who, to their great commendations be it spoken, spared no pains, night nor day, but with abundance of toil and hazard of their own health ... did all the homely & necessary offices for them, which dainty & queasy stomachs cannot endure to hear named; and all this willingly & cheerfully, without any grudging in the least, showing herein their true love unto their friends & brethren. A rare example & worthy to be remembered. Two of these seven were Mr. William Brewster, their Reverend Elder, & Myles Standish, their Captain & military commander, unto whom myself & many others, were much beholden in our low & sick condition [Bradford 77].

In the winter of 1622, Captain Standish was to go to Massachusetts Bay, but was twice driven back by high winds, the latter time being sick with a "violent fever" [Good News 299–300]. The Governor took his place and the meeting occurred as intended; Standish recovered within the month [Good News 304].

Lyford and Oldham, in their derogatory letters to England about the early settlement at Plymouth, said "Captain Standish looks like a silly boy, and is in utter contempt" [Bradford 156]. Standish had a facility with language, but one editor remarked that "Standish, though 'the best linguist among them,' in the Indian dialects, was more expert with the sword than the pen" [Young's Pilgrim Fathers 115].

In early 1623, Captain Standish went to trade with the Indians. On meeting some of greater number than his little band, he soon missed some beads, and taking his men "set them on their guard about the sachem's house ... threatening to fall upon them without further delay if they would not forthwith restore them, signifying ... that as he would not offer the least injury, so he would not receive any at their hands, which should escape without punishment or due satisfaction" [Good News 309]. This bold stance won respect as well as the return of the beads.

In a 1623 trip to the area near what would be Boston, Captain Standish warned the men there of the Indians' violent intentions. When a number arrived to trade, Standish boldly faced them down and averted a skirmish, but not without suffering some personal slights:

Also Pecksuot, being a man of greater stature than the Captain, told him, though he were a great captain, yet he was but a little man; and, said he, though I be no sachem, yet I am a man of great strength and courage. These things the Captain observed, yet bare with patience for the present [Good News 338].

In a running conflict in spring of 1623, Standish and a small troop took the high ground and, as one assailant drew his bow to fire at Standish, Standish and one other fired at him and broke his arm, "whereupon they fled into a swamp. When they were in the thicket, they parleyed, but to small purpose, getting nothing but foul language. So our Captain dared the sachem to come out and fight like a man, showing how base and woman-like he was in tonguing it as he did, but he refused, and fled" [Good News 341].

In late 1625 Captain Standish was sent to England with letters and instructions

> both to their friends of the company ... and also the Honorable Council of New England to the company to desire that seeing that they meant only to let them have goods upon sale, that they might have them upon easier terms, for they should never be able to bear such high interest.... But he came in a very bad time, for the State was full of trouble, and the plague very hot in London, so as no business could be done, yet he spake with some of the Honored Council, who promised all helpfulness to the plantation which lay in them ... yet with much ado he took up £150 (& spent a good deal of it in expences) at 50 per cent, which he bestowed in trading goods & such other most needful commodities as he knew requisite for their use, and so returned passenger in a fishing ship [Bradford 177–79].

In 1627, pursuant to the renegotiation of the financial agreement between the London merchants and the Plymouth settlers, Myles Standish became one of the eight Undertakers who agreed to oversee the liquidation of Plymouth Colony's debts [Bradford 194–96; Bradford LB 38–40].

In 1628, Captain Standish was sent to capture Thomas Morton by force. Coming upon Morton's dwelling, Standish found him to be well armed and locked within. Fortunately, they were "over armed with drink" and, coming out of the house

> they were so steeled with drink as their pieces were too heavy for them, [Morton] ... with a carbine ... had thought to have shot Captain Standish; but he [Standish] stepped to him, & put by his piece, & took him. Neither was there any hurt done to any of either side, save that one was so drunk that he ran his own nose upon the point of a sword that one held before him as he entered the house; but he lost but a little of his hot blood [Bradford 209–10].

In 1634 when John Alden was imprisoned in Massachusetts Bay, Captain Standish was sent to free him [Bradford 264–65].

BIBLIOGRAPHIC NOTE: In 2007 the General Society of Mayflower Descendants issued Volume Fourteen of the Five Generations Project, compiled by Russell L. Warner and covering the descendants of Myles Standish.

The last clause of the will of Myles Standish, in which he complains of being "surruptuously detained" from his rightful inheritance and then lists a number of estates, has spawned a great amount of research into the English origin of this immigrant.

In 1914 Thomas Cruddas Porteus published "Some Recent Investigations Concerning the Ancestry of Capt. Myles Standish" [NEHGR 68:339–69]. Porteus transcribed many estate documents and came to the tentative conclusion that Myles Standish descended from a certain Huan Standish of the Isle of Man.

In 1933 Merton Taylor Goodrich prepared a study of "The Children and Grandchildren of Capt. Myles Standish" [NEHGR 87:149–60]. Goodrich touches only briefly on the matter of the Standish ancestry; the most important part of his article is a careful study of both wives and each of the children of Myles Standish, dealing in detail with a number of matters of chronology and proof. This article is the bedrock on which all later work is based.

In the 1980s G. V. C. Young tackled the problem of the ancestry of Myles Standish and has advanced our knowledge greatly. In 1984 Young presented an extended argument that Myles Standish was born on the Isle of Man and that he was the son of a John Standish of Ellanbane on the Isle of Man [*Myles Standish: First Manx American* (Isle of Man 1984)]. This John Standish was son of another John Standish, who was son of a Huan Standish of Ellanbane, the very man proposed by Porteus in 1914. Although this conclusion is well argued, the proof is not yet complete; nevertheless, Young's identification is highly probable.

In 2006 Jeremy Dupertuis Bangs attacked the problem of the birthplace of Myles Standish. He analyzed a series of articles published in 1999 and 2000 by Helen Moorwood which argued for Croston, Lancashire, as the solution to problem, but determined that this conclusion was based on a confusion regarding place names and other misunderstandings. Bangs also reviewed the earlier work of Porteus and Young and concluded that the former "succeeded in finding the Manx-Lancashire branch of the Standish family to which Myles somehow must have belonged" [MQ 72:133–59]. In other words, the ancestry of Myles Standish must have run through the Isle of Man branch of the family and does not come directly from Lancashire. Even so, given the remaining uncertainties, and in particular our ignorance of the identity and place of residence of Myles's father, we cannot be certain that Myles Standish was born on the Isle of Man.

Young has published two brief supplements to this work: *More About Pilgrim Myles Standish* (Isle of Man 1987) and *Ellanbane Was the Birthplace of Myles Standish* (Isle of Man 1988).

Two recent treatments of the life of Myles Standish have been published by Jeremy D. Bangs [Strangers and Pilgrims 177–201] and by Caleb H. Johnson [Mayflower Passengers 210–31].

In 2014 Caleb Johnson reported on "The Long-lost Portrait of Myles Standish Rediscovered" [MD 63:138–49]. An inscription on this painting states "Aetatis suae 38. Anno 1625." If the identification of the portrait is correct, then it was probably painted when Standish was on his mission to London in 1625 and 1626 and also gives a probable birthdate for Standish as about 1587.

ELIAS STORY

Mr. Edward Winslow, Elizabeth his wife and two men-servants called George Soule and Elias Story; also a little girl was put to him called Ellen, the sister of Richard More.

Mr. Edward Winslow his wife died the first winter, and he married with the widow of Mr. White and hath two children living by her, marriageable, besides sundry that are dead. One of his servants died, as also the little girl, soon after the ship's arrival. But his man, George Soule, is still living and hath eight children.

ORIGIN: Leiden (as servant of *EDWARD WINSLOW*).
MIGRATION: 1620 on the *Mayflower*.
FIRST RESIDENCE: Plymouth.

OCCUPATION: Servant to *EDWARD WINSLOW*.

BIRTH: Born say 1600.
DEATH: Early 1621 at Plymouth.
MARRIAGE: None.
CHILDREN: None.

COMMENTS: Caleb Johnson comments on the distribution of the surname in England [Mayflower Passengers 232].

EDWARD THOMSON

Mr. William White and Susanna his wife and one son called Resolved, and one born a-shipboard called Peregrine, and two servants named William Holbeck and Edward Thompson.

Mr. White and his two servants died soon after their landing.

ORIGIN: Amsterdam (as servant of *WILLIAM WHITE*).
MIGRATION: 1620 on the *Mayflower*.
FIRST RESIDENCE: Plymouth.

OCCUPATION: Servant to *WILLIAM WHITE*.

BIRTH: Born say 1600.
DEATH: Provincetown Harbor 4 December 1620 "[d]ies Edward Thomson, servant of Mr. White, the first that dies since their arrival" [Prince 165].
MARRIAGE: None.
CHILDREN: None.

EDWARD TILLEY

Edward Tilley and Ann his wife, and two children that were their cousins, Henry Sampson and Humility Cooper.

Edward Tilley and his wife both died soon after their arrival, and the girl Humility, their cousin, was sent for into England and died there. But the youth Henry Sampson is still living and is married and hath seven children.

ORIGIN: Leiden [NEHGR 143:208].
PREVIOUS RESIDENCES: Henlow, Bedfordshire.
MIGRATION: 1620 on the *Mayflower*.
FIRST RESIDENCE: Plymouth.

OCCUPATION: Serge weaver [NEHGR 143:208].
FREEMAN: On 11 November 1620, Edward Tilley signed the Mayflower Compact [Morton 26].

BIRTH: Baptized Henlow, Bedfordshire, 27 May 1588 (as "Edmond"), son of Robert and Elizabeth (_____) Tilley [TAG 52:203].
DEATH: Early 1621 at Plymouth.
MARRIAGE: Henlow 20 June 1614 Agnes Cooper [TAG 52:205]. She died at Plymouth in early 1621.
CHILDREN: None known.
ASSOCIATIONS: *JOHN TILLEY* was Edward Tilley's elder brother. *HUMILITY COOPER* and *HENRY SAMSON* were niece and nephew of Agnes (Cooper) Tilley [TAG 52:198–208].

PREMIGRATION BIOGRAPHY: Edward Tilley was born at Henlow, Bedfordshire, in 1588, son of Robert Tilley and his wife Elizabeth. In his will of 1612, Robert Tilley described himself as a yeoman [TAG 52:201], which usually indicated a landowner who held enough land to earn a living above the subsistence level, and so his son Edward would have grown up in a relatively affluent household.

In 1614 Edward married at Henlow Agnes Cooper, daughter of Edmund Cooper of the same place [TAG 52:206]. No further record of Edward Tilley and his family has been found at Henlow, and by 1618 they had moved to Leiden. On 25 April 1618 [NS], Edward Tilley of Leiden agreed to allow his apprentice Robert Hagges to return to England from Leiden to collect an inheritance; Hagges had already served two years of a five-year contract. Among the witnesses to this agreement was Robert Cooper, brother-in-law of Edward Tilley and father of Humility Cooper [Strangers and Pilgrims 441–42; NEHGR 143:208].

COMMENTS: On 15 November 1620, soon after landing in Provincetown Harbor, sixteen men were equipped with musket, sword, and corslet, under the command of Capt. Myles Standish "unto whom was adjoined, for counsel and advice, William Bradford, Stephen Hopkins, and Edward Tilley"; this party explored the outer Cape for three days [Mourt 19–24]. Edward Tilley also joined the expedition of 6 December 1620 along the inner coastline of Cape Cod with nine others, under the leadership of Myles Standish; this exploratory party found and selected the settlement site which became the town of Plymouth [Mourt 32]. The voyage along the coast was bitterly cold and on the first day "Edward Tilley had like to have sounded [swooned] with cold" [Mourt 32].

BIBLIOGRAPHIC NOTE: In 1976 Robert Leigh Ward explored the English origin of the Tilley family at Henlow, Bedfordshire, and the close connections with Humility Cooper and Henry Samson [TAG 52:198–208]. In 1985 Ward further extended the ancestry of this group of immigrants [TG 6:166–86].

JOHN TILLEY

John Tilley and his wife, and Elizabeth their daughter.

John Tilley and his wife both died a little after they came ashore. And their daughter married with John Howland and hath issue as is before noted.

ORIGIN: Leiden.
PREVIOUS RESIDENCES: Henlow, Bedfordshire.
MIGRATION: 1620 on the *Mayflower.*
FIRST RESIDENCE: Plymouth.

FREEMAN: On 11 November 1620, John Tilley signed the Mayflower Compact [Morton 26].
ESTATE: In the 1623 Plymouth land division, the deceased John Tilley and his wife, along with their daughter Elizabeth, were included in the household of John Howland [MQ 40:10].

BIRTH: Baptized Henlow, Bedfordshire, 19 December 1571, son of Robert and Elizabeth (_____) Tilley [TAG 52:203].
DEATH: Early 1621 at Plymouth.
MARRIAGE: Henlow 20 September 1596 Joan (Hurst) Rogers [TAG 52:199]. She had married (1) Thomas Rogers. She died at Plymouth in early 1621.
CHILDREN:

> i ROSE TILLEY, bp. Henlow 23 October 1597 [TAG 52:198]; no further record.
>
> ii JOHN TILLEY, bp. Henlow 26 August 1599 [TAG 52:198]; no further record.
>
> iii ROSE TILLEY, bp. Henlow 28 February 1601/2 [TAG 52:198]; no further record.
>
> iv ROBERT TILLEY, bp. Henlow 25 November 1604 [TAG 52:198]; m. St. Paul, Bedford, Bedfordshire, 1 November 1632 Mary Hawkins [MQ 65:322–25; St. Paul, Bedford, PR].
>
> v ELIZABETH TILLEY, bp. Henlow 30 August 1607 [TAG 52:198]; m. about 1625 *JOHN HOWLAND.*

ASSOCIATIONS: John Tilley was the elder brother of *EDWARD TILLEY.*

PREMIGRATION BIOGRAPHY: John Tilley was born at Henlow, Bedfordshire, in 1571, son of Robert Tilley and his wife Elizabeth. In his will of 1612, Robert Tilley described himself as a yeoman [TAG 52:201], which usually indicated a landowner who held enough land to earn a living above the subsistence level, and so his son John would have grown up in a relatively affluent household.

In 1596, at the age of twenty-five, John married at Henlow a young widow, Joan (Hurst) Rogers, widow of Thomas Rogers. John and Joan had five children born at Henlow between 1597 and 1607, after which the family is not further recorded at Henlow. There is however a tantalizing record which indicates that John Tilley may have been residing at Wootton, Bedfordshire, in 1613, although this is far from certain [TAG 60:172–73]. John's brother Edward Tilley was certainly in Leiden by 1618, if not earlier, and John may have joined him there before migrating to New England.

COMMENTS: John Tilley joined the expedition of 6 December 1620 along the inner coastline of Cape Cod with nine others, under the leadership of Myles Standish; this exploratory party found and selected the settlement site which became the town of Plymouth [Mourt 32].

Thomas Rogers, the first husband of John Tilley's wife, was not the *Mayflower* passenger of that name.

BIBLIOGRAPHIC NOTE: In 1976 Robert Leigh Ward explored the English origin of the Tilley family at Henlow, Bedfordshire, and the close connections with Humility Cooper and Henry Samson [TAG 52:198–208]. In 1985 Ward published some additional biographical information on John Tilley [TAG 60:171–73].

In 1999 Joy Forster found the marriage of Robert Tilley and Mary Hawkins and demonstrated that Joan Rogers, daughter of Joan Hurst and Thomas Rogers and Robert's older half-sister, married Edward Hawkins, brother of Robert's wife [MQ 65:322–25].

In 2010 Caleb Johnson published manorial records from Henlow pertaining to the Tilley, Cooper, and Hurst families [MQ 76:125–34].

In 2011 Eugene Cole Zubrinsky explored the ancestry of Joan (Hurst) (Rogers) Tilley, the wife of John Tilley [TAG 85:1–8]. In 2014 and again in 2018 Randy A. West further extended our knowledge of that ancestry [TAG 87:25–28; MD 66:10–13].

THOMAS TINKER

Thomas Tinker and his wife and a son.

Thomas Tinker and his wife and son all died in the first sickness.

ORIGIN: Leiden.
MIGRATION: 1620 on the *Mayflower*.
FIRST RESIDENCE: Plymouth.

OCCUPATION: Wood sawyer [Leiden Pilgrims 252].
FREEMAN: "Thomas Stincker [*sic*], Englishman, wood sawyer," was admitted a citizen of Leiden on 6 January 1617 [NS]; his guarantors were Abraham Grey and John Keble [Leiden Pilgrims 252].

On 11 November 1620, Thomas Tinker signed the Mayflower Compact [Morton 26].

BIRTH: By about 1596 (assuming he was 21 when made a citizen of Leiden).
DEATH: Early 1621 at Plymouth.
MARRIAGE: By 1620 _____ _____. She died at Plymouth in early 1621.
CHILD:

       i Son TINKER, b. by 1620; d. Plymouth in the winter of 1620–1 "in the first sickness."

COMMENTS: The dates of Thomas Tinker's birth and marriage and the birth of his son could have been some years earlier; the dates given above merely provide a *terminus ante quem*.

Caleb Johnson notes the marriage of Thomas Tinker, carpenter, and Jane White at Thurne, Norfolk, on 25 June 1609, who may be the *Mayflower* couple [Mayflower Passengers 239]. Banks suggested two quite different origins for Thomas Tinker, without any basis other than identity of name [English Homes 89].

WILLIAM TREVOR

There were also other two seamen hired to stay a year here in the country, William Trevor, and one Ely. But when their time was out they both returned.

ORIGIN: England.
MIGRATION: 1620 on the *Mayflower*.
FIRST RESIDENCE: Plymouth.
RETURN TRIPS: Returned to England in 1621 on the *Fortune* [Bradford 108].

OCCUPATION: Mariner.

BIRTH: Born say 1600.
DEATH: After 1650.
MARRIAGE: None known.
CHILDREN: None known.

COMMENTS: On 27 April 1650, William Trevor was in Massachusetts Bay, presumably as a transient visitor, and deposed that "'Thompsons Island' is 'the' formerly called 'Island of Trevour' which I took possession of in 1619 and declared the same (as the effect of my proceedings) to Mr. David Thompson in London; on which information the said Thompson obtained a grant and patent for peaceable and quiet possession of said island to him and heirs forever; I being in the Company's service at the said time" [NEHGR 9:248, abstracting the original deposition, presumably at the Massachusetts Archives]. In his edition of Bradford, Charles Deane argued that this episode must have taken place in the fall of 1621, not long before Trevor returned to England, and that Trevor, three decades after the event, misremembered the date. DAVID THOMSON {1623, Piscataqua} was awarded his patent in late 1622 [William Bradford, *History of Plymouth Plantation*, ed. Charles Deane (Boston 1856) 208–9; GMB 3:1807–9].

When the *Fortune* returned to England late in 1621, two of the passengers were William Trevor and Robert Cushman. The ship was captured and detained by the French. Cushman later wrote to Bradford about the plans made by Thomas Weston to establish a plantation in New England, and that "William Trevore hath lavishly told [Weston] but what he knew or imagined of Capawack [Martha's Vineyard], Mohegan and the Narragansetts"

[Bradford 107–8; William Bradford, *Of Plymouth Plantation*, ed. Caleb Johnson (n.p. 2006) 529–30].

Given his known maritime occupation, William Trevor of the *Mayflower* may have been "Mr. Trevore, master" of the *William* which arrived about 22 February 1632/3 "at Plymouth, with some passengers and goods for the Massachusetts Bay, but she came to set up a fishing at Scituate & so to go to trade at Hudson's River" [WJ 1:119].

JOHN TURNER

John Turner and two sons; he had a daughter came some years after to Salem, where she is now living.

John Turner and his two sons all died in the first sickness. But he hath a daughter still living at Salem, well married and approved of.

ORIGIN: Leiden.
PREVIOUS RESIDENCES: England.
MIGRATION: 1620 on the *Mayflower.*
FIRST RESIDENCE: Plymouth.

OCCUPATION: Merchant [Leiden Pilgrims 264].
CHURCH MEMBERSHIP: Member of the Leiden congregation by 1620.
FREEMAN: On 27 September 1610, John Turner, Englishman, merchant, was admitted as a citizen of Leiden [Leiden Pilgrims 264].

On 11 November 1620, John Turner signed the Mayflower Compact [Morton 26].

BIRTH: By 1589 (based on date of Leiden citizenship).
DEATH: Early 1621 at Plymouth.
MARRIAGE: By about 1615 _____ _____. She did not come over in 1620 and was dead by 1622, when her orphaned daughter Elizabeth was residing in the Leiden household of Anthony Clement.
CHILDREN:

> i Son TURNER, b. say 1615; d. Plymouth in early 1621 [Bradford 446].
> i Son TURNER, b. say 1617; d. Plymouth in early 1621 [Bradford 446].
> iii ELIZABETH TURNER, b. say 1619; m. and living in Salem in 1650 (see **COMMENTS**).

PREMIGRATION BIOGRAPHY: John Turner was born in England and first appeared at Leiden in 1610 when he was admitted as a citizen, which would indicate that he was born no later than 1589. He could well have been born some years earlier, especially if he underwent an extensive apprenticeship before becoming a merchant.

Given the lack of evidence, the actual birth dates for Turner's children might be some years earlier than those given above, so we do not know whether he was already married when he arrived at Leiden, or whether he married there.

On 11 June 1620, Robert Cushman, then in England, addressed a letter to the leaders of the Leiden congregation informing them that "I received your letter yesterday, by John Turner" and that "[y]ou shall hear distinctly by John Turner, who I think shall come hence on Tuesday night" [Bradford 365–66]. The fact that John Turner was entrusted with letters passing between these prominent members of the Leiden congregation suggests that Turner himself was a member of that body, and probably had been for some years.

COMMENTS: In 1976 Robert S. Wakefield presented evidence indicating that the daughter of John Turner who came to New England after 1620 (probably in 1629 or 1630) was "Lysbet Turner" who appears in the 1622 poll tax list for Leiden in the household of Anthony Clement (the same household in which resided the widow and children of Thomas Rogers). Wakefield argued that she was the Elizabeth Turner who witnessed a deed in Salem on 8 October 1635 and joined the church there on 28 December 1637 [TAG 52:110–13].

In 2016 Christopher Challender Child attempted to identify the daughter Elizabeth who went to Salem [MD 64:151–73]. Child undertook a close analysis of the Salem church records and concluded that the Elizabeth Turner who witnessed a deed at Salem in 1635 and joined the church there in 1637 was not the daughter of the *Mayflower* passenger. Child's annotations of the church records supply clues that may lead to the correct identification of the husband of the *Mayflower* passenger's daughter.

RICHARD WARREN

Mr. Richard Warren, but his wife and children were left behind and came afterwards.

Mr. Richard Warren lived some four or five years and had his wife come over to him, by whom he had two sons before [he] died, and one of them is married and hath two children. So his increase is four. But he had five daughters came over with his wife, who are all married and living, and have many children.

ORIGIN: London [Mourt 32].
PREVIOUS RESIDENCES: Great Amwell, Hertfordshire.
MIGRATION: 1620 on the *Mayflower*.
FIRST RESIDENCE: Plymouth.

FREEMAN: On 11 November 1620, Richard Warren signed the Mayflower Compact [Morton 26].
ESTATE: In the 1623 Plymouth division of land Richard Warren received an uncertain number of acres (perhaps two) as a passenger on the *Mayflower*, and five acres as a passenger on the *Anne* (presumably for his wife and children) [PCR 12:4–6; MQ 40:12]. In the 1627 Plymouth division of cattle Richard Warren, his wife Elizabeth Warren, Nathaniel Warren, Joseph Warren, Mary Warren, Anna Warren, Sarah Warren, Elizabeth Warren, and Abigail Warren were the first nine persons in the ninth company [PCR 12:12].

Richard Warren was one of the Purchasers, those who acquired the rights to land distributions in Plymouth Colony as a consequence of the agreement made between the London merchants and the Plymouth settlers in 1627 [Ford 282–88].

In the 25 March 1633 Plymouth tax list Widow Warren was assessed 12s., and in the list of 27 March 1634, 9s. [PCR 1:10, 27].

On 1 July 1633, "Mrs. Warren and Rob[er]t Bartlet" were allowed to mow where they did the previous year, and again on 14 March 1635/6 [PCR 1:15, 41].

On 28 October 1633, "a misted [messuage] that was granted formerly to Richard Warren, deceased, & forfeited by a late order, for want of building, the said misted was granted to Mr. Raph Fog & his heirs forever, provided the said Raph within twelve months build a dwelling house upon the same, & allow widow Warren so much for her fence remaining thereon as Rob[er]t Heeks [Hicks] & Christopher Wadsworth shall think it may be serviceable to the said Raph" [PCR 1:18].

On 7 March 1636/7, "it is agreed upon, by the consent of the whole Court, that Elizabeth Warren, widow, the relict of Mr. Richard Warren, deceased, shall be entered, and stand, and be purchaser instead of her said husband, as well because that (he dying before he had performed the said bargain) the said Elizabeth performed the same after his decease, as also for the establishing of the lots of lands given formerly by her unto her sons-in-law Richard Church, Robert Bartlett and Thomas Little, in marriage with their wives, her daughters" [PCR 1:54, 2:177].

On 2 February 1637[/8], "Mrs. Elizabeth Warren of the Eele River, widow, for and in consideration of a marriage already solemnized betwixt John Cooke the younger of the Rockey Noocke and Sarah her daughter doth acknowledge that she has given … unto the said John Cooke one lot of land lying at Eele River containing eighteen acres or thereabouts and lying on the north side of Robert Bartlett's lot formerly also given the said Robert in marriage with Mary another of the said Mrs. Warren's daughters" [PCR 12:27; see also PCR 12:28].

On 9 January 1639[/40], "Mrs. Elizabeth Warren, widow, for and in consideration of a marriage already consummate betwixt Anthony Snow & Abigail her daughter hath freely & absolutely given … unto the said Anthony Snow all that her house situate near the place called Wellingsly (alias) Hobs Hole with the eight acres of lands thereunto adjoining" [PCR 12:53–54].

On 5 May 1640, "Richard Church, Rob[er]te Bartlett, Thomas Little, & Mrs. Elizabeth Warren are granted enlargements at the heads of their lots to the foot of the Pyne Hills, leaving a way betwixt them and the Pyne Hills, for cattle and carts to pass" [PCR 1:152].

On 11 June 1653, as the result of a disagreement between Mrs. Elizabeth Warren and her son Nathaniel, and a petition offered in court by Mrs. Jane Collier on behalf of her grandchild, Sarah, wife of Nathaniel Warren, the court chose four indifferent men to settle the matter of access to lands [MD 2:64, citing PCLR 2:73].

On 4 March 1673/4, Mary Bartlett, wife of Robert Bartlett, came into this court and owned "that she hath received full satisfaction for whatsoever she might claim as due from the estate of Mistress Elizabeth Warren, deceased, and John Cooke, in the behalf of all her sisters, testified the same before the court; and the court doth hereby settle the remainder of the said estate on Joseph Warren" [PCR 5:139–40].

BIRTH: By about 1585 (based on date of marriage).

DEATH: Plymouth 1628. ("This year died Mr. Richard Warren, who hath been mentioned before in this book, and was an useful instrument; and during his life bore a deep share in the difficulties and troubles of the first settlement of the plantation of New-Plymouth" [Morton 89].)

MARRIAGE: Great Amwell, Hertfordshire, 14 April 1610 Elizabeth Walker, daughter of Augustine Walker. She was baptized at Baldock, Hertfordshire, in September 1583 [TAG 78:81–86]. "Mistress Elizabeth Warren, an aged widow, aged above 90 years, deceased [at Plymouth] on the second of October, 1673, who, having lived a godly life, came to her grave as a shock fully ripe. She was honorably buried on the 24th of October aforesaid" [PCR 8:35].

CHILDREN:

    i MARY WARREN, b. about 1611 (d. Plymouth 27 March 1683 "in her 73d year" [PChR 1:250]); m. say 1629 ROBERT BARTLETT {1623, Plymouth} [PM 42] (date based on estimated age of children at their marriages).

    ii ANN WARREN, b. about 1612 (deposed 6 June 1672 "aged sixty years or thereabouts" [MD 2:178, citing PCPR 3:1:40]); m. Plymouth 19 April 1633 THOMAS LITTLE {1632, Plymouth} [PCR 1:13; PM 305].

    iii SARAH WARREN, b. by 1613 (named in grandfather's will of 19 April 1613 [TAG 78:83, citing Commissary Court of London, Essex and Herts, D/ABW 41/186]); m. Plymouth 28 March 1634 John Cooke Junior [PCR 1:29], son of *FRANCIS COOKE*.

    iv ELIZABETH WARREN, b. say 1615; m. by 7 March 1636/7 [PCR 1:54; TAG 60:129–30] (and probably by 14 March 1635/6 [PCR 1:41, 56, 152]) RICHARD CHURCH {1630, Weymouth} [PM 105] (he shared mowing land with Mrs. Warren 14 March 1635/6 [PCR 1:41]).

    v ABIGAIL WARREN, b. say 1619; m. Plymouth 8 (or 9) November 1639 ANTHONY SNOW {1637, Plymouth} [PCR 1:134].

    vi NATHANIEL WARREN, b. Plymouth about 1624 (deposed 15 October 1661 "aged thirty-seven years or thereabouts" [MD 2:178–79, citing PCLR 2:2:56]); m. Plymouth 19 November 1645 Sarah Walker [PCR 2:94]. (See WILLIAM COLLIER {1633, Plymouth} for discussion of her possible ancestry [PM 128].)

   vii JOSEPH WARREN, b. Plymouth by 1627; m. by 1653
   Priscilla Faunce (eldest child b. Plymouth 23 September
   1653 [PCR 8:33]), daughter of JOHN FAUNCE {1623,
   Plymouth} [PM 201–3].

PREMIGRATION BIOGRAPHY: Richard Warren was born about 1585
and was married at Great Amwell, Hertfordshire, in 1610. His first five children were born in England prior to 1620, but no records have been found
for any of their baptisms. Soon after arrival in New England he was said to
be of London, but no records placing him in that city have been discovered,
although he had connections with the city by marriage [TAG 78:274–75].
Morton's statement that he "was an useful instrument; and during his life
bore a deep share in the difficulties and troubles of the first settlement of
the plantation of New-Plymouth" and his being addressed as "Mr." suggest
that he was one of the London merchants who provided financing for and
was involved in the planning of the voyage to New England [Morton 89].

COMMENTS: Richard Warren was in the party that explored Cape Cod in
early December 1620; he was described at that time as being "of London"
[Mourt 32].

   On 5 July 1635, Thomas Williams, servant of Widow Warren, confessed that "there being some dissention between him and his dame, she,
after other things, exhorted him to fear God & do his duty, he answered,
he neither feared God, nor the devil" [PCR 1:35]. Williams was reproved
and released [PCR 1:35]. On 5 January 1635/6, Widow Warren paid 30s. to
Thomas Clarke for borrowing his boat, and although returning it to a place
of usual safety, an extraordinary storm wrecked it [PCR 1:36]. On 3 June
1639, "Mr. Andrew Hellot" was ordered to pay Mrs. Warren 10s. to settle
an account between them [PCR 7:12].

BIBLIOGRAPHIC NOTE: The Five Generations Project of The General
Society of Mayflower Descendants has treated the descendants of Richard
Warren as Volume Eighteen in the Five Generation Project, in three parts.
The first part, covering the first four generations, compiled by Robert S.
Wakefield, and revised by Judith H. Swan, appeared in 2004 (third edition)
[MF 18:1]. The second and third volumes, covering the fifth-generation
descendants and prepared by Judith H. Swan, were published in 2011 (second edition) and 2001.

   In 1938 L. Effingham deForest published a thorough study of Richard
Warren [Moore Anc 561–70]. In 2003 Edward J. Davies published two articles that present the evidence for the marriage of Richard Warren and for
some of his wife's family [TAG 78:81–86, 274–75].

WILLIAM WHITE

Mr. William White and Susanna his wife and one son called Resolved, and one born a-shipboard called Peregrine, and two servants named William Holbeck and Edward Thompson.

Mr. White and his two servants died soon after their landing. His wife married with Mr. Winslow, as is before noted. His two sons are married and Resolved hath five children, Peregrine two, all living. So their increase are seven.

ORIGIN: Amsterdam.
PREVIOUS RESIDENCES: Wisbech, Cambridgeshire.
MIGRATION: 1620 on the *Mayflower*.
FIRST RESIDENCE: Plymouth.

FREEMAN: On 11 November 1620, William White signed the Mayflower Compact [Morton 26].
ESTATE: In the 1623 Plymouth division of land William White received five acres as a passenger on the *Mayflower* [PCR 12:4; MQ 40:12]. (Robert Wakefield argued that these five acres were the shares of the deceased William White, his two sons, and his two servants. An acre for his remarried widow is included in the grant to her second husband, Edward Winslow [MQ 40:12].)

In the 1627 Plymouth division of cattle Resolved White and Peregrine White were the tenth and eleventh persons in the third company [PCR 12:10].

BIRTH: Baptized 25 January 1586/7 at Wisbech, Cambridgeshire, son of Edward and Thomasine (Cross) (May) White [TAG 89:81–94, 168–88].
DEATH: Plymouth 21 February 1620[/1] [Prince 184].
MARRIAGE: By about 1615, probably at Amsterdam, Susanna Jackson, born about 1594, daughter of Richard and Mary (Pettinger) Jackson of Scrooby, Nottinghamshire [TAG 89:241–64]. She married (2) Plymouth 12 May 1621 *EDWARD WINSLOW* [Bradford 86].

CHILDREN:

    i RESOLVED WHITE, b. about 1615, probably at Amsterdam (deposed 4 July 1674 "aged about 59 years" [MD 33:99]; deposed 5 November 1678 "aged about sixty-three years" [EQC 7:112]); m. (1) Scituate 8 April 1640 Judith Vassall [PCR 8:19], daughter of WILLIAM VASSALL {1630, Boston} [WF 653–57]; m. (2) Salem 5 October 1674 Abigail (_____) Lord, widow of WILLIAM LORD {1635, Salem} [GM 2:4:334–40].

    ii PEREGRINE WHITE, b. late November aboard the *Mayflower* in Provincetown Harbor ("Whilst some were employed in this discovery [of a good harbor], it pleased God that Mistress White was brought abed of a son, which was called Peregrine" [Mourt 31; TAG 89:187]); m. by 6 March 1648/9 Sarah Bassett, daughter of WILLIAM BASSETT {1621, Plymouth} [PCR 2:183; PM 48].

ASSOCIATIONS: William White was uncle of Dorothy (May) Bradford, first wife of *WILLIAM BRADFORD* [TAG 89:241–64].

PREMIGRATION BIOGRAPHY: William White was baptized at Wisbech, Cambridgeshire, on 25 January 1586/7 and resided there until he reached his majority in 1608. Although nothing is known of his religious beliefs or practices before that time, he was born into a family which in the 1570s had been involved with the sect known as the Family of Love. In March of 1608, barely two months after his twenty-first birthday, William White was awarded £10 in a financial settlement at a session of the Wisbech Barton manorial court [TAG 89:186]. Within two months, by May 1608, he had established residence at Amsterdam, where he joined the Ancient Church, the English separatist church that had been organized there in the 1590s. White's elder half-siblings Henry and Jacomine May had joined him in the move from Wisbech to Amsterdam, and on 5 May 1609 he had accompanied Jacomine at her marriage with Jan l'Ecluse [TAG 89:83]. About 1615, presumably at Amsterdam, William White married Susanna Jackson, daughter of Richard Jackson of Scrooby, Nottinghamshire; although no record has been found for the Jackson family in Amsterdam, Richard had been a member of the separatist congregation at Scrooby and was probably not residing in England at the time of this marriage [TAG 89:251–56]. No further record for William White has been found at Amsterdam, and none of the records for men of this name at Leiden seem to pertain to William White of Amsterdam. Caleb Johnson argues that William White's placement in Bradford's list of *Mayflower* passengers makes it likely that he was not from Leiden [TAG 89:88–90]. It appears that he and his family remained at Amsterdam until 1620 and then joined members of the Leiden congregation when they boarded the *Speedwell* on the first leg of their journey to the New World.

COMMENTS: On 30 October 1623, Edward Winslow wrote from London to "his much respected Uncle Mr. Robert Jackson" who was clerk of the sewers at Spalding, Lincolnshire. In his letter he wrote that "almost two years since I wrote to my father-in-law declaring the death of his son White & the continued health of his daughter and her two children; also how that by God's providence she was become my wife.... My wife hath had one child by me, but it pleased him that gave it to take it again unto himself; I left her with child at my departure (whom God preserve) but hope to be with her before her delivery" [NEHGR 109:242–43]. For decades this was the only evidence for the origin of Edward Winslow's second wife, who was the widow of William White. Finally, in 2017, the team of Sue Allan, Caleb Johnson, and Simon Neal discovered additional evidence which identified her as Susanna Jackson, daughter of Richard Jackson of Scrooby, Nottinghamshire [TAG 89:241–64 (which includes a discussion of earlier attempts to solve this problem)].

BIBLIOGRAPHIC NOTE: In 1997 the General Society of Mayflower Descendants published an updated account of William White and his descendants as Volume Thirteen of the Five Generations Project, compiled by Robert S. Wakefield [MF 13]. (This supersedes an earlier version, prepared by Robert M. and Ruth W. Sherman and issued as part of the first volume of the Five Generations Project [MF 1:95–187].)

In 2017 Caleb Johnson, Sue Allan, and Simon Neal published the evidence and argumentation that establish the origin of William White and his connection with the May family of Wisbech, Cambridgeshire [TAG 89:81–94, 168–88].

ROGER WILDER

Mr. John Carver, Katherine his wife, Desire Minter, and two manservants, John Howland, Roger Wilder. William Latham, a boy, and a maidservant and a child that was put to him, Jasper More.

Also, his man Roger and the little boy Jasper died before either of them, of the common infection.

ORIGIN: Leiden (as servant of *JOHN CARVER*).
MIGRATION: 1620 on the *Mayflower*.
FIRST RESIDENCE: Plymouth.

OCCUPATION: Servant to *JOHN CARVER*.

BIRTH: Born say 1600.
DEATH: Early 1621 at Plymouth.
MARRIAGE: None.
CHILDREN: None.

COMMENTS: Caleb Johnson presents evidence for a Roger Wilder who was baptized at Rotherwicke, Hampshire, on 28 December 1595 who, although probably too old to be the *Mayflower* passenger, may provide a clue to discovering the correct origin [Mayflower Passengers 249].

THOMAS WILLIAMS

Moses Fletcher, John Goodman, Thomas Williams, Digory Priest, Edmund Margesson, Peter Browne, Richard Britteridge, Richard Clarke, Richard Gardiner, Gilbert Winslow.

Moses Fletcher, Thomas Williams, Digory Priest, John Goodman, Edmund Margesson, Richard Britteridge, Richard Clarke, all these died soon after arrival in the general sickness that befell. But Digory Priest had his wife and children sent hither afterwards, she being Mr. Allerton's sister. But the rest left no posterity here.

ORIGIN: Leiden.
MIGRATION: 1620 on the *Mayflower*.
FIRST RESIDENCE: Plymouth.

FREEMAN: On 11 November 1620, Thomas Williams signed the Mayflower Compact [Morton 26].

BIRTH: Born by about 1599 (assuming he was twenty-one when he signed the Mayflower Compact).
DEATH: Early 1621 at Plymouth.
MARRIAGE: None known.
CHILDREN: None known.

COMMENTS: In his analysis of Bradford's passenger list, Caleb Johnson places Thomas Williams as a member of John Robinson's Leiden congregation [TAG 80:99]. Johnson also suggests that this immigrant was baptized at Great Yarmouth, Norfolk, on 12 August 1582, son of John and Judith (Short) Williams [Mayflower Passengers 250; MQ 75:290–91].

The *Mayflower* passenger Thomas Williams should not be confused with the Thomas Williams who had settled at Plymouth by 1635 [GM 2:7:435–39].

EDWARD WINSLOW

Mr. Edward Winslow, Elizabeth his wife and two men-servants called George Soule and Elias Story; also a little girl was put to him called Ellen, the sister of Richard More.

Mr. Edward Winslow his wife died the first winter, and he married with the widow of Mr. White and hath two children living by her, marriageable, besides sundry that are dead. One of his servants died, as also the little girl, soon after the ship's arrival. But his man, George Soule, is still living and hath eight children.

ORIGIN: Leiden.
PREVIOUS RESIDENCES: Droitwich, Worcestershire; London.
MIGRATION: 1620 on the *Mayflower*.
FIRST RESIDENCE: Plymouth.
REMOVES: Marshfield by 1643.
RETURN TRIPS: Made many trips to England on personal and colony business. Sailed for England in 1646 and never returned to New England.

OCCUPATION: Merchant.
FREEMAN: On 11 November 1620, Edward Winslow signed the Mayflower Compact [Morton 26].

As governor, appears at head of 1633 the list of Plymouth freemen [PCR 1:3]. In the list of Plymouth Colony freemen of 7 March 1636/7 [PCR 1:52]. In Plymouth section of the 1639 Plymouth Colony list of freemen [PCR 8:173], then erased and entered in Marshfield section of same list [PCR 8:177, 195].

EDUCATION: Attended the King's School of Worcester Cathedral from April 1606 until April 1611 [Edward Winslow 2]. Apprenticed to "John Beale, citizen and stationer, for the term of eight years," on 19 August 1613, but left his master in 1617 [Edward Winslow 3–4]. On a return trip to London in 1635 Winslow obtained his freemanship from the Stationers' Company [unpublished research of Caleb Johnson].

Winslow had a hand in writing *Mourt's Relation* and also authored three other important pamphlets: *Good Newes from New England, or A Relation of Things Remarkable in That Plantation* (1624); *Hypocrisie Unmasked* (1646); and *New England's Salamander* (1647).

OFFICES: Plymouth Colony governor, 1 January 1632/3, 5 January 1635/6, 5 June 1644 [PCR 1:5, 36, 2:71]. Assistant, 1 January 1633/4, 1 January 1634/5, 3 January 1636/7, 6 March 1637/8, 2 March 1640/1, 1 March 1641/2, 7 March 1642/3, 4 June 1645, 1 June 1647, 7 June 1648, 4 June 1650 [PCR 1:21, 32, 48, 79, 2:8, 15, 33, 40, 52, 56, 83, 115, 123, 153].

In Marshfield section of the 1643 Plymouth Colony list of men able to bear arms [PCR 8:196].

ESTATE: In the 1623 Plymouth division of land Edward Winslow was granted four acres as a passenger on the *Mayflower* [PCR 12:4; MQ 40:12]. In the 1627 Plymouth division of cattle Edward Winslow, Susanna Winslow, Edward Winslow, and John Winslow were the sixth through the ninth persons in the third company [PCR 12:10].

Edward Winslow was one of the Purchasers, those who acquired the rights to land distributions in Plymouth Colony as a consequence of the agreement made between the London merchants and the Plymouth settlers in 1627 [Ford 282–88].

On 25 June 1631, Edward Winslow purchased three adjacent lots of land: three acres from John Winslow, four acres from Francis Eaton, and two acres from Myles Standish [PCR 12:16]. (These lots were those distributed in the land division of 1623.)

In the 25 March 1633 Plymouth tax list "Edward Wynslow, Gov[erno]r," was assessed £2 5s., and the same amount in the list of 27 March 1634 [PCR 1:9, 27).

In his will, dated 18 December 1654 and proved 16 October 1655, "Edward Winslowe of London, Esquire, being now bound in a voyage to sea in the service of the commonwealth," bequeathed to "Josia my only son" the entire estate "he allowing to my wife a full third part thereof for her life"; to "the poor of the Church of Plymouth in New England £10 and to the poor of Marshfield where the chiefest of my estate lies £10"; "my linen which I carry with me to sea to my daughter Elizabeth"; residue to "my son Josias, he giving to each of my brothers a suit of apparel"; "son Josias my executor"; "my four friends Dr. Edmond Wilson, Mr. John Arthur, Mr. James Shirley & Mr. Richard Floyd" overseers "for the rest of my personal estate in England" [MD 4:1–2; Waters 179, citing PCC 377 Aylett].

BIRTH: Born Droitwich, Worcestershire, 18 October 1595, and baptized there 20 October 1595, son of Edward and Magdalen (Oliver) Winslow [MQ 75:137–38].

DEATH: At sea near Hispaniola 8 May 1655 "aged 59 years, 6 months, and 18 days" [NEHGR 4:297].

MARRIAGE: (1) Leiden 12 May 1618 [NS] Elizabeth Barker [Plooij XXXV; Leiden Pilgrims 290; MD 22:66–67], b. probably in late 1591 or early 1592, daughter of Samuel Barker of East Bergholt and Chattisham, Suffolk [NEHGR 173:5–17 (and see **COMMENTS**)]. She died at Plymouth on 24 March 1620/1 [Prince 189].

(2) Plymouth 12 May 1621 Susannah (Jackson) White, daughter of Richard and Mary (Pettinger) Jackson of Scrooby, Nottinghamshire, and widow of *WILLIAM WHITE* ("The first marriage in this place, is of Mr. Edward Winslow to Mrs. Susanna White, widow of Mr. William White" [Prince 190]). She died after 18 April 1656 [Edward Winslow 400–1].

CHILDREN:

With second wife

    i Child WINSLOW, b. and d. 1622 or 1623 (in a letter dated 30 October 1623, Edward Winslow wrote that "[m]y wife hath had one child by me, but it pleased him that gave it to take it again unto himself; I left her with child at my departure ... but hope to be with her before her delivery" [NEHGR 109:243]).

    ii EDWARD WINSLOW, b. say 1624; living in 1627; no further record (but perhaps the child who died shortly before 28 January 1640/1 [WP 4:312]). (This was the child Susanna (Jackson) (White) Winslow was carrying in October 1623.)

    iii JOHN WINSLOW, b. say 1626; living in 1627; no further record (but perhaps the child who died shortly before 28 January 1640/1 [WP 4:312]).

    iv JOSIAH WINSLOW, b. after 22 May 1627 (not in cattle division); m. by 1658 Penelope Pelham, daughter of HERBERT PELHAM {1637, Cambridge} (eldest known child b. Marshfield 13 March 1658 [MarVR 5]; in his will of 1 January 1672/3, Herbert Pelham makes bequests to "my daughter Penelope Winslow" and "my son Josias Winslow" [NEHGR 33:291, 293; TAG 18:144]).

    v ELIZABETH WINSLOW, b. say 1631; m. (1) St. Olave Hart Street, London, 9 March 1655/6 Robert Brooks [MD 1:238–40, 60:27–29]; m. (2) Salem 22 September 1669 GEORGE CURWEN {1638, Salem} (called "loving sister Corwin" in brother Josiah's will [MD 1:238–40, 5:82– 85; NEHGR 150:193]).

ASSOCIATIONS: Brother of *GILBERT WINSLOW*, JOHN WINSLOW {1621, Plymouth}, JOSIAH WINSLOW {1631, Plymouth}, and KENELM WINSLOW {1631, Plymouth} [PM 507–21].

PREMIGRATION BIOGRAPHY: Edward Winslow was born at Droitwich, Worcestershire, in 1595. After attending the King's School of Worcester Cathedral from 1606 to 1611, he was apprenticed to John Beale, stationer and citizen of London, "for the term of eight years, from the 19th day of August, 1613." In 1617 Winslow removed to Leiden where he worked with William Brewster in his publishing ventures and joined John Robinson's congregation [Edward Winslow 3–5].

As members of the Leiden congregation began to make plans for their removal to the New World, Edward Winslow was also active in those affairs. In late 1619 or early 1620 he and his wife were in England where they disposed of land Elizabeth had inherited at Chattisham, Suffolk [NEHGR 173:5–6]. In a letter written from Leiden on 10 June 1620, Samuel Fuller, Edward Winslow, William Bradford, and Isaac Allerton wrote to John Carver and Robert Cushman, then in England, regarding some final details of the business arrangements for the voyage [Bradford 360–61].

COMMENTS: Edward Winslow was a member of the exploratory party that left Provincetown Harbor on 6 December 1620 and selected the site for the town of Plymouth [Mourt 32].

In 1627, pursuant to the renegotiation of the financial agreement between the London merchants and the Plymouth settlers, Edward Winslow became one of the eight Undertakers who agreed to oversee the liquidation of Plymouth Colony's debts [Bradford 194–96; Bradford LB 38–40].

Edward Winslow was a valued agent for Plymouth Colony (as is evident from the pages of Bradford's history) and for Massachusetts Bay Colony as well. Winslow left Plymouth for London in 1646 and never returned. He rose rapidly in the service of Cromwell's Commonwealth and was part of Cromwell's expedition to the West Indies when he died in 1655. All these aspects of Edward Winslow's life are portrayed in great detail in Jeremy Dupertuis Bangs's biography of the man.

We suggest a slight adjustment in the estimated birth date of Elizabeth Barker, Edward Winslow's first wife. Sue Allan and her team give her birthdate as "c. 1593" based on her first appearance on the Diocese of Norwich recusant list on 13 March 1607/8 and the assumption that this indicates that she had by then attained the age of fourteen [NEHGR 173: 9, 16].

However, it is likely that this recusant list was compiled in compliance with the 1593 Act Against Puritans, which was aimed at all persons aged sixteen and older. Elizabeth Barker was not on the recusant list dated 21 July 1607 but was on the list of 13 March 1607/8. If her sixteenth birthday occurred between these two dates, then she would have been born in late 1591 or early 1592.

BIBLIOGRAPHIC NOTE: In 1850 Lemuel Shattuck published a "Genealogical Memoir of the Descendants of Edward Winslow, Governor of Plymouth Colony," which included in a footnote a list of birth and baptismal dates for Edward and his siblings [NEHGR 4:297–303]. Savage objected to this list of dates [Savage 4:598–99], but in 1866 William S. Appleton examined the original parish registers of Droitwich and in 1867 published the results of his research, which were in agreement with the 1850 article [NEHGR 21:209–11]. In 2009 Caleb Johnson further addressed the issue of the dates of Edward Winslow's birth and baptism [MQ 75:137–38].

From 1965 through 1970 John G. Hunt published seven short, intriguing articles on the Winslow family, examining the ancestry of the five brothers, both on the paternal and maternal sides [TAG 41:168–75, 42:52–55, 186–87, 43:239–41; NEHGR 121:25–29, 122:175–78, 124:182–83]. In 2000 Kenneth W. Kirkpatrick (*nom de plume* of Marshall Kirk) extended one line of this research [NEHGR 154:78–108].

The standard genealogy of the Winslows, now considerably out of date, was published in 1887 and 1888 by David P. and Frances K. Holton [*The Winslow Memorial*, 2 volumes (New York 1877, 1888)]. The bulk of these two volumes is devoted to the descendants of Kenelm Winslow, who had far more posterity in the male line than his four brothers combined.

Edward Winslow has been treated by Ruth C. McGuyre and Robert S. Wakefield in the fifth volume of the Five Generations series of the General Society of Mayflower Descendants [MF 5:3–27]. Susan Hardman Moore included Edward Winslow in her study of Great Migration immigrants who returned to reside in England [Abandoning 324–26].

In 2004 Jeremy Dupertuis Bangs published *Pilgrim Edward Winslow: New England's First International Diplomat, A Documentary Biography* [Boston 2004], replete with complete transcriptions of many of Winslow's writings. Nearly half of this volume covers the very active last decade of Winslow's life, after he left Plymouth.

GILBERT WINSLOW

Moses Fletcher, John Goodman, Thomas Williams, Digory Priest, Edmund Margesson, Peter Browne, Richard Britteridge, Richard Clarke, Richard Gardiner, Gilbert Winslow.

Gilbert Winslow, after diverse years' abode here, returned into England and died there.

ORIGIN: Droitwich, Worcestershire.
MIGRATION: 1620 on the *Mayflower.*
FIRST RESIDENCE: Plymouth.
RETURN TRIPS: Returned to England by 1627 [Abandoning 351].

FREEMAN: On 11 November 1620, Gilbert Winslow signed the Mayflower Compact [Morton 26].
ESTATE: In the 1623 Plymouth division of lands "Gilbard Winslow" received one acre as a passenger on the *Mayflower* [PCR 12:4; MQ 40:12]. His name does not appear in the 1627 Plymouth division of cattle.

On 1 June 1663, Plymouth Court acknowledged "Gilbert Winslow, deceased, who was one of the first comers, to have a right of land, and do allow his heirs to look out and propose to the Court some parcel of land that the Court may think meet to accommodate them in" [PCR 4:40]. The inventory of the estate of his brother KENELM WINSLOW, dated 12 September 1672, included "one-half of the portion of land granted by the Court to him [Kenelm Winslow] and his brother Josias Winslow upon the account of their brother Gilbert Winslow as he was a first comer" [MD 24:42, citing PCPR 3:1:56].

On 24 December 1631, Edward Winslow (who was in England at the time) was appointed administrator of the estate of Gilbert Winslow. His estate came to £30 6s. 6d. [TAG 81:246, citing PCC Admons, 1631-33, f. 71].

BIRTH: Baptized Droitwich, Worcestershire, 29 October 1600, son of Edward and Magdalen (Oliver) Winslow [NEHGR 4:297, 21:210].
DEATH: Buried Ludlow, Shropshire, 11 October 1631 [TAG 81:246].
MARRIAGE: None known.
CHILDREN: None known.
ASSOCIATIONS: Brother of *EDWARD WINSLOW*, JOHN WINSLOW {1621, Plymouth}, JOSIAH WINSLOW {1631, Plymouth}, and KENELM WINSLOW {1631, Plymouth} [PM 511–21].

PREMIGRATION BIOGRAPHY: In his youth Gilbert Winslow undoubt-edly resided at Droitwich with his family. There is no evidence that he joined his brother Edward in Leiden, nor do we know where he was living when he decided to sail for New England in 1620, when he would have been nineteen years old.

INDEX SECTION

This final section contains four indices, three of a familiar variety and one that is experimental. The three familiar ones are of surnames, places, and ships. The unusual index is a rearrangement of the surname index, by first name, instead of last.

INDEX OF SURNAMES

This index lists all persons in this volume who were alive in the seventeenth century. Modern authors, historians, and genealogists are not indexed.

INDEX OF FIRST NAMES

While the Index of First Names is derived from the Index of Surnames, there are a number of differences that should be noted. In the first place, this index is intended not for assistance in finding one's place in the text, but for providing clues to further research. As a result, this index has been simplified, with each entry including only one of the surnames used by a married woman during her life. All surnames are included, but in a different form than in the Index of Surnames. For example, a woman who was married twice will appear in the Index of Surnames three times, as "Smith, Mary," as "Jones, Mary (Smith)," and as "Brown, Mary (Smith) (Jones)." In the Index of First Names she will also appear three times, but now as "Mary, Smith," as "Mary, Jones," and as "Mary, Brown."

George Ernest Bowman conceived the idea of an Index of First Names more than a century ago, but he never implemented it in print. There are many ways in which such an index might be useful, some of them unexpected. When the first version of this index was printed, it became obvious that such an arrangement of names would be a useful proofreading tool; all occurrences of "Willaim" instead of "William" would be grouped together and could be corrected at the same time.

Beyond this aid to index production, the Index of First Names should be helpful to researchers in a number of ways. Anyone searching for an unidentified wife with an unusual first name might want to look at all the entries for "Prudence," for example. Or an onomastic argument for identity, dependent on name usage within a family and on the relative frequency of use of a name, should be assisted by this index. Resourceful genealogists will undoubtedly find more uses for this unusual variety of index.

This Index of First Names has already borne fruit. In the second volume of the second Great Migration series, Melinde Lutz Byrne was writing the sketch of PENELOPE DARLOE {1635, Boston} [GM 2:2:285–86] and used the list of Penelopes in the index to *The Great Migration Begins* to identify her as the wife of ROBERT TURNER {1633, Boston} [GMB 3:1851–55].

INDEX OF PLACES

Because so many town names are common to old and New England, these names are followed, so far as possible, by the English counties or New England colonies to which they belonged. Localities within towns, such as field names and neighborhoods, are generally not indexed.

INDEX OF SHIPS

Most of the entries in this index are for the ships that brought passengers to Plymouth Colony.

INDEX OF SURNAMES

INDEX OF FIRST NAMES

INDEX OF PLACES

INDEX OF SHIPS